A &
Pl S

FO RS

First United States of America edition published in 1999
by Barron's Educational Series, Inc.
Adapted from *500 Popular Annuals & Perennials for Australian Gardeners*.
© Copyright 1998 by Random House Australia.
Photo Library © Copyright 1998 by Random House Australia.

Editor   Loretta Barnard

Consultants   Geoff Bryant
                Sarah Guest
                Maureen Heffernan

Page Layout   Joy Eckermann

All inquiries should be addressed to:
Barron's Educational Series Inc.
250 Wireless Boulevard
Hauppauge, NY 112788
http://www.barronseduc.com

International Standard Book Number 0-7641-1177-9
Library of Congress Catalog Card Number 99-72099

Printed in Hong Kong by Sing Cheong Printing Co. Ltd
987654321

CONTENTS

Introduction

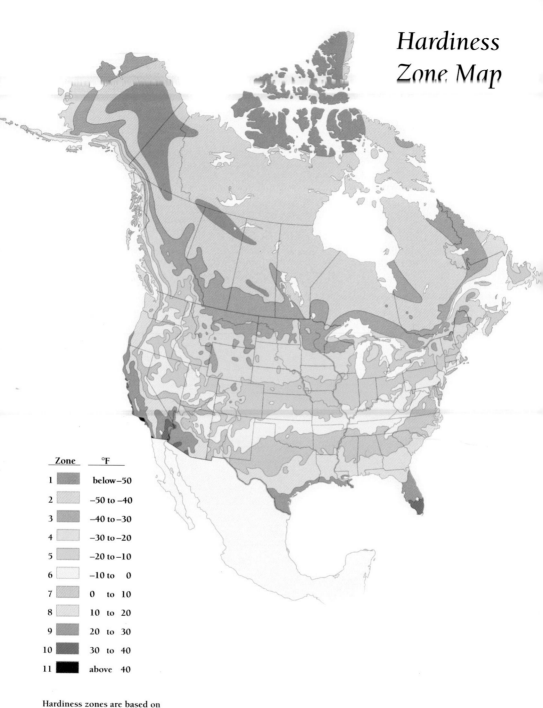

Hardiness Zone Map

Zone	°F
1	below −50
2	−50 to −40
3	−40 to −30
4	−30 to −20
5	−20 to −10
6	−10 to 0
7	0 to 10
8	10 to 20
9	20 to 30
10	30 to 40
11	above 40

Hardiness zones are based on
the average annual minimum
temperature for each zone.

Annuals and perennials give a garden more than the occasional splash of bright color. In many cases they 'make' a garden—giving it its essential character, its atmosphere and sense of place. Few gardens seem complete without the presence of these plants and their flourish of flowers mark the seasons as surely as the weather.

Often what begins with a few tentative purchases and trial runs leads to a lifetime of happy, harmless plant collecting. Friendships are cemented and remembered with personal gifts of such plants. In some families plants become 'family' plants when they move from place to place and between the generations with 'their' family. For some, just the scent or sight of a particular plant will bring back treasured affections and experiences of the past. Whether the gardener has the space and time for a stunning pair of matched herbaceous borders or is limited to a couple of tubs on a porch, the presence of annuals and

perennials can give great pleasure and add a personal touch to the common-place.

Both annuals and perennials have the unwarranted reputation of being time-consuming, space-consuming, money-consuming and water-consuming. But the key issue is, of course, how the available resources are used. The possession of unlimited resources will not necessarily make for the creation of

The stately *Agapanthus* prefers full sun.

You can put your own stamp on a garden by selecting the colors you like, such as the strong colors of *Tagetes erecta*, *Tagetes patula* and *Salvia viridis*.

Even after flowering, the attractive seed heads of this poppy complement the scarlet flowers of the *Penstemon*.

For a continuous effect, group them with perennials, staggering the flowering times of the plants so that when a small pocket of annuals is nearly past its prime a perennial just behind is about to flower. This complementary display can take a few seasons to achieve, as many perennials need two years to bloom, but don't give up, as experimenting in this way is one of the most rewarding aspects of gardening.

Apart from color combinations within a garden, try to tie in the house color to that of a garden display so they complement one another: a red or red-orange toned house looks good surrounded by bright oranges, yellows, rusty reds and creams, while a white or pastel painted house blends well with soft blue, mauve, pink and white flowers plus masses of silver foliage.

Just as important as linking the house to the garden, is the overall siting of the garden beds. Most annuals demand full sun to flower well so be sure to choose an aspect where the plants will receive as much light, particularly morning sun, as possible. Give them generously wide beds ensuring the colorful display will not be overwhelmed by shrub foliage or robbed of nutrients by the roots of nearby permanent plants.

a lovely garden filled with annuals and perennials. It can help, but a little plant knowledge, a little know-how, a few good friends and some good books are far more effective.

Planting combinations

By combining perennials with annuals in a more informal manner, the garden loses that 'all or nothing' effect which is so evident when a bed of annuals has 'finished' and is again planted out with tiny seedlings. By placing clumps of perennials beside drifts of annuals the eye is drawn from one accent to another, say from a group of low-growing annuals in front to the taller perennial flower spikes behind. Annuals are marvelous for providing a festive welcome to an entrance or a splash of color to a shrub border when the garden is to be used for a special event.

🌿 **Outstanding Perennials with a Long Flowering Season** 🌿	
Catananche caerulea	*Hemerocallis* 'Stella D'Oro'
Centranthus rubra	*Oenothera speciosa*
Convolvulus sabatius	*Nepeta faassenii*
Coreopsis grandiflora	*Perovskia atriplicifolia*
Dianthus latifolius	*Rudbeckia hirta*
Echinacea purpurea	*Scaevola* 'Mauve Clusters'
Galliardia × *grandiflora*	

Instant color effects

One of the most welcome developments in recent years has been the increase in

With their long spikes of large, brilliant, strongly colored flowers, lupins are a joy in any garden.

the number of annuals and perennials available in 'instant color' pots and flats. Once red geraniums were the only available way to provide a splash of color in early spring; now, right through the seasons a pot or tray of mature flowering annuals can be purchased to add instant color to a garden dead spot or patio. And don't overlook hanging baskets filled with annuals to highlight a garden color scheme. If potting up seedlings to make a basket full of your own instant color, take care to choose plants that will fall gracefully over the edge of the basket. If you are using large pots or tubs, both uprights and sprawling plant types can produce a very decorative display.

Annuals, by their very nature, aim to set as many seeds as possible within a very short life span. Gardeners can extend the flowering period by cutting the blooms for indoor use or pinching or deadheading faded flowers before they seed and so decide it's all over for

another year. If you follow this procedure, remember it is good practice to provide regular nourishment to the plants in the form of a quick-acting fertilizer designed to promote flowers rather than foliage growth.

Plant names
Species
What we call a species is the form in which a plant was found in the wild. The membership of a particular genus is denoted by the first word in a plant's name while the subsequent word usually refers to some aspect of the plant's appearance, native habitat or to the person who discovered or introduced the plant to gardeners. These two botanical names are, by custom, written in italics.

Cultivars
Following these two names there is often a name contained in quotation marks and written in normal print. This is the

name of what is called a cultivar—or selection—and denotes a particular form of the species. The cultivar's name is often of great significance to gardeners as these plants have particular and recognizable characteristics. They may display larger flowers than the common wild form, or the flowers and leaves may be in different shades and have different markings. The scent may be more pronounced, the plant larger, smaller, fatter, thinner, be more upright, more spreading, have a neater appearance or a longer flowering season. In other words, these named cultivars are worth knowing about. Plant breeders regularly introduce new named strains and cultivars.

Hybrids

Hybrids are plants which are bred by crossing one species with another and their presence is indicated by the use of the symbol '×' or the words 'Hybrid', 'hybridus' or 'hybrida'. Hybrids are bred to increase the vigor and splendor of plants and to alter their appearance. Most hybrids do not grow true from seeds.

Common names

Today, with gene therapy rapidly becoming a part of normal plant breeding, the gardener can expect many interesting developments in plant appearance and behavior.

Common names are like nicknames. Some are so well known as to make those who use botanical names in ordinary conversation appear pretentious! Others are now obscure to the point of being more or less obsolete. However, as many plants bear the same or very similar common names, they are of limited use. Botanical names may appear a little daunting when first encountered but they are essential tools in the processes of identifying and buying plants.

Definitions
Perennials

A perennial is a plant with a life cycle longer than two growing seasons. During each year of a perennial's life a plant will flower and set seed in the season which is appropriate to a particular climate and situation. Perennials which survive the tough times by becoming dormant and spending the season below ground are referred to as 'herbaceous perennials'. Those which are on view throughout the year are referred to as 'evergreen perennials'.

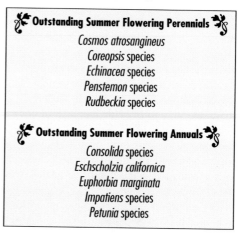

Outstanding Summer Flowering Perennials

Cosmos atrosangineus
Coreopsis species
Echinacea species
Penstemon species
Rudbeckia species

Outstanding Summer Flowering Annuals

Consolida species
Eschscholzia californica
Euphorbia marginata
Impatiens species
Petunia species

Annuals

Plants which live for a single season and die after flowering are called annuals. In cold climates this definition is clear cut as these plants, once they have flowered, die with the first frosts of winter. In climates where no hard frosts occur, these distinctions become a little blurred as some so-called annuals are, in point of fact, frost tender short-lived perennials which have been selected and bred for use as flowering annuals in colder climates. (For example, *Nicotiana sylvestris* is a true open-pollinated annual which appears in spring, flowers, sets seed and dies as winter approaches. Whereas the *N. alata* derivatives found on seedling benches appear to have the potential for a longer life. They can also be propagated through division.)

However, it is worth remembering that some of these so-called annuals were bred to provide one quick display and while they may prove capable of survival for several years they may also fail to perform with any flamboyance in their second and subsequent seasons.

> ### Outstanding Spring Flowering Perennials
> Aubrieta deltoida
> Aquilegia species
> Dicentra spectabilis
> Phlox subulata
> Primula species
>
> ### Outstanding Spring Flowering Annuals
> Clarkia hybrids
> Lathyrus odoratus
> Myosotis alpestris
> Nigella damascena
> Papaver nudicaule
> Viola × wittrockiana

Biennials

A biennial is a plant with a life cycle that spans two growing seasons; establishing a rootstock in the first then flowering, setting seed and dying in the second. Many biennials evolved in cold regions and often react to mild climates by flowering in their first year.

Buying and choice

When choosing plants the first thing to do is to find out which plants grow well in your locality, to acquire those with appeal, and to learn how to get the best from them.

Then, when ready to experiment,

A display of annuals and perennials like these *Nicotiana*, *Begonia*, *Verbena* and *Ageratum* can take a lot from the soil. You must nourish the soil if you want to repeat the display season after season.

Be careful when buying plants, and only choose happy, healthy specimens.

When purchasing annuals the choice usually lies between buying a tray of seedlings or a packet of seeds. Highly bred and hybridized annuals such as the latest impatiens and petunias are best bought in trays as seedlings. Many require careful handling during infancy and this is best left to those with the right equipment and knowledge. Yet the home gardener can achieve pleasing results by buying seeds designed for the home market.

Open-pollinated annuals are valued for their ability to self-sow. These are fleeting easy care plants of tremendous charm which, if conditions suit their needs, have the grace to reappear year after year often choosing the most impossible of situations and often making a success of their chosen situation. The seeds of open-pollinated annuals are easily bought, stored and grown.

🌿 Outstanding Open-pollinated Annuals 🌿	
Antirrhinum majus	Eschscholzia californica
Ammi majus	Lathyrus odorata
Anchusa capensis	Myosotis alpestris
Calendula officinalis	Nicotiana sylvestris
Cosmos bipinnatus	Nigella damascena
Cynoglossum amabile	Papaver rhoeas

explore other plants which enjoy similar climates and conditions and add a few to your collection. Knowing the native locations of desirable plants will do much to help the beginner to match plants to climates and conditions. Suburban nurseries often acquire their plants from a variety of sources, with the result that not all their flowery offerings will thrive in the garden next door unless nurtured by an expert. It really does pay to do your homework.

As confidence, experience and enthusiasm builds, the gardener will learn to mimic the growing conditions found in situations bearing little resemblance to their local climate and will achieve success with many such 'foreign' plants.

If novice gardeners follow these stages, they will save both money and heartache and, from the very beginning, will enjoy the pleasures of growing flourishing annuals and perennials.

When buying the seeds, inspect the packaging and the use-by date stamp. Those which have been hermetically sealed into foil packs should last for years but their deterioration will begin as soon as the packet is opened. Those packaged in paper or stored at home are best sown within 12 months of their purchase. If storing unopened or leftover seed, make sure it is kept in a cool, dry spot.

Many annuals can be bought either as seedlings or seeds and many gardeners, nervous of using seeds, stick with seedlings, thereby missing much of the joy

A colorful hanging basket placed in the lattice work makes a charming addition to a courtyard or patio.

Many annuals and perennials grow wonderfully well in containers. This glorious display of lobelia proves that!

provided by the old-fashioned, easy-care, open-pollinated, or newest hybrid annuals.

Perennials should always be bought from reputable growers who take pride, among other things, in endowing their plants with the correct names and cultivation notes.

Plants bearing the name of a particular cultivar should always be propagated using vegetative methods—division, cuttings or tissue culture. Plants produced using these methods will automatically grow true to their parents' appearance. Odd self-sown descendants may prove charming and thrifty but they should not be given the name of their parental cultivar as these wildlings rarely replicate their parents' characteristics.

The lists provided by out of town growers who provide mail order services are also well worth inspection by plant enthusiasts. Their advertisements are to be found in reputable gardening magazines. Botanical gardens are another good source for finding information on reputable plant sources.

If possible when buying from suburban nurseries or supermarkets buy soon after the plants have arrived. Many so-called 'bargains' will have been exposed to unsuitable overcrowded conditions for too long, and are pot bound and

Outstanding Autumn Flowering Perennials

Anemone japonica
Aster species
Echinacea purpurea
Helenium species
Rudbeckia lanciniata

Outstanding Autumn Flowering Annuals

Cleome spinosa
Helianthus annuus
Rudbeckia 'Indian Summer'
Salvia 'Victoria'
Zinnia species

---

diseased. Only buy what look, at least superficially, like healthy happy plants

Planting, maintenance and nurture

Prepare and plant well and you will save yourself a heap of trouble. Many seeds can be sown directly into the soil, and others do better if they are first nurtured in containers.

Raising seedlings

To raise happy, healthy plants in containers, it is important to use a good soil mix. It should be open and friable, and, of course, well-drained. Some coarse sand, leaf mold or other garden compost should be added. There are also very good seed-raising mixtures available from nurseries and garden centers.

Sprinkle the seeds over the surface of a shallow container, such as a seedling tray, and then lightly cover the seeds with a little seed-starting mixture. Covering the container with a sheet of glass or plastic ensures that moisture loss is kept to a minimum. Now place the container in a warm spot. Don't forget to moisten the soil.

The seeds will soon germinate; but do not be in a hurry to prick out the seedlings and plant into the garden. Make sure soil is evenly moist but not water-logged, to prevent disease problems. When they have grown a little larger, gently pick the seedlings up by their leaves — not the stem — loosening the soil if necessary. They are then ready to be planted straight into a decorative pot for the balcony or porch, or straight into the garden bed. For annuals, wait until all

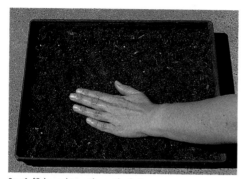

Step 1: fill the seed tray with a good soil mix.

Step 2: sprinkle the seeds over the surface of the soil.

Step 4: cover with glass or plastic.

Step 3: cover the seeds with a little seed-starting mixture.

Step 5: remove the cover when the seedlings have germinated.

Gently loosen the soil around the seedling before transplanting.

Make the holes larger than the seedling's root mass.

Place the seedling in the hole, firm it down and water immediately.

danger of frost has passed before planting out into the garden.

Tray-grown seedlings should be carefully separated and planted into a fine, well-prepared soil in holes at least twice the size of their existing root mass. Specially designed slow-release fertilizer granules can be added to the holes prior to planting, or sprinkled around the base of the plants after planting. The little plants should be watered immediately and kept evenly moist during the early stages of their establishment. The young growth of seedlings is the favored fare of snails and slugs and the wise gardener acts accordingly. (Tomorrow morning almost always proves too late.)

Seed beds

If you want to raise many seedlings, a seed bed is probably the best way of

going about it. Find a warm, sheltered location in the garden, ensure that drainage is efficient, and check that the soil is suitable. Sandy soils need the added moisture of compost; clay soils need to have some coarse sand added. Dig the bed over, adding fertilizer. Seedlings in the garden will need protection from direct sunlight. Shade cloth or some other light covering suspended on a frame is quite suitable.

Dig a hole slightly larger than the root base, separate the seedlings and place gently into the prepared hole. Some seeds are very small and stick together and an even distribution may be easier to obtain if the seeds are first dusted with talcum powder.

Water the seedlings well. The seed bed will need protection from snails, slugs and birds, and should never be allowed to dry out completely or be kept in an over-soggy condition during the early stages of plant growth. If the seedlings look over-crowded a few can be pulled out and discarded. When the seedlings are large enough to transplant into the garden, carefully separate the plants, and gently place into the garden bed. Water well.

Preparing garden beds

To ensure strong growth and maximum flowering, prepare your garden beds

To prepare the garden bed, fork over the soil and add compost.

Rake over the soil to ensure a smooth, even surface.

Sow the seeds, cover with a fine layer of soil, and gently firm down.

soundly. If the area to be planted has not been dug over before, it is a good idea to double dig. This means that the topsoil, say to a fork's depth, is weeded and put aside and the soil under this layer is dug over to the depth of a fork. Humus, such as well-rotted manure, leaf mold, or compost can be added to this layer to help break up heavy clay particles or to add moisture-retentive qualities to sandy soils. The result should be a loose, easily worked substance. This double digging is particularly beneficial to perennials which may be left in the same position for some years.

Replace the top layer of soil and prepare this surface in accordance with your planting needs. If planting perennials, a dressing of well-rotted manure or compost or a complete fertilizer can be added while roughly digging the soil over; if hardy annual seeds are to be sown directly into the soil in temperate areas, this top layer needs to be well dug over to remove any clods, then raked evenly to ensure a smooth, even surface.

Then check that water drains away quickly and freely. If there is any doubt dig a deep hole and fill it with water. If water is still visible the following morning then the drainage should be attended to before planting. Most drainage problems can be improved with the simple addition of coarse sand, small stones or some similar gritty material. If the problem persists the addition of an agricultural drain should be considered.

Problem soils, both clay and sandy soils, will benefit if well-rotted compost, as much as can be obtained, is deeply dug through the bed and when worms are encouraged to take up residence.

Generally speaking, a neutral to slightly acidic soil will prove best for the ordinary growing of most annuals and perennials. If there are any doubts a testing kit can be purchased. A more acid soil (one with a pH level falling below 6.5) can be treated with lime or gypsum to raise the pH. An alkaline soil, or a soil with a pH over 7, or one where a lack of trace elements is suspected, may need to have sulphur or considerable amounts of organic matter incorporated into it, to help lower the pH. To properly test and/ or alter your soil's pH, consult with your local county extension agency for exact recommendations and safe applications of materials.

While the bed is in this initial pre-planting phase it may be wise to check the ways in which extra water can be provided during dry spells, bearing in mind that hand-held hoses and sprinklers waste water, encourage mildews and molds and often flatten small plants. A drip system is the usual domestic choice and, while the bed is bare, the layout can be checked so that an even, deep delivery can be achieved.

If this initial preparation is done thoroughly it will be years before deep digging need be done again. Any further nutrition can be laid on the soil's surface and the work of conveying it down to the roots left to worms and water.

In many areas the local climate determines when and if seeds can be planted directly into the ground. If a late frost is a possibility, a much greater success rate is ensured if seeds are sown indoors in a greenhouse or on a warm, weather-proof porch, under indoor grow lights, near a sunny window or other sheltered well-lit spots. This guarantees that the seedlings are ready to be transplanted as soon as weather permits.

Annuals are grown from seed each season, but there are various ways to propagate perennials. Many can be grown from seed; however it usually takes longer for blooms to form. If established crowns or rhizomes are divided, new plants, true to form, are generally established more quickly and often produce flowers the following season.

For gardeners in all climatic zones, annuals provide welcome displays of color, especially in early spring, while perennials put on a color parade at least once a year, often as a bonus to distinctive foliage. What's more, perennials pay handsome dividends, providing the gardener with a source of plant material with which to experiment with design and color combinations each season.

These mature seedlings are ready to be planted.

Pack the soil around the plants and water immediately.

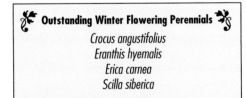

Outstanding Winter Flowering Perennials
Crocus angustifolius
Eranthis hyemalis
Erica carnea
Scilla siberica

Planting perennials
Dig a hole about three times the depth and width of the container. At the bottom of the hole, make a small hump, and add a few slow-release fertilizer

granules. Then ease the plant from its container; slightly loosen the roots; spread them over the hump; and refill the hole steadying the plant as you go. The level at which the plant material meets the soil's surface should be the same as it was when the plant was in its container. Gently firm the soil and water gently but thoroughly. Do not apply liquid feed at this point.

Ideally perennials are planted while dormant and just before their seasonal growth spurt. However many perennials are container grown and sold while in flower. These can be planted while flowering provided adequate aftercare is given. However, if conditions are demanding or the plant looks in any way stressed, it will be wise to trim the plants and to remove all the flowering stems. If there are any doubts keep the plant in its container until the appropriate season.

Mail order plants should be exposed to the light and air as soon as they arrive and allowed a small period of rest and recuperation before being planted.

Plants that are pot bound should be soaked for a few hours and the roots spread with care and lightly pruned before they are planted.

Some perennials will prove to have been grown in soil very different from the local soil. These should have all the existing soil gently washed from the roots prior to planting and may take a little longer than usual to adjust to their new environment. A hormone designed to stimulate root growth may assist.

Some perennials dislike root disturbance, and should be planted into their prepared holes gently and carefully. Paeonies are an example.

Water and watering

Most garden plants have been bred or selected for growth in places where the precipitation is evenly distributed throughout the growing season and many will prove unable to survive without help from a hose when grown in drier climates and under the usual crowded garden conditions.

A watering regime should be carefully thought through if plants are to put their roots down and thrive and the gardener is to maintain a sensible lifestyle. Waste through evaporation will be minimized if water is applied during the cooler night hours and applied directly to the soil through some form of drip system. A timer will also minimize waste. One or two deep soakings every week should be sufficient and is infinitely preferable to daily squirtings from hand-held hoses. Such squirtings will save plant lives but such rescue remedies rarely lead to lush, long term, good health.

The problems associated with artificial watering have led to a growing interest and enthusiasm for wild gardens and gravel gardens where suitable species are planted, nurtured for a few weeks and then permitted to do or die without further help or hindrance from the gardener.

Mulch and nutrition

Perennial beds are usually treated to an annual top dressing of well-rotted organic mulch. (The contents of the compost bin, straw, leaf mold, or any compost designed for use with perennials are recommended.) The purpose of this mulch is to suppress weeds, to conserve water and to supply nutrition. The mulch should be spread around the plants in spring or late winter before growth begins and/or in autumn when the plants are tidied up and prepared for dormancy and their next season of growth. If the soil is healthy the worms will take the nutrients down to the plants' roots. Many gardeners get superb results when using a good mulch—one which contains a little animal matter and a lot of vegetable matter—as the sole supplier of plant nutrition.

In places where the growing season is prolonged a second flowering or pro-longed flowering may be a possibility. In such conditions the usual mulch can be supplemented with slow release fertilizer granules and/or the occasional light liquid feed half way through the season.

Fine water-conserving nutritional mulches are also used with annuals. They should be dug through the bed prior to planting and, in the case of seed beds, not laid on top of the soil's surface where they can form an impenetrable crust. In gravel gardens the stones themselves provide the water-preserving weed-suppressing substance and all nutritional needs must be supplied from above. A very few granules of slow-release fertilizer or the occasional light

liquid feed will suffice as, generally speaking, the plants which grow and thrive in gravel gardens are modest feeders and well capable of scraping a living from a bit of dirt and a stony surface.

General maintenance

During the growing season weeds should be removed as they appear. A good mulch and some healthy top growth will prevent this chore from becoming overly arduous.

Spent flowers and leaves should be cleared away as soon as they lose their visual appeal and the beds kept clear of withered or rotting vegetation.

Hybrid annuals should be cleared away as soon as their visual appeal fades. Open-pollinated annuals, if seed collection is intended, must be left until the seeds have set and ripened.

Some perennials will require staking. This depends on the choice of plant, the situation and the climate. Spikes of flowers like delphiniums are usually

A well-mulched garden such as this will help to control weeds, conserve water and add nutrition.

It's easy to see that these violas have been lovingly tended.

staked individually whereas mounding plants, which require support, are grown through 'mushrooms' of wire or networks of strong twigs. The trick is to provide just enough support to hold the flowering mass upright in rough weather. Too little by way of support and the plants may go down like dominoes. Too much and a flower bed will look messy. In situations where massive plant support is required many people prefer to use sticks, twigs and natural string rather than multi-hued metal and/or plastic contraptions.

Some flowering perennials (and petunias and impatiens) benefit from a minor mid-season cut back. All perennials which enjoy a period of summer growth are cut back as winter approaches and flower production ceases.

Those which have grown over-large or are becoming scraggly in the center are dug up and divided in such a way as to reduce the mass and then replanted. Excess and poor or decaying material is conveyed to the compost heap. When the winter comes a perennial bed should look somewhat bare, neat and clean, and allow space for the winter flowering perennials such as hellebores to spread their decorative leaves and flowers.

❦ Outstanding Perennials for Cutting ❦

Achillea filipendulina
Iris reticulata
Delphinium species
Paeonia species
Zantedeschia species

❧ Outstanding Annuals for Cutting ❧

Centaurea cyanus
Consolida species
Gaillardia pulchella
Lathyrus odoratus
Papaver nudicaule

In spring, when the summer flowering perennials emerge from their hibernation, the new shoots will need protection from snails and slugs. The fresh new growth of annuals certainly will. The foliage of some annuals and perennials is also prone to attack by caterpillars. If applied regularly, a simple, harmless pyrethrum spray or powder should control the problem and will be most effective if the undersides of the leaves are also coated with the mixture.

In drier sub-tropical climates the popular perennials and annuals of colder climates can often be grown successfully. Some will bloom in winter and die back in summer, in which case the seasonal maintenance program is reversed.

Division and propagation

Division

Large well-established perennials can (and should) be lifted and divided with a sharp clean knife while dormant in winter. In areas with hard winter frosts, it is often better to leave dividing until late winter or very early spring, in order to lessen the exposure of the young divisions to severe cold.

Each subdivision should be comprised of clean healthy-looking roots and a few shoots. These subdivisions can be planted directly back into the garden or potted and cherished for future use.

The process of lifting and dividing winter or early spring flowering perennials is exactly the same but is usually performed just after the plants have flowered.

Cuttings

Many perennials and a few of the so-called annuals, including petunias, nasturtiums, and wall flowers, can be grown from soft cuttings. A mature-looking shoot of manageable size can be taken. This 'cutting' or 'heel' can then be dipped into a hormone mixture designed for soft cuttings (this is not an essential procedure) and 'planted' into a pot filled with a free draining propagating mix. While these cuttings are taking root they must not be exposed to extremes of temperature or allowed to become over-dry or over-wet. Specially designed home propagators are available but many home gardeners develop their own ingenious methods of maintaining an even temperature and moisture level.

Plants propagated by these two methods will probably bloom in their first season and will be exact clones of their parent plant. Plants grown from seed may present in a variety of shapes and shades and have characteristics which vary from that of the parent plant.

When taking soft cuttings, be sure to take a mature-looking shoot, and plant it in a good propagating mix.

The seemingly careless habit of *Erigeron karvinskianus* adds real character to this small courtyard.

Many perennials when grown from seed do not bloom in their first year of garden growth.

Seed collection and propagation

Seeds to be collected for propagation should be allowed to remain with the parent plant until the pod is on the verge of bursting and the seeds are ripe. The easiest way to collect the seeds is by cutting the stems so that the pods, with their burden of seeds, fall directly into a container. The seeds are then removed from the pods, spread on a tray, and sun dried for a few days in a still spot. They can then be packaged, labeled and stored in a dry place. Seed grown plants do not necessarily grow true to the parent plant's appearance.

Design, placement and usage

Whether the intention is to recreate a grand English border, a cottage garden, a wild or gravel garden, to adorn a doorway or to fill a few gaps, a little forethought and planning will go a long way towards achieving a satisfactory and attractive planting. For example a deciduous plant, which looks fabulous when in flower, may leave a huge hole in the vegetation for many months and, while this may be of little account in a large garden, in a smaller one it can prove an eyesore. And no matter how much a particular plant may be desired, if the situation is unfavorable the gardener should consider the time and money it will take to nurture this favored plant.

Annuals and perennials can be used in a variety of ways either to enhance an existing design or to make and hold the design itself. Commercially produced annuals are used (petunias in sunny spots and impatiens in shady ones) when the designer seeks to establish bright blocks of color or when an entrance is perceived to be in need of some form of welcoming decoration. At the height of their glory these bright flowers can add to both structure and color. However as their flowering season is usually followed by a season of bare earth, some gardeners prefer to use evergreen perennials such as agapanthus, hedera (ivy), ajuga, sedum, hostas, hellebores and iberis. In comparison to the well-known annuals, these plants may have shorter, less flamboyant flowering periods, but their decorative foliage remains to hold the eye and carry the design. It is all a matter of choice and of knowing exactly what one is hoping to achieve—and for how long.

Herbaceous borders

Herbaceous borders are the apotheosis of gardening with perennials. These borders are usually arranged on a north/south axis and are either backed by a wall or hedge or paired on either side of a path. While they are a challenge to design they are less demanding of time than might be imagined, provided the gardener has a clear idea of expected plant behavior in their particular situation.

In Britain, the home of grand herbaceous borders, the fabulous flowery display is of limited duration—two to three months at most. But the border is usually designed so that one grouping of plants succeeds another as the season progresses. In milder climates the intention is often to have something on show throughout the year and these flower borders often appear sparser than a classic British border in full flower.

In herbaceous borders perennials are arranged in a harmonious manner and identical plants are usually planted together in groups of three, five or seven. Taller plants are placed behind the shorter ones in borders which can only be viewed from one side, and along the spine in borders which are visible from all sides. Plants which display upright spikes of flowers are placed in contrast to those with mounding forms.

Great attention is given to harmonious color arrangements and to the way in which the foliage of one grouping will enhance the appearance of its near neighbors. Recognized color schemes include those which follow a segment of the colors found in the rainbow. For example the chosen theme might be scarlet, yellow, orange and bronze; or ruby-red, hot-pink, purple and sapphire blue; or lavender, silver, pink and mauve. The tonal strengths are co-ordinated and contrasted too. For example ruby-red, purple and sapphire-blue when diluted become the softer silvery shades of pale-pink, mauve lavender and baby-blue. Often, to provide visual focus, small flicks of clear scarlet or white are used to break the harmony of these careful schemes. Purists do not advocate the use of annuals in herbaceous borders but many gardeners fill the gaps created when some plant has failed to live up to expectations with annuals.

These borders in their classic form are beyond the scope of most gardeners but they are worth some study as many of their characteristics can be copied in smaller gardens and to great effect. The adoption of a harmonious color scheme for example will do much to give a small garden a spacious well-integrated feeling. Attention to the visual relationship between foliage and flower will add to its charm and architecture. And the grouping or massing of plants will prevent spotty over-busy effects.

Cottage gardens

The arrangement of annuals and perennials in modern cottage gardens is more relaxed. The easy going intention is to create an abundant flowery garden where nature has gone slightly out of control. Perennials are usually established as single plants and, if they spread beyond their allotted space, all well and good. Open-pollinated annuals are used to great effect with half their charm coming, as the years pass, from the random placements which only a plant can find for itself. A single packet of mixed open-pollinated seeds will soon give a 'cottage' effect.

Sometimes a slight air of formality is introduced with a formal planting on either side of a front path, or through a balanced arrangement of containers near a doorway. However, in general, the joy in cottage gardening comes from the abundance of flowers and fruit rather than from carefully controlled plant arrangements.

Gravel gardens

In gravel gardens plants which enjoy poor soils, good drainage and sunlight (gravel can get horribly stained when used in damp shady spaces) are planted and allowed and encouraged to come and go as they will. Some gardeners cover the entire garden with gravel; others combine paving stones with gravel. Some prefer to cover much of the

The joy in cottage gardening comes from the abundance of colorful flowers and fruit.

surface with tough spreading low-growing evergreen plants such as gazania and thymus while yet others prefer a more flexible open arrangement in which some of the gravel can always be seen. In these open arrangements more upright plants such as *Valeriana officinalis*, *Linaria purpurea*, *Lychnis coronaria* and verbascums are used. Open-pollinated annuals are also permitted to find the odd niche.

The trick in a gravel garden is to pull out unwanted plants as soon as they appear in such a way as to give an uncontrolled natural impression.

Wild gardens

In wild gardens annuals and/or perennials are established in great drifts and waves and allowed to get on with the job of decorating the scenery. Usually the mass is arranged so that it follows and enhances the natural contours of the land. Sometimes a single easy-care species, usually one with a long flowering season, such as corcopsis, is relied on to adorn a large area. Wild gardens are usually low maintenance gardens with a single season of splendor. Yet a little ingenuity can provide decorative effects throughout the year. In cold climates, for example, frosted seed heads can prove enormously decorative.

Small suburban gardens

The design and plant arrangements in small suburban gardens can reflect any of these recognized styles. It is all a matter of picking up on a few basic and appropriate design characteristics and, as always, matching the plants to the local conditions and climate. However, in small suburban gardens it is more usual and often just as effective to use annuals and perennials to add color, to fill gaps and to provide structure as and when they are required. A single row of

Because it can tolerate heat, salt air and poor soil, *Pericallis* × *hybrida* is a popular garden annual.

agapanthus, hosta, daylily, liriope or ornamental grasses when used to edge a wall, fence or garden subdivision will do much to give the area a sophisticated spacious-looking trim and will enhance any existing architectural features.

Some final points

Some annuals are described as 'frost hardy annuals'. This does not necessarily indicate that these plants will perform over several years but that their seeds can be sown in autumn or early spring. If these plants are true annuals they will then die after flowering in the common way. The term 'hardy plant' refers to frost hardy plants and not to a plant's capacity to withstand drought or heat.

Poor drainage and hot humidity are as big a danger to annuals and perennials when grown in warm temperate climates as frost is in colder climates.

Generally speaking plants with gray or

Wallflowers can be in bloom for months, and add vibrancy to any size garden.

silvery leaves are well-adapted to hot, sun-scorched situations.

Mark the place as perennial plants retreat into dormancy. It is all too easy to forget the position of a precious plant and to put a spade through it.

Most of the popular ornamental perennials and annuals bloom during the warmer months. However many of those plants described as 'summer blooming' will adapt their life cycle and bloom during the sunny but cooler winter months.

Every gardener must take on the responsibility of not introducing invasive plants to a neighborhood. What will or will not prove invasive in a particular area is beyond the scope of this book. Contact the relevant government agency, such as your local county extension agency, and be observant and be vigilant—if only for your own sake.

A

Acaena 'Blue Haze'

Acanthus mollis

ACAENA

Around 100 species make up this genus of low-growing evergreen perennials from the southern hemisphere. They have thin, creeping stems or buried rhizomes that bear at intervals tufts of small pinnate leaves with toothed margins. Flowers are insignificant, green or purple-brown, in dense stalked heads or spikes, and are followed by small dry fruit with barbed hooks. Acaenas make good rock garden plants. Some more vigorous species are regarded as weeds.

Cultivation

These tough plants thrive in exposed places and poor soil, but do demand good drainage and summer moisture. Propagate from seed or by division.

Acaena 'Blue Haze'

Thought probably to be a form of *Acaena magellanica*, from the southern Andes of South America and subantarctic islands, this vigorous creeper can spread to an indefinite size, the stems rooting. The crowded leaves with roundish, toothed leaflets are an attractive pale blue-gray, and in summer it sends up 4 in (10 cm) high purplish flowerheads followed in autumn by red-spined fruit. A useful

ground cover, it will spill over rocks or retaining walls. *Zones 7–10.*

ACANTHUS
Bear's breeches

Around 30 species of perennials and shrubs make up this genus. The deeply lobed and toothed leaves of *Acanthus mollis* and *A. spinosus* have lent their shape to the carved motifs seen on Corinthian columns. Only the more temperate perennial species have been much cultivated. They have erect spikes of bracted, curiously shaped flowers, which appear in spring and early summer.

Cultivation

Frost hardy, they do best in full sun or light shade. They prefer a rich, well-drained soil with adequate moisture. Watch for snails and caterpillars. Propagate by division in autumn, or from seed.

Acanthus mollis

This species is somewhat variable, the form grown in gardens having broader, softer leaves and taller flowering stems than most wild plants. It is more of a woodland plant than other acanthuses,

Achillea 'Coronation Gold'

Acanthus spinosus

Achillea 'Moonshine'

appreciating shelter and deep, moist soil. The large leaves are a deep, glossy green and rather soft. Flower spikes can be over 6 ft (1.8 m) tall, the purple-pink bracts contrasting with the crinkled white flowers. Spreading by deeply buried rhizomes, it can be hard to eradicate. *Zones 7–10.*

Acanthus spinosus
This eastern Mediterranean species has large leaves that are deeply divided, the segments having coarse, spine-tipped teeth. In summer it sends up flower spikes to about 4 ft (1.2 m) high; the individual flowers and bracts are similar to those of *A. mollis. Zones 7–10.*

ACHILLEA
Yarrow, milfoil, sneezewort
There are about 85 species of *Achillea* from the temperate northern hemisphere. The foliage is fern-like and aromatic. Most species bear masses of large, flat heads of tiny daisy flowers from late spring to autumn in shades of white, yellow, orange, pink or red. They suit massed border plantings and rockeries. This genus is named after Achilles, who, in Greek mythology, used the plant to heal wounds.

Cultivation
These hardy perennials tolerate poor soils, but do best in sunny, well-drained sites in temperate climates. They multiply rapidly by deep rhizomes and are easily propagated by division in late winter or from cuttings in summer.

Achillea 'Coronation Gold'
This vigorous hybrid cultivar originated as a cross between *Achillea clypeolata* and *A. filipendulina*. It has luxuriant grayish green foliage and flowering stems up to 3 ft (1 m) tall with large heads of deep golden yellow in summer and early autumn. *Zones 4–10.*

Achillea 'Moonshine'
A cultivar of hybrid origin, this plant bears pretty flattened heads of pale

sulfur yellow to bright yellow flowers throughout summer. It has delicate, feathery, silvery gray leaves and an upright habit, reaching a height of 24 in (60 cm). Divide regularly in spring to promote strong growth. *Zones 3–10.*

Achillea tomentosa
Woolly yarrow

Native to southwestern Europe, this is a low, spreading plant with woolly or silky haired, finely divided gray-green leaves and flowerheads of bright yellow on 12 in (30 cm) stems. Tolerating dry conditions and hot sun, it is excellent in the rock garden or as an edging plant. *Zones 4–10.*

ACONITUM
Aconite, monkshood, wolfsbane

The 100 or so species of this genus from the northern hemishpere are renowned for the virulent poisons contained in the

Aconitum napellus

sap. From ancient times until quite recently they were widely employed for deliberate poisoning. The poison has also been used medicinally in controlled doses. The flowers are mostly in shades of deep blue or purple or less commonly white, pink or yellow, with 5 petals of which the upper one bulges up into a prominent helmet-like shape.

Cultivation

Monkshoods prefer deep, moist soil and a sheltered position, partly shaded if summers are hot and dry. Propagate by division or from seed.

Aconitum napellus
Aconite, monkshood

Of wide distribution in Europe and temperate Asia, this is also the monkshood species most widely grown in gardens. The stems are erect, to 4 ft (1.2 m) or so high, with large leaves divided into very narrow segments and a tall, open spike of deep blue to purplish flowers. A vigorous grower, it likes damp woodland or stream bank conditions. *Zones 5–9.*

ACTAEA
Baneberry

Only 8 species of frost-hardy perennials belong to this genus, which occurs in

Achillea tomentosa

Actaea alba

Actaea rubra

Europe, temperate Asia and North America, mostly in damp woodlands and on limestone outcrops. They have large compound leaves springing from a root crown; the leaflets are thin and broad with strong veining and sharp teeth. Flowers are in short, feathery spikes or heads, the individual flowers smallish with many white stamens among which the narrow petals are hardly detectable. The fruits are white, red or black berries, often on a stalk of contrasting color. All parts of the plants are very poisonous.

Cultivation
Requiring a cool, moist climate, these plants grow best in sheltered woodland conditions or in a damp, cool spot in a rock garden. Propagate from seed or by division.

Actea alba
White baneberry
From the eastern USA, this summer-flowering perennial is most notable for its handsome berries, though its flowers and foliage are attractive too. It forms a clump of fresh green, divided leaves with a spread of 18 in (45 cm), from which rise the fluffy white flowers on stems up to 3 ft (1 m) high. By late summer they have developed into spires of small, gleaming white berries on red stalks. *Zones 3–5.*

Actaea rubra
Red baneberry, snakeberry
This North American species grows to 24–30 in (60–75 cm) tall and wide and has 6–18 (15–45 cm) wide leaves. The mauve-tinted white flowers are about ¼ in (6 mm) in diameter and clustered in round heads on wiry stems. The berries are bright red. *Actaea rubra* f. *neglecta* is a taller-growing form with white berries. *Zones 3–9.*

ADIANTUM
Maidenhair fern
Maidenhairs are renowned for their billowy fronds of many delicate, membranous, almost circular fresh green leaflets, each connected by a very fine blackish stalk to a repeatedly branched main stalk which is also smooth and black. Spore cases appear as tiny indentations with curled-over 'lips' around the edges of leaflets. The genus, consisting of over 200 species in all but the coldest parts of the world (the majority in the American tropics), is very varied: some species have larger, thicker, oblong or triangular leaflets without individual stalks.

Cultivation
The hardier species will thrive outdoors in shady areas, spreading by deep or

Adiantum pedatum f. billingsiae

Aegopodium podagraria 'Variegatum'

shallow rhizomes, but dislike transplanting. Tropical species, most with fronds in dense tufts, are usually grown indoors, and like strong light but not direct sun, and high humidity. Propagate from spores.

Adiantum pedatum
American maidenhair

The most frost hardy species, this ranges in the wild across cooler parts of North America, also temperate East Asia and the Himalayas. The fronds, up to 2 ft (60 cm) high, are distinctive, with wedge-shaped leaflets arranged in neat rows along radiating 'spokes' from the main stalk. Its rhizomes can spread to form a large, dense patch in a shady spot. *A. pedatum* f. *billingsiae*, a cultivated form, has broader, slightly ruffled segments of a bluish green hue. *Zones 4–9.*

AEGOPODIUM

Consisting of 5 species of perennials in the carrot family, native to Europe and Asia, this genus is known in cool-

temperate gardens only in the form of the common ground elder or goutweed—a moderately handsome plant, but detested for its rampant spread by underground rhizomes and the difficulty of eradicating it. Resembling a lower-growing version of parsnip, it has compound leaves with large, toothed leaflets and rounded umbrels of white flowers. Ground elder was once thought effective against gout, and its young shoots can be used as a green vegetable.

Cultivation

Growing ground elder is very easy. It is an effective ground cover where space allows, smothering other weeds. It does best in moist soil and partial shade. Any piece of root will grow.

Aegopodium podagraria
Ground elder, goutweed

Spreading to an indefinite width, and up to 3 ft (1 m) high, ground elder sends up its pure white umbels of bloom in summer. 'Variegatum' is sometimes grown as a ground cover: its leaflets are neatly edged white and it is slightly smaller and less aggressive than the normal green form. *Zones 3–9.*

Agapanthus praecox subsp. orientalis

Agastache foeniculum

AGAPANTHUS
African lily, agapanthus, lily-of-the-Nile
Native to southern Africa, these strong-growing perennials have fine foliage and showy flowers produced in abundance over summer. Arching, strap-shaped leaves spring from short rhizomes with dense, fleshy roots. Flowers are shades of blue (white in some cultivars) in many flowered umbels, borne on a long erect stem, often 3 ft (1 m) or more tall.

Cultivation
Agapanthus enjoy full sun but tolerate some shade, and will grow in any soil as long as they get water in spring and summer. Remove spent flower stems and dead leaves at winter's end. Propagate by division in late winter, or from seed in spring or autumn.

Agapanthus praecox
This is the most commonly grown of the 10 species. Its glorious starbursts of lavender-blue flowers appear in summer, and its densely clumped evergreen foliage is handsome in the garden all year round. It is also available in white. *Agapanthus praecox* subsp. *orientalis* has large dense umbels of blue flowers. It prefers full sun, moist soil and is marginally frost hardy. *Zones 9–11.*

AGASTACHE
This genus of some 20 species of perennials is from China, Japan and North America. Most are upright with stiff, angular stems clothed in toothed-edged, lance-shaped leaves. Heights range from 18 in–6 ft (45 cm–1.8 m) tall. Upright spikes of tubular, 2-lipped flowers develop at the stem tips in summer. Flowers are usually white, pink, mauve or purple with the bracts that back the flowers being of the same or a slightly contrasting color.

Cultivation
They like moist, well-drained soil and a sunny spot. Hardiness varies, but most tolerate occasional frosts to 20°F (–7°C). Plants can be propagated from seed or cuttings.

Agastache foeniculum
syn. *Agastache anethiodora*
Anise hyssop
This 18 in–4 ft (45 cm–1.2 m) tall, soft-stemmed North American species makes a clump of upright stems with 3 in (8 cm) leaves. Often treated as an annual, it is primarily grown for the ornamental value of its purple flower spikes. The anise-scented and flavored foliage is used to make a herbal tea or as a flavoring. *Zones 8–10.*

AGERATUM
Floss flower

While best known for the annual bedding plants derived from *Ageratum houstonianum*, this genus includes some 43 species of annuals and perennials mostly native to warmer regions of the Americas. They are clump-forming or mounding plants up to 30 in (75 cm) tall with felted or hairy, roughly oval to heart-shaped leaves with shallowly toothed or serrated edges. The flowerheads are a mass of fine filaments, usually dusky blue, lavender or pink and crowded in terminal clusters.

Cultivation

They prefer full sun and moist, well-drained soil. Propagate by spring-sown seed, either raised indoors in containers or sown directly in the garden.

Ageratum houstonianum

Native to Central America and the West Indies, this annual ageratum is popular

as a summer bedding plant. It is available in tall (12 in [30 cm]), medium (8 in [20 cm]) and dwarf (6 in [15 cm]) sizes and forms clumps of foliage with fluffy flowers in an unusual dusky blue. Pink and white forms are also available. *Zones 9–11.*

AJUGA
Bugle

About 50 species of low-growing annuals and perennials make up this genus, which ranges through Europe, Asia, Africa and Australia, mainly in cooler regions. Rosettes of soft, spatulate leaves lengthen into spikes of blue, purple or pink (rarely yellow) 2-lipped flowers. In most perennial species the plants spread by runners or underground rhizomes. They make attractive ground covers.

Cultivation

These are frost-hardy, trouble-free plants requiring moist soil and shelter from strong sun, though the bronze and variegated forms develop best color in sun. Propagate by division.

Ajuga reptans
European bugle, common bugle, blue bugle

The commonly grown ajuga spreads by surface runners, making a mat of leafy rosettes only 2–3 in (5–8 cm) high and indefinite spread. In spring it sends up spikes of deep blue flowers, up to 8 in (20 cm) high in some cultivars. The most

Ajuga reptans 'Atropurpurea'

Ajuga reptans

Ageratum houstonianum

familiar versions are: 'Atropurpurea' (syn. 'Purpurea') which has dark purple to bronze leaves; 'Burgundy Glow', with cream and maroon variegated leaves; 'Multicolor', with white, pink and purple leaves; and 'Variegata', with light green and cream leaves. *Zones 3–10.*

ALCEA
Hollyhock
Native to Turkey and the eastern Mediterranean, hollyhocks were originally called holy hock or holy mallow; it is said that plants were taken to England from the Holy Land during the Crusades. There are about 60 species in the genus. They bear flowers on spikes which may be 6 ft (1.8 m) or more high; 'dwarf' cultivars grow to 3 ft (1 m) tall.

Cultivation
They are frost hardy but need shelter from wind, benefiting from staking in exposed positions. They prefer sun, a rich, heavy well-drained soil and frequent watering in dry weather. Propagate from seed. Rust disease can be a problem; spray with fungicide.

Alcea rosea
syn. *Althaea rosea*
Hollyhock
This biennial or perennial has tall spikes of flowers which appear in summer and early autumn. Colors range from pink, purple, cream to yellow; they can be either single, flat circles 4 in (10 cm) across, or so lavishly double that they are like spheres of ruffled petals. Foliage is roundish and the plants may be as much as 10 ft (3 m) tall, erect and generally unbranched. The Chater's Double Group of cultivars have peony-shaped, double flowers. *Zones 4–10.*

ALCHEMILLA
Lady's mantle
There are some 300 species of herbaceous perennials in this Eurasian genus, as well as a few alpine species in Australia and New Zealand. They form clumps of palmate or rounded, lobed, gray-green leaves often covered in fine hairs. Branched inflorescences of tiny yellow-green flowers develop in summer. Their sizes range from 6–30 in (15–75 cm) tall and wide. Many species have styptic and other medicinal properties.

Cultivation
These hardy plants are easily grown in any well-drained soil in afternoon shade. Propagate from seed or by division.

Alchemilla mollis
Lady's mantle
Sometimes sold as *Alchemilla vulgaris*, this is the most widely cultivated species in the genus. It is a low-growing perennial ideal for ground covers, the front of borders or for rock gardens. It is clump-forming, growing to a height and spread

Alcea rosea

Alchemilla mollis

Allium giganteum

Alchemilla vetteri

Allium moly

of 16 in (about 40 cm). It has decorative, wavy edged leaves, and in summer, it bears masses of small sprays of greenish yellow flowers, similar to *Gypsophila*. Zones 4–9.

Alchemilla vetteri

This is a small species from the mountains of southwest Europe. Its flowering stems rarely exceed 8 in (20 cm) tall and the foliage clump is usually less than 12 in (30 cm) wide. The leaves have 7 to 9 lobes with toothed edges. Zones 4–9.

ALLIUM

This large genus consists of more than 700 species of bulbous perennials and biennials occurring in temperate regions of the northern hemisphere and ranging in height from 4 in–5 ft (10 cm–1.5 m). Some species are edible, including onions, garlic and chives. The ornamental species mostly come from west and central Asia. All have flowers in an umbel terminating on a small, erect stalk and sheathed in bud by membranous bracts. Bulbs can be very fat or quite slender but generally produce new bulbils at the base, sometimes also in the flower stalks.

Cultivation

They prefer a sunny, open position in fertile, well-drained, weed-free soil. They are susceptible to onion fly, stem eelworm, rust and onion white rot. Propagate from seed or bulbils.

Allium giganteum
Giant allium

Among the tallest of flowering alliums, this species has 4–6 ft (1.2–1.8 m) stems topped with dense, 4–6 in (10–15 cm) diameter umbels of violet to deep purple flowers in mid-summer. The leaves are gray-green, 18 in (45 cm) or more long. Zones 6–10.

Allium moly
Golden garlic

Native to southern Europe, in some parts of which its appearance in a garden was regarded as a sign of prosperity, *Allium moly* grows to 15 in

Allium schoenoprasum

Aloysia triphylla

(45 cm). Broad, gray-green basal leaves surround stems which each bear an umbel of up to 40 flowers. The bright yellow, star-shaped flowers appear in summer. *Moly* was the classical name of a magical herb, fancifully applied to this species by Linnaeus. *Zones 7–9.*

Allium schoenoprasum
Chives

The narrow, cylindrical leaves of this perennial plant are used for flavoring and garnishing savory dishes. Growing to 10 in (25 cm) in small, neat clumps, it bears numerous balls of mauve flowers in late spring and summer which are edible. Plant in full sun or part-shade and keep well-watered. Propagate from seed or division of small bulbs. Lift and divide the clumps every 2 or 3 years to invigorate the tufts. Chives make an attractive edging for the herb garden and can be grown in window boxes, troughs and flower pots. *Zones 5–10.*

ALOYSIA

This genus consists of around 40 species of evergreen shrubs from North, Central and South America, grown for their aromatic foliage. The branches are soft and cane-like with leaves arranged in opposite pairs or in whorls of three. Tiny flowers are borne in panicles terminating the branches.

Cultivation

They prefer a well-drained, loamy or light-textured soil and plenty of summer watering. Tolerant of only mild frosts, they do best in sunny positions in warm, coastal environments. In cold areas they should be planted out new each year. Remove dead wood in early summer and prune well in late winter. Propagate by semi-hardwood cuttings in summer or soft-tip cuttings in spring.

Aloysia triphylla
syn. *Lippia citriodora*
Lemon-scented verbena

Grown for its heavily lemon-scented, crinkly pale to mid-green leaves, this shrub has an open, rather straggling habit and reaches a height and spread of 10 ft (3 m). Racemes of dainty, light lavender flowers appear in summer and autumn. It needs regular pruning to improve its shape. Oil of verbena is produced from the leaves. *Zones 8–11.*

ALSTROEMERIA
Peruvian lily

These tuberous and rhizomatous plants with about 50 species are among the finest of perennials for cutting, but they do drop their petals. Erect, wiry stems bear scattered, thin, twisted leaves concentrated on the upper half, and terminate in umbels of outward-facing

Alstroemeria psittacina

Alstroemeria aurea

Alstroemeria, Ligtu Hybrid

flowers, usually with flaring petals that are variously spotted or streaked. They flower profusely from spring to summer.

Cultivation

All grow well in sun or light shade in a well-enriched, well-drained acidic soil. Propagate from seed or by division in early spring. Although frost hardy, dormant tubers should be covered with loose peat or dry bracken in cold winters.

Alstroemeria aurea
syn. *Alstroemeria aurantiaca*
Native to Chile and the most easily grown species, this has heads of orange flowers, tipped with green and streaked with maroon. Leaves are twisted, narrow and lance-shaped. 'Majestic' and 'Bronze Beauty' have deep orange flowers; they grow to 2–3 ft (0.6–1 m) with a similar spread. *Zones 7–9.*

Alstroemeria, Ligtu Hybrids
The well-known Ligtu Hybrids first appeared in Britain in the late 1920s, when *Alstroemeria ligtu* was crossed with *A. haemantha*. They come in a range of colors from cream to orange, red and yellow, but have been overshadowed in recent years as cut flowers by other hybrid strains derived from *A. aurea*. The plants die down soon after flowering. *Zones 7–9.*

Alstroemeria psittacina
syn. *Alstroemeria pulchella*
New Zealand Christmas bell
Though native to Brazil, *Alstroemeria psittacina* gets its common name from its popularity in New Zealand, where its crimson and green flowers are borne at Christmas. The well spaced stems, about 24 in (60 cm) high, spring from tuberous roots. Easily grown in warm-temperate climates, it can spread rapidly and be difficult to eradicate. *Zones 8–10.*

AMARANTHUS
The 60 or so species of annuals and short-lived perennials in this genus from tropical and warm-temperate areas are grown for their brilliant foliage, curious flowers and adaptability to hot, dry conditions. The minute flowers are borne in drooping tassel-like spikes.

Cultivation
They need a sunny, dry position with protection from strong winds, and a fertile, well-drained soil, mulched during hot weather. Propagate from seed.

Amaranthus caudatus
Love-lies-bleeding, tassel flower

This species, growing to 4 ft (1.2 m) or more high, has oval, dull green leaves and dark red flowers in long, drooping cords, their ends often touching the ground. Flowers appear in summer through to autumn. In many old gardens this plant was used to give height in the center of circular beds. *Zones 8–11.*

Amaranthus tricolor

Native to tropical Africa and Asia, this quick-growing annual has given rise to many cultivated strains, some used as leaf vegetables (Chinese spinach), others as bedding plants with brilliantly colored leaves. They are bushy annuals, reaching about 3 ft (1 m) high and 18 in (45 cm) wide. Tiny red flowers appear in

Amaranthus caudatus

Ammi majus

summer. 'Joseph's Coat' has brilliant bronze, gold, orange and red variegated 8 in (20 cm) long leaves which retain their coloring into late autumn. *Zones 8–11.*

AMMI

Six species of carrot-like perennials belong to this genus, occurring wild in the Mediterranean region, western Asia and the Canary Islands. They are fairly typical umbellifers with large, ferny basal leaves and flowering stems bearing large umbels of numerous small white flowers. *Ammi* was the classical Greek and Latin name for a plant of this type, though its exact identity is uncertain.

Cultivation

Usually treated as annuals, they are easily grown in a sheltered but sunny position in any reasonable garden soil, kept fairly moist. Propagate from seed in spring. They usually self-seed once established.

Ammi majus
Bishop's weed

Native to the Mediterranean region and western Asia, this species has become widely naturalized in other continents. It grows to about 24–36 in (60–90 cm) tall, producing a succession of large, lacy flowering heads in summer and autumn. The cut flowers are sometimes sold in florists' shops. *Zones 6–10.*

Amaranthus tricolor 'Joseph's Coat'

AMPELOPSIS

This is a genus of about 5 species of deciduous vines in the grape family, occurring wild in temperate Asia and North America. Climbing by tendrils, they have leaves that are compound with radiating leaflets, or simple and toothed. Insignificant flowers are followed by small, rather dry berries, mostly bluish or blackish.

Cultivation

Grow in a sunny or partially shaded position in a moisture-retentive, but well-drained soil. They are fully hardy, grow rapidly and need strong support with plenty of room to spread. Cut back hard to the main branches when berries have finished. Propagate from cuttings in summer or by layering in fall.

Ampelopsis brevipedunculata

syns *Ampelopsis heterophylla, Vitis heterophylla*

Turquoise-berry vine, porcelain vine

This vigorous climber will twine, with the aid of tendrils, 15 ft (4.5 m) or more. It has grape-like, lobed leaves, small greenish flowers in summer, and in autumn bunches of berries like minia-

ture grapes that ripen from pale green to turquoise, bright blue and violet. The leaves of *A. brevipedunculata* var. *maximowiczii* are variable and larger than the species. The cultivar *A. b.* 'Elegans' has white and pink marbled leaves. *Zones 4–9.*

AMSONIA

Blue star

This genus of around 20 species of perennials and subshrubs, native to southern Europe, western Asia, Japan and North America, grow to around 3 ft (1 m) tall and have bright to deep green, narrow, lance-shaped leaves. The flowers, borne mainly in summer, are tubular with widely flared mouths. They are carried in phlox-like heads at the stem tips.

Cultivation

Amsonias are easily grown in any moist, well-drained soil. Plant in full sun or part-shade. They are moderately to very frost hardy and generally die back to the rootstock in winter. Propagation is from seed, early summer cuttings or by division.

Amsonia tabernaemontana

Blue star, blue dogbane

This delightful perennial from northeastern and central USA has stiff stems, 24–36 in (60–90 cm) tall, which are topped by pyramidal clusters of small,

Amsonia tabernaemontana

Ampelopsis brevipedunculata

Anaphalis margaritacea

Anchusa azurea 'Lodden Royalist'

star-shaped flowers of pale blue from late spring to summer, flowering along with peonies and irises. The leaves are narrow to elliptical. It needs minimal care if given moist, fertile soil in full sun to light shade, and suits a perennial border or damp wildflower meadow. *Zones 3–9.*

ANAPHALIS
Pearl everlasting
This genus of around 100 species of gray-foliaged perennials has narrow, lance-shaped leaves which are often clothed in cobwebby hairs attached directly to upright stems. Panicles on clusters of papery white flowerheads terminate the stems in summer or autumn. Heights range from 6–30 in (15–75 cm) depending on the species. They are good cut flowers, and the foliage and flowers are just as decorative when dried.

Cultivation
Plant in light, gritty, well-drained soil in full sun. They do not like being wet but when in active growth the soil should not be allowed to dry out. Prune in winter. Propagate from seed or division.

Anaphalis margaritacea
syn. *Anaphalis yedoensis*
Pearl everlasting
Native to North America, Europe and Asia, this perennial has papery, small yellow flowers which can be dried. It has lance-shaped, silvery gray leaves and the

flowers are borne on erect stems in late summer. Bushy in habit, it grows to about 24–30 in (60–75 cm) high and about 24 in (60 cm) wide. It prefers a sunny situation (but will grow in part-shade). *Zones 4–9.*

ANCHUSA
Alkanet, summer forget-me-not
This genus consists of about 50 species of annuals, biennials and perennials. Many have a weedy habit and undistinguished foliage, but they bear flowers of a wonderful sapphire blue, which are carried in clusters over a long spring and early summer season. They suit herbaceous borders, beds and containers.

Cultivation
Frost hardy, they like a sunny spot in deep, rich, well-drained soil. In hot areas planting in part-shade helps maintain flower color. Feed sparingly; water generously. Propagate perennials by division in winter, annuals and biennials from seed in autumn or spring.

Anchusa azurea
syn. *Anchusa italica*
Italian alkanet
Occurring wild around the Mediterranean, and the Black Sea, this species is

Androsace sarmentosa

Anchusa capensis 'Blue Angel'

an upright perennial up to 3–4 ft (1–1.2 m) high and 24 in (60 cm) wide. It has coarse, hairy leaves and an erect habit with tiers of brilliant blue flowers borne in spring to summer. Cultivars differ in their precise shade of blue: rich blue 'Morning Glory', light blue 'Opal' and the intense deep blue of 'Loddon Royalist'. *Zones 3–9.*

Anchusa capensis
Cape forget-me-not

From southern Africa, this species is biennial in cool climates, but in warm-temperate gardens it can be sown very early in spring to bear intense blue flowers in summer. It grows to 15 in (40 cm) tall and wide. 'Blue Angel' reaches a height and spread of 8 in (20 cm) bearing shallow, bowl-shaped sky-blue flowers in early summer. *Zones 8–10.*

ANDROSACE
Rock jasmine

This genus consists of around 100 species of annuals and perennials from cooler regions of the northern hemi-sphere. The low-growing perennials form dense mats or cushions no more than 4 in (10 cm) high. Most have light green or silvery gray, loose rosettes of foliage crowded along prostrate stems, topped with umbels of small white or pink 5-petalled flowers in spring and summer.

Cultivation

They like sunny, well-drained scree or rock garden conditions with free-draining gravel-based soil and additional humus. Most are quite frost hardy. Propagate from seed, cuttings or self-rooted layers.

Androsace carnea

This 2 in (5 cm) high, cushion-forming evergreen perennial from the mountains of southern Europe has fine, pointed leaves with hairy edges. Short-stemmed heads of pink flowers develop in spring. It is an excellent container or alpine house plant. *A. carnea* subsp. *laggeri* has deep pink flowers on longer stems. *Zones 5–9.*

Androsace sarmentosa

This is a Himalayan perennial species that spreads by runners. It forms patches of rosettes of small, oval leaves with a covering of fine silvery hairs. Large heads of yellow-centered, pink flowers on 4 in (10 cm) stalks are borne in spring. 'Brilliant' has darker mauve-pink flowers. *Zones 3–8.*

ANEMONE
Windflower

There are over 100 species of perennials in this genus and all have tufts of basal leaves that are divided in palmate fashion into few to many leaflets. The starry or bowl-shaped flowers have 5 or more petals. They can be divided into the autumn flowering species with fibrous roots, such as *A. hupehensis* and *A. × hybrida*, and the tuberous and rhizomatous types, usually spring flowering, which include the ground-hugging *A. blanda* and *A. nemorosa*. Replace tuberous-rooted types every 1–2 years.

Cultivation
Most are frost hardy and do well in rich, moist yet well-drained soil in a lightly shaded position. Propagate from seed planted in summer or divide established clumps in early winter.

Anemone blanda
This delicate-looking tuberous species is frost hardy. Native to Greece and Turkey, it grows to 8 in (20 cm) with crowded tufts of ferny leaves. White, pink or blue star-shaped flowers appear in spring. It self-seeds freely and, given moist, slightly shaded conditions, should spread into a beautiful display of flowers. Popular cultivars include 'Atrocaerulea', with deep blue flowers; and 'Radar' with white-centered magenta flowers. *Zones 6–9.*

Anemone coronaria
Wind poppy, florist's anemone
This frost hardy species dies back to small woody tubers; these are sold in

Anemone coronaria St. Brigid Group

packets, the plants being treated almost as annuals. They grow to about 10 in (25 cm) high, and the poppy-like flowers range in color from pink to scarlet, purple or blue. The St Brigid Group has double flowers. It is excellent as a cut flower. *Zones 8–10.*

Anemone hupehensis
Japanese wind flower
This species from central and western China (long cultivated in Japan), can be almost evergreen in milder climates where, if conditions suit, it may spread and provide good ground cover, producing its single white to mauve flowers on tall, openly branched stems during early autumn. *Anemone hupehensis* var. *japonica* is taller and has more petals than the wild Chinese plants. It includes 'Prinz Heinrich' (Prince Henry) with 10 or more deep rose-pink petals, paler on the undersides. Most of the cultivars ascribed to this species are now placed under *Anemone × hybrida*. *Zones 6–10.*

Anemone × hybrida
These popular hybrids have flowers in all shades from white to deepest rose, the petals numbering from 5 to over 30. They generally lack fertile pollen. The robust plants may reach heights of 5 ft (1.5 m) in flower. There are over 30

Anemone blanda 'Atrocaerulea'

cultivars, including 'Honorine Jobert' with pure white, 6–9-petaled flowers and dark green leaves. *Zones 6–10*.

ANETHUM
Dill

This well-known herb genus includes two species occurring wild in Europe and temperate Asia. The commonly cultivated dill *(Anethum graveolens)* is an annual, the other a biennial. Dill has a long, wiry root from which develops an upright, hollow stem with ferny foliage. Umbels of tiny bright yellow flowers develop at the stem tip and are followed by the pungent seeds. Dill is widely used in pickling and fish dishes. The foliage is best used before flowering. It also has medicinal uses, these days most notably as an indigestion remedy.

Cultivation
Only moderately frost hardy, dill is easliy grown in any moist well-drained, humus-rich soil in sun. The seed is best sown in spring where it is to grow, as seedlings are difficult to transplant. Dill often self-sows.

Anethum graveolens
Dill

Originally from southwestern Asia, this deliciously aromatic annual grows to about 3 ft (1 m) high with leaves divided into thread-like, fragile segments. Yellow

flowers are borne in summer followed by the pungent dill seeds. Both leaves and seeds are used for flavoring. *Zones 5–10*.

ANGELICA

This genus of 50 or so northern hemisphere species has a bold palm-like leaf structure. The bunches of pale green flowers on tall stems have a pleasant aroma.

Cultivation
They prefer moist, well-drained, rich soil in sun or shade. Angelica will self-sow or can be propagated from seed.

Angelica archangelica
A fast-growing, robust biennial, this species was valued for centuries for its medicinal uses — to relieve toothache, to dispel 'phrenzies of the head', and to protect against plague. The young stems are used, and are most familiar as a candied green garnish for sweet dishes. It grows to 6 ft (1.8 m). Cut back flowerheads to ensure leaf production. It has deeply divided, bright green leaves and umbels of small flowers in late summer, and does best in filtered sunlight. Protect from strong winds. *Zones 4–9*.

ANIGOZANTHOS
Kangaroo paw
These evergreen Western Australian perennials have unique bird-attracting,

Angelica archangelica

Anemone × hybrida 'Honorine Jobert'

tubular flowers, the outsides coated with dense shaggy hairs and opening at the apex into 6 'claws', the whole resembling an animal's paw. Foliage is grass-like, and species can range in height from 1–6 ft (0.3–1.8 m). Flowers come in many colors including green, gold, deep red and orange-red.

Cultivation
They prefer warm, very well-drained sandy or gravelly soil and a hot, sunny, open position. Water well during dry seasons. Most tolerate light frosts and drought. Propagate by division in spring or from fresh seed. Plants are often affected by ink disease, a fungus which blackens the foliage.

Anigozanthos Bush Gems Series
The best of the kangaroo paws for their resistance to ink disease, the Bush Gems hybrids are mostly of compact size, with flowers ranging from yellow, gold and green through to orange, red and burgundy. 'Bush Heritage' is a cultivar of 12–20 in (30–50 cm) high with flowers of burnt terracotta and olive green. 'Bush Twilight' has prolific flowers in muted orange, yellow and green tones. 'Bush Gold' has golden yellow flowers. *Zones 9–11.*

Anigozanthos 'Regal Claw'
One of the many striking cultivars with parents listed as *Anigozanthos preissii* and *A. flavidus*, 'Regal Claw' is a dwarf plant with flowers of orange with a red felted overlay. *Zones 9–11.*

ANTENNARIA
Cat's ears, ladies' tobacco
A genus of around 45 species of ever-green to near-evergreen perennials of the daisy family from temperate regions of the northern hemisphere, most species form dense mats of leaf rosettes that root

Anigozanthos 'Regal Claw'

Anigozanthos Bush Gems Series, 'Bush Gold'

as they spread; a few are mounding and up to 15 in (38 cm) tall. The narrow, crowded leaves are usually bracts surrounding a disc of petal-less florets, the heads clustered on short stems.

Cultivation
Most species are very frost hardy and are best grown in moist, well-drained soil in full sun or morning shade. Propagate from seed or division.

Antennaria dioica
Catsfoot
A stoloniferous perennial occurring wild in the colder parts of the northern hemi-

Anthemis tinctoria

Antennaria dioica 'Australis'

sphere. It forms a mat of rosettes of narrow spatula- to lance-shaped leaves, dark green above but white-woolly on the undersides. In summer, strong 8 in (20 cm) tall flower stems develop bearing clusters of white, pink or yellow flowerheads. Catsfoot is unusual among composites (daisies) in having different sexes on different plants (dioecious), the female flowerheads larger than the male. An attractive ground cover or rock garden plant, it also has some medicinal uses. *Antennaria dioica* 'Australis' has silvery gray stems topped with clusters of white flowers. *Zones 5–9.*

ANTHEMIS

There are 100 or so species of this genus of annuals and perennials. Belonging to the larger daisy family, the flowerheads have the typical daisy shape and are generally white, cream or yellow with distinctive contrasting disc florets. Most species have somewhat aromatic, finely dissected foliage in shades of green or silver gray, which makes them ideal in the mixed border or rock garden.

Cultivation

They flower best in full sun and like well-drained soil. The perennials can be short-lived and often become untidy, but cutting back after flowering ensures a more shapely plant. They are easily replaced by cuttings taken in summer or by division in fall or spring. Annual species can be grown from seed.

Anthemis tinctoria
Dyer's chamomile, golden Marguerite

Native to Europe and western Asia, this is a very hardy, easily grown perennial that is covered in late spring and summer with a dazzling display of daisy flowers above fern-like, crinkled green leaves. The plant mounds to as much as 3 ft (1 m) high if supported on a rockery or a bank. The flowers of this species were once used to make a yellow dye. The cultivar 'E. C. Buxton' has subtle soft yellow blooms blending beautifully with the fine foliage. *Zones 4–10.*

ANTIGONON
Coral vine

This is a Mexican and Central American genus of three species of tendril climber, only one of which is widely cultivated. They are tender evergreens that behave as deciduous perennials in cold-winter areas if the roots are protected from freezing. The leaves are dark green and heart-shaped with wavy edges. The dense foliage canopy is decked with trailing sprays of clustered racemes of small flowers, appearing over a long season. Only the heart-shaped sepals, tightly pressed together, provide the color, which ranges from the deepest coral to quite pale pink or even white.

Cultivation

They thrive in any well-drained soil in a warm spot but require ample summer moisture. The top dies back at temperatures just below freezing and the roots die if the soil freezes. Propagate from seed, cuttings or divsion of the rootstock.

Antigonon leptopus
Coral vine, chain of love

This is a fast growing, showy creeper that may grow to 25 ft (8 m) or more. It bears masses of deep pink, heart-shaped flowers from early summer to autumn, and is ideal for trellises, pergolas and arbors where a light cover is desirable. *Zones 9–11.*

ANTIRRHINUM
Snapdragon

The resemblance of snapdragon flowers to the face of a beast was noted by the ancient Greeks, who called them *Antirrhinon*, nose-like. In French they are *gueule de loup*, wolf's mouth, and in German and Italian the name means lion's mouth. The genus consists of about 40 species, most from the western Mediterranean region but with a few from western North America. They include annuals, perennials and evergreen subshrubs. The garden snapdragon (*A. majus*) is a perennial but many treat it as an annual.

Antigonon leptopus

Cultivation

They prefer fertile, well-drained soil in full sun. Propagate from seed.

Antirrhinum majus
Garden snapdragon

This bushy short-lived perennial bears showy flowers from spring to autumn. The many named cultivars, usually grown as annuals, have a spread of 12–18 in (30–45 cm) and range from tall: 30 in (75 cm); to medium: 18 in (45 cm); to dwarf: 10 in (25 cm). Treat garden snapdragons as annuals—they rarely flower well after the first year, and old plants often succumb antirrhinum rust. Deadhead to prolong flowering and pinch out early buds to increase branching. The Coronette Series of F1 hybrids exemplifies some of the qualities plant geneticists are injecting into their breeding programs. These include tolerance of bad weather, extra large blooms on heavy spikes and uniformity from seedling stage. Two popular cultivars of *A. majus* are 'Flower Carpet' and 'Madame Butterfly'. *Zones 6–10.*

AQUILEGIA
Columbine

These clump-forming perennials have spurred, bell-shaped—single and double

Antirrhinum majus

forms—flowers in a varied color range, and fern-like foliage. Some make good cut flowers, and the dwarf and alpine species make good rock-garden plants. They flower mostly in late spring and early summer, and look best in bold clumps.

Cultivation

Frost hardy, they prefer a well-drained light soil, enriched with manure, and a sunny site protected from strong winds. In cold climates columbines are perennials and need to be cut to the ground in late winter. Propagate by division or from seed in autumn and spring; many of them self-seed readily.

Aquilegia canadensis
American wild columbine

This native of eastern North America produces masses of nodding, red and yellow flowers with medium-length spurs, on 18–24 in (45–60 cm) stems in late spring and early summer. It tolerates full sun, provided there is plenty of moisture. It also tolerates heat if some shade is provided. *Zones 3–9.*

Aquilegia 'Crimson Star'

These long-spurred aquilegias usually face their flowers upwards, in contrast to the pendent flowers of the short-spurred granny's bonnets. The nectar spurs, which in other aquilegias normally match the color of the petals of which they are a prolongation, match the crimson of the sepals in this cultivar. *Zones 3–10.*

Aquilegia McKana Hybrids

The McKana Hybrids are derived chiefly from *Aquilegia caerulea*, *A. chrysantha* and *A. formosa*. They bear flowers in a variety of colors in late spring and early summer. Whatever the color of the sepals, the 5 petals that carry the spurs are usually white or yellow. Pinching off spent flowers will prolong the season. The plants grow to 3 ft (1 m) or more. *Zones 3–10.*

Aquilegia vulgaris
Granny's bonnets, columbine

This European columbine grows to 3 ft (1 m) high with a spread of 18 in (45 cm) or more. On long stems from the center of a loose rosette of gray-green foliage, it bears funnel-shaped, short-spurred flowers, typically dull blue in wild plants but ranging through pink, crimson,

Aquilegia canadensis

Aquilegia 'Crimson Star'

Aquilegia McKana Hybrid

Aquilegia vulgaris 'Nora Barlow'

Arabis caucasica

Arabis blepharophylla

white and purple in garden varieties. 'Nora Barlow' has curious double flowers, with many narrow, greenish sepals and pink petals. *Zones 3–10.*

ARABIS
Rock cress

Over 120 species make up this northern hemisphere genus of annuals and perennials, the latter mostly evergreen. Although some can reach as much as 3 ft (1 m) in height, species grown in gardens are dwarf, often mat-forming perennials suited to the rock garden, dry walls and crevices. They spread by short rhizomes, producing crowded tufts of spatula-shaped leaves. Short sprays of delicate, 4-petaled flowers are held above the foliage in spring and summer.

Cultivation

They grow best in well-drained soil in a sunny position. Propagate from seed or cuttings in summer, or by division.

Arabis blepharophylla
California rock cress

This is a moderately frost-hardy species native to California, where it grows at low altitudes. Forming a compact clump 4–6 in (10–15 cm) high, it has tufts of toothed green leaves that extend into short, leafy spikes of pink to purple flowers during spring. It is best planted in a rockery or crevice where it will not be overrun. The cultivar 'Frühlingzauber' ('Spring Charm') has rich, rose-purple flowers. *Zones 7–10.*

Arabis caucasica
syn. *Arabis albida*
Wall rock cress

This tough, evergreen perennial is sometimes used to overplant spring-flowering bulbs. It forms dense clusters of thick foliage up to 6 in (15 cm) high with a spread of 18 in (45 cm). In spring it has white flowers on loose racemes above gray-green leaf rosettes. There are various forms, such as 'Pinkie', *A. c.* var. *brevifolia* and double-flowered forms such as 'Flore Pleno'. *Zones 4–10.*

ARCTOTIS
syns *Venidium*, × *Venidio-arctotis*
African daisy

The stems and leaves of this South African genus of about 50 species of

Arctotis fastuosa

Arctotis Hybrid, 'Apricot'

annuals and evergreen perennials, are coated in matted downy hairs, giving them a gray-green or silvery gray color. The flowers are typical of the daisy family. They need the sun to open fully, and colors range from creamy yellow through orange to deep pinks and claret reds. Growth habit varies from compact and shrubby to prostrate.

Cultivation
Given plenty of space in full sun and well-drained, sandy soil, arctotises may be used as bedding plants or to cover a large area of dry bank. Propagate from seed or cuttings.

Arctotis fastuosa
syn. *Venidium fastuosum*
Cape daisy, monarch of the veld
This adaptable perennial can be treated as an annual in colder regions. It will grow 24 in (60 cm) high, with silvery green, lobed leaves and glistening orange flowerheads with purple zones at the base of each of the many ray petals and a black central disc. It is a colorful choice for a sunny position in the garden. *Zones 9–11.*

Arctotis Hybrids
These plants are grown as annual bedding plants in frost-prone areas but will overwinter in milder climates. Growing to a height and spread of around 18 in (45 cm), they have gray, lobed leaves that are quite downy

beneath. In summer and autumn they produce a long succession of showy blooms, to 3 in (8 cm) across in a very wide range of colors, often 2-toned. 'Gold Bi-Color', 'Apricot', 'Dream Coat' and 'Wine' are among the more popular named hybrids. *Zones 9–11.*

ARENARIA
Sandwort
This genus consists of some 160 species of mainly mound-forming or ground cover perennials, some of which become shrubby with age. They are widespread in the northern hemisphere, with a few southern hemisphere species too. The plants commonly develop a dense mass of fine stems clothed with tiny, deep green or gray-green leaves and small, usually white, flowers in spring or summer. The flowers may be borne singly or in small clusters.

Cultivation
They are easily grown in any moist, well-drained soil in full sun. They are ideal rock garden or tub plants and are generally very frost hardy. Propagate from seed, self-rooted layers or small tip cuttings.

Arenaria montana
This species from southwest Europe is larger than most arenarias in both leaves and flowers. It has gray-green leaves up to 1½ in (35 mm) long and mounds to about 6 in (15 cm) tall. Its flowering stems tend to be rather upright and

extend slightly above the foliage clump. The abundant flowers are pure white with yellow-green centers. *Zones 4–9.*

ARISAEMA
Jack in the pulpit

This genus of the arum family consists of around 150 species of tuberous or rhizomatous perennials found in temperate to tropical parts of the northern hemisphere. Their foliage is variable and they often have only one or two leaves per shoot. The leaves are usually divided, sometimes finely, and make a frilled base to the erect, flowering stem that emerges through the center of the foliage. The flowering stems carry a single flower spike in spring or early summer. The bloom has a central spadix of minute, fleshy flowers surrounded by a greenish spathe. Heads of fleshy red fruit follow the flowers.

Cultivation

Most tolerate moderate to severe frosts and prefer woodland conditions with moist, humus-rich soil and dappled shade. Propagate from seed or offsets.

Arisaema triphyllum

This distinctive wildflower of North America's northeastern woodlands flowers in spring before the trees leaf.

Arenaria montana

One or two medium green leaves, each divided into 3 leaflets, expand to a height of about 12 in (30 cm) after the flowers fade. The slender spadix is enclosed by a spathe of pale green to purple-brown. For best results, gardeners should only buy plants that have been nursery-propagated. *Zones 4–9.*

ARMERIA
Thrift, sea pink

This genus of about 35 species of low-growing, tufted, early summer-flowering perennials is found in a wide variety of environments in temperate Eurasia, Africa and the Americas—from salt marshes and storm-swept headlands of the seashores to alpine meadows. The plants have crowded, narrow, mostly evergreen leaves, usually forming a dense mound, and small flowers crowded into globular heads, each atop a slender stalk.

Cultivation

They suit rock gardens or borders and prefer exposed, sunny positions and rather dry soil with good drainage. They are generally frost hardy. Propagate from seed or cuttings.

Arisaema triphyllum

Armeria maritima
Common thrift, sea pink

Native around much of the northern hemisphere and consisting of many wild races, thrift was in cultivation as early as 1578. Growing to 4 in (10 cm) high and spreading to 8 in (20 cm), it has a mound-like mass of narrow, dark green leaves, and dense flowerheads of small, white to pink flowers are produced in spring and summer. Most *Armeria* cultivars are derived from this species. 'Vindictive' has vibrant rose-pink flowers. 'Alba' has small white flowers. *Zones 4–9.*

ARTEMISIA
Wormwood

This large genus of some 300 species of perennials and shrubs is native to temperate regions of the northern hemisphere, many from arid and semi-arid environments. They have decorative foliage which is often aromatic and sometimes repellent to insects; in many species it is coated with whitish hairs. It makes an attractive addition to a flower border. The small yellowish flowerheads are not showy. There are both evergreen and deciduous species.

Cultivation

Mostly quite frost hardy, they prefer an open, sunny situation with light, well-drained soil. Prune lightly in spring. Propagate from cuttings in summer or by division in spring.

Armeria maritima

Artemisia ludoviciana
syn. *Artemisia purshiana*
Western mugwort, white sage

Native to western North America and Mexico, this rhizomatous species has lance-shaped, sometimes coarsely toothed leaves, which are densely white-felted beneath and gray- to white-haired above. Bell-shaped, grayish flowerheads are produced in summer. A spreading, invasive species, it reaches a height of 4 ft (1.2 m) and is very frost hardy. *Zones 4–10.*

Artemisia 'Powis Castle'

This assumed hybrid between *Artemisia absinthium* and *A. arborescens* has finely dissected, silvery leaves, a gentle, 24–36 in (60–90 cm) mounding habit and because it seldom flowers, it remains more compact than other species; older plants benefit from a hard cutting back in early

Artemisia 'Powis Castle'

Artemisia ludoviciana

Arum italicum

Aruncus dioicus

spring. In cold climates, grow indoors over winter for planting out in spring. *Zones 6–10.*

ARUM

Although many plants are called arums, only a few truly belong to this genus, consisting of some 25 species from the Mediterranean region and western Asia. Only 2 or 3 are widely available. They are tuberous perennials with broad, fleshy leaves, usually arrow-shaped and often variegated with a paler green along the veins. The true flowers are minute, carried in the finger-like spadix that terminates the thick flower stalk; the spadix in turn is encircled by the more conspicuous spathe, or bract.

Cultivation
The species described below is easily grown in part shade in moist but well-drained, humus-rich soil, and requires no attention. Propagate by division after the foliage dies back, or from seed in autumn.

Arum italicum
Italian arum
Growing to 12 in (30 cm), this species from Europe and North Africa has

broad, arrow-shaped, marbled leaves in autumn. Appearing in early spring, the flower spike has a light green, hooded spathe with a yellowish spadix standing erect in the center. It is followed by orange berries that last until late summer. *Zones 7–10.*

ARUNCUS
Goat's beard
There are 3 species in this genus of rhizomatous perennials, occurring widely over temperate and subarctic regions of the northern hemisphere. Their appearance is like the giant astilbe, with ferny basal leaves up to 3 ft (1 m) long and summer plumes of tiny cream flowers in 8–18 in (20–45 cm) long, pyramidal panicles carried on wiry stems that hold them well above the foliage.

Cultivation
They prefer sun or part-shade and moist, humus-rich, well-drained soil around edges of ponds. It is frost hardy. Propagate from seed or by division.

Aruncus dioicus
syns *Aruncus sylvestris*, *Spiraea aruncus*
A graceful, woodland perennial, this clump-forming plant produces a mass of

Asarum caudatum

Asarum europaeum

rich green, fern-like foliage and arching plumes of tiny, greenish or creamy white flowers in summer. It grows 6 ft (1.8 m) tall and 4 ft (1.2 m) wide. Cut flowering stems back hard in autumn. 'Kneiffii' reaches about 3 ft (1 m) and has cream-colored flowers. *Zones 3–9.*

ASARUM
Wild ginger

This genus consists of over 70 species of rhizomatous perennials, both evergreen and deciduous, distributed widely through temperate areas of the northern hemisphere but most numerous in Japan and the USA. They are better known for their use in traditional medicine than as ornamental plants, though the foliage can make an attractive ground cover in shaded woodland gardens. The leaves are either kidney- or heart-shaped, and the small, bell-shaped flowers, which are usually hidden below the leaves, are mostly dull brownish or purplish and open at the mouth into 3 sharply reflexed sepals.

Cultivation

They prefer a shady site in moist, well-drained soil and can be planted out at any time between autumn and spring. They spread rapidly; divide the clumps every few years in spring, or propagate from seed.

Asarum caudatum
British Columbia wild ginger

Native to the coastal mountains of western North America, this ground-hugging, evergreen perennial grows in relatively deep shade on the forest floor. Spreading by rhizomes, it forms irregular, open patches and flowers from late spring into summer. Large, 6 in (15 cm) long, kidney-shaped leaves rise to 8 in (20 cm) above ground, hiding the brownish purple blooms. *Zones 6–9.*

Asarum europaeum
Asarabacca

Widely distributed in European woodlands, this species has conspicuous shaggy hairs on both the creeping rhizomes and the 4–6 in (10–15 cm) long leaf stalks. The deep-green, glossy leaves are kidney-shaped to almost circular, up to 3 in (8 cm) wide. The dull purplish flowers, hidden under the leaves, are insignificant, only about $\frac{1}{2}$ in (12 mm) long. Asarabacca was formerly used medicinally and as an ingredient of snuff powders, but it is moderately toxic. *Zones 6–9.*

ASCLEPIAS
Milkweed

Found naturally in the Americas, this genus consists of over 100 species of

Asclepias speciosa

Asperula arcadiensis

perennials, subshrubs and (rarely) shrubs and includes both evergreen and deciduous plants. Most have narrow, pointed elliptical to lance-shaped leaves and all have milky white sap. The small flowers are borne in stalked clusters arising from the upper leaf axils. They have 5 reflexed petals below a waxy corona. Elongated seed pods with silky plumes follow. The sap is poisonous.

Cultivation
They grow in any well-drained soil in full sun. Hardiness varies with the species. Some shorter-lived perennials may be treated as annuals, and are usually raised from seed. Some hardier North American species require a cool climate and will not survive where winters are too warm. Propagate from seed or semi-ripe cuttings.

Asclepias speciosa
A 3 ft (1 m) tall perennial from eastern North America, this species has oval leaves up to 6 in (15 cm) long. The flowers are dull pinkish red and white and up to 1 in (25 mm) in diameter. The fruit have soft spines. *Zones 2–9.*

Asclepias tuberosa
Butterfly weed
One of North America's brightest meadow wildflowers, this widely

distributed, 24–36 in (60–90 cm), mounding perennial with a tuberous rootstock produces broad heads of small orange (sometimes yellow or red) flowers during summer. It is very popular with butterflies. *Zones 3–9.*

ASPERULA
Woodruff
There are around 100 species of annuals, perennials and subshrubs in this European and Asian genus. Most are densely foliaged mat- or tuft-forming perennials with tiny, narrow leaves arranged in whorls of 4 or more on fine stems. In spring and summer the plants may be smothered in tiny flowers, usually white, pale pink, sometimes yellow. Most spread by under-ground runners and a few woodland species grow to about 24 in (60 cm) high.

Cultivation
They like gritty, well-drained soil and full sun. Propagate from seed, from small rooted pieces removed from the clump, or by division.

Asperula arcadiensis
This perennial Greek species makes a woody based tuft of foliage up to 6 in (15 cm) high. The narrow leaves are gray and downy, $^1/_2$ in (12 mm) or so long. The tiny flowers are pink to pale purple. *Zones 5–9.*

ASTER
Michaelmas or Easter daisy, aster

This genus of perennials and deciduous or evergreen subshrubs contains over 250 species, ranging in height from miniatures to 6 ft (1.8 m) giants. Showy, daisy-like flowerheads are usually produced in late summer or autumn in a wide range of colors, including blue, violet, purple, pink, red and white, all with a central disc of yellow or purple.

Cultivation
They prefer sun (or part-shade in hot areas) in a well-drained soil. Keep moist, and shelter from strong winds. Cut the long stems down to ground level and tidy the clumps when the flowers have faded. Propagate by division in spring or late fall, or from softwood cuttings in spring. Divide plants every 2 to 3 years.

Aster ericoides
Heath aster
The specific name means 'with leaves like those of *Erica*', the heath genus, and indeed this American species has small, narrow leaves, at least on the upper stems. With flowering stems rising up to 3 ft (1 m) high from tufted basal shoots towards mid-summer and into autumn, it provides a lovely display of massed, small, white flowerheads as does one of its more compact cultivars, 'White Heather'. *Zones 4–10.*

Aster ericoides 'White Heather'

Aster × frikartii
A garden hybrid between *Aster amellus* and the Himalayan *A. thomsonii*, the original areas with very large, violet-blue flowerheads is still popular despite the addition of a number of newer cultivars. It is a rather narrowly clumping plant about 30 in (75 cm) high. 'Mönch' is a very free-flowering plant to 15 in (38 cm) with clear blue, long-lasting blooms; 'Wunder von Stäfa' is taller, to 24 in (60 cm) with lavender blue blooms. *Zones 5–9.*

Aster novae-angliae
New England aster
Originally native over a wide area of the eastern and central USA, this species is represented in cultivation by many cultivars, showing much variation in form and color of blooms. Vigorous clumps of mostly vertical, 3–5 ft (1–1.5 m) stems are likely to lean with the weight of large, loose clusters of daisies, making staking necessary. Cultivars include the late-blooming, clear pink 'Harrington's Pink'; and the rose-pink, mildew-resistant 'Barr's Pink'. *Zones 4–9.*

Aster novi-belgii
New York aster
Novi-belgii is Linnaeus' attempt to translate New Amsterdam (now New

Aster novae-angliae 'Barr's Pink'

Aster novi-belgii 'Ernest Ballard'

York) into Latin; the Belgii were the tribe encountered by Julius Caesar in the Low Countries. The New York aster in its wild form is native to the east coast, from Newfoundland to Georgia. It has given rise to innumerable garden forms in colors ranging from the palest mauve to violet and deep pink, and with varying degrees of 'doubling' of the flowerheads. They are among the most useful plants for the perennial border in cooler-temperate climates. 'Ernest Ballard', named for a leading aster breeder, grows to 3 ft (1 m) with large, purple-red blooms. *Zones 3–9.*

ASTILBE
False spiraea

The 14 species in this genus of early to late summer perennials have basal tufts of ferny, compound leaves, the leaflets usually sharply toothed. Pointed, plume-like panicles of tiny, white to pink or red flowers rise above the foliage. Most usual in cultivation are the *Astilbe × arendsii* hybrids, though there are many recent hybrid cultivars of different parentage. The name 'spiraea' was mistakenly attached to this genus when they were introduced to England in the 1820s.

Cultivation

They need a lightly shaded place with rich, leafy soil that never dries out, though they do not like being flooded. Cooler climates suit them best. They make good cut flowers and indoor plants. Propagate by division in winter.

Astilbe, Arendsii Hybrids

This attractive hybrid group, derived from four east Asian species, is named after German horticulturalist Georg Arends (1863–1952) to whom many of the finest cultivars are credited. Heights vary from 18–48 in (0.45 cm–1.2 m),

Astilbe, Arendsii Hybrid 'Europa'

with a spread of 18–30 in (45–75 cm). They produce feathery spikes in a wide color range from late spring to early summer. Cultivars are available in a range of colors from red through pink to white, and include 'Amethyst', with pale purple to pink flowers; 'Fanal' with long-lasting scarlet flowers; 'Rheinland' with deep rose flowers; and 'Europa', with pale pink flowers. *Zones 6–10.*

ASTRANTIA
Masterwort

All 10 species of this genus, an unusual member of the carrot family, are herbaceous perennials that occur in mountain meadows and woodlands of Europe and western Asia. They have delicate flowerheads surrounded by a collar of pointed bracts, carried on wiry stems above clumps of deeply toothed, lobed foliage of soft mid-green.

Cultivation

They prefer moist, fertile, woodland conditions, or near the edges of streams or ponds. As long as the roots are kept moist they will tolerate full sun; indeed the variegated species color much better in sun. In a suitable position they will build up clumps. They can be propagated by division in early spring or from seed.

Astrantia major

Astrantia major

Native to central and eastern Europe, this species has deeply lobed, palmate leaves forming a loose mound of foliage 18 in (45 cm) tall from which rise nearly bare stems to 24 in (60 cm) or more, each topped by intricately formed, soft pink or white, daisy-like flowerheads, surrounded by petal-like bracts in the same colors. The flowers are produced almost throughout summer. 'Rosea' is slightly taller, with blooms of rich rose pink. *Zones 6–9.*

Athyrium nipponicum 'Pictum'

ATHYRIUM
Lady fern

Consisting of around 180 species ranging through most of the world's lands, lady ferns can be found in temperate, tropical and even in alpine regions. Those from cooler climates are deciduous but many of the tropical and subtropical ones are evergreen. They have creeping rhizomes and upright, simple to tripinnate fronds with grooved stems.

Cultivation

These ferns thrive in a humid atmosphere, so do not allow to dry out. They need shade, moisture and fertile soil that is slightly acidic and rich in humus. Propagation is by spores or division.

Athyrium nipponicum 'Pictum'
Japanese painted fern

Prized for its soft, metallic-gray new fronds suffused with bluish or reddish hues, this Japanese native grows to 18 in (45 cm) in height. Locate in humus-rich loam with adequate moisture in a semi-sunny exposure; this will ensure the richest foliage color. *Zones 4–9.*

Aubrieta deltoidea

AUBRIETA
Rock cress

These mountain flowers make carpets of color in the front of flowerbeds, or down retaining walls. Not very tall — 6 in (15 cm) or so at most — they will happily sprawl to several times their height and in spring cover themselves with 4-petaled flowers, mainly in shades of purple. The plants most often seen in gardens are hybrids mainly derived from *Aubrieta deltoidea*. The genus name honors the French botanical painter Claude Aubriet (1668–1743).

Cultivation

They are easy to grow in cool-temperate climates (flowering is erratic in warm ones), in fertile, well-drained soil. They are short lived and cuttings should be taken in summer every 3 or 4 years. They are also propagated by division of the rhizomatous rootstock.

Aubrieta deltoidea

Native to southeastern Europe and Turkey, this compact, mat-forming

Aurinia saxatilis

perennial has greenish gray leaves and masses of starry, mauve-pink flowers borne in spring. The species itself is now rare in gardens, most cultivated plants being hybrids now known collectively as *Aubrieta × cultorum*, though they are often listed as *A. deltoidea*. *Zones 4–9*.

AURINIA

This is a genus of 7 species of biennials and evergreen perennials native to Europe, Turkey and the Ukraine. They are mainly small, spreading, mound-forming plants. The leaves are initially in basal rosettes, mostly fairly narrow. They bear elongated sprays of tiny yellow or white flowers in spring and summer.

Cultivation

Plant in light, gritty, well-drained soil in full sun. They suit rock gardens, rock crevices or dry-stone walls. Most species are frost hardy and are propagated from seed or small tip cuttings; they will self-sow in suitable locations.

Aurinia saxatilis

syn. *Alyssum saxatile*

Basket of gold, yellow alyssum

This commonly grown species has hairy, gray-green leaves, and forms rather loose mounds to 10 in (25 cm) high. It is smothered in bright yellow flowers in spring and early summer. It is very popular as a rock garden or wall plant. There are a number of cultivars, including 'Argentea' with very silvery leaves; 'Citrina' with lemon-yellow flowers; 'Gold Dust', up to 12 in (30 cm) mounds with deep golden-yellow flowers; and 'Tom Thumb', a 4 in (10 cm) high dwarf with small leaves. *Zones 4–9*.

Baptisia australis

BAPTISIA
False indigo

Baptisia is a genus of 20–30 species of pea-flowered perennials from eastern and central USA. The common name arises from the former use of some species by dyers as a substitute for true indigo (*Indigofera*). Most are shrubby in habit, and the leaves are divided into 3 leaflets like a clover. The blue, purple, yellow or white pea-flowers are borne in terminal spikes over summer.

Cultivation
They prefer full sun and neutral, well-drained soil. They are not bothered by frost, or very dry conditions in summer. They should not be transplanted or disturbed. Propagation is from seed in autumn or by division.

Baptisia australis
False indigo
This summer-flowering perennial is attractive in both flower and foliage. The leaves are blue-green and form a loose mound up to about 4 ft (1.2 m) high and 3 ft (1 m) across. The lupin-like flowers are borne on erect spikes from early to mid-summer and are an unusual shade of purplish blue. The seed pods can be dried for indoor decoration. *Zones 3–10.*

BEGONIA
There are over 1,500 known species of begonias. From tropical and sub-tropical areas they have beautifully colored and textured foliage and showy flowers. Mostly evergreen, they have usually asymmetrical leaves of rather brittle and waxy texture. Begonias are divided into a number of classes depending on growth habit and type of rootstock. Cane-stemmed begonias are erect growers, with usually pendent clusters of flowers; shrubby begonias have a more closely branched habit; winter-flowering begonias bear profuse and colorful flowers that peak in winter; rhizomatous begonias are a large and varied class, with leaves arising directly from creeping, knotty rhizomes—they include the Rex begonias with colorfully variegated leaves; and the tuberous begonias, which die back to tubers in winter and bear large, often double flowers in summer.

Cultivation
Many of the cane-stemmed, winter-flowering, shrubby and rhizomatous types can be grown outdoors in frost-free climates. As indoor plants they need standard potting mix with peat moss or leafmold added. Grow in bright to moderate light, with good ventilation and above-average humidity. Tuberous begonias need special treatment: tubers must be forced into growth in early spring at 65°F (18°C) in peat moss or sphagnum, and kept in a cool, well-ventilated greenhouse for the flowering season. After flowering, plants die back and tubers are lifted in mid-autumn and stored dry. Propagate from tubers in the case of tuberous begonias. Propagate other begonias from stem or leaf cut-tings, or by division of rhizomes, or from seed.

Begonia grandis subsp. evansiana
Hardy begonia
Native to China, southern Japan and the highlands of Southeast Asia, this

Begonia Tuberhybridia Group

Begonia Semperflorens-cultorum Group

tuberous subspecies is the only begonia that can be expected to survive moderately cold winters outdoors. It is a low, bushy plant with red stems, growing to 24 in (60 cm) tall. The broad, pale green, fleshy leaves are flushed coppery red on the undersides. Fragrant pink flowers about 1 in (25 mm) across are produced in nodding clusters all summer. Preferring semi-shade, the plant dies back in winter. *Zones 7–11.*

Begonia Tuberhybrida Group

These well-known tuberous begonias bear glorious large blooms in almost every color except blues, as singles or doubles, with many variations of frills and ruffles. They are derived from a number of species native to the Andean region of South America. The tubers sprout in mid-spring, producing weak, brittle stems up to about 24 in (60 cm) long with rather sparse, mid-green leaves. The summer flowers can weigh down the stems, which may need staking. After flowering, plants enter their dormant stage and the tubers are normally lifted in mid-autumn and stored dry. There are several subgroups, based on growth form and flower type: most numerous are the Camellia-flowered and Rose-flowered cultivars, with very large, mostly double flowers up to 6 in (15 cm) across or even larger. Picotee group cultivars are mostly double blooms with petal edges washed

in contrasting or deeper shades of the flower color. Cultivars of the Multiflora type are usually single-flowered and do not need bud removal. The Pendula Group of hybrids carry their flowers in pendent sprays; they look best cascading from hanging baskets. *Zones 9–11.*

Begonia Semperflorens-cultorum Group
Bedding begonia, wax begonia

These dwarf, shrubby begonias are often grown as bedding annuals, for example, 'Ernst Benary', or for borders, and are also popular as potted plants. Freely branching plants with soft, succulent stems, they have rounded, glossy green leaves (bronze or variegated in some cultivars). The flowers are profuse, opening progressively at the branch tips over a long summer and early autumn season (most of the year in warmer climates). The numerous cultivars include singles and doubles in colors of bright rose pink, light pink, white or red. Pinch out growing tips to encourage bushy growth. *Zones 9–11.*

BELAMCANDA

This genus, native to southern and eastern Asia and belonging to the iris family, contains only 2 species. The plants are perennials but of weak growth and short lived, with flattened fans of thin-textured leaves arising from thin rhizomes. Slender flowering stems terminate in a few rather small flowers with 6 narrow petals; these are followed by seed pods which split widely to reveal rows of shiny black seeds, like small berries, which are popular for dried flower arrangements.

Cultivation
These plants need sunshine and rich, well-drained soil. Water well in summer. In cold climates dormant plants need protection from heavy frosts. Propagate by division or from seed, which should be sown every second or third year.

Belamcanda chinensis
Leopard lily, blackberry lily
This 24–36 in (60–90 cm) tall plant has something of the habit of an iris but the summer flowers do not look like irises. Up to 2 in (5 cm) across, they come in a range of colors from cream to yellow, apricot or deep orange-red, usually with darker spotting, hence the common name leopard lily. The seed pods open to reveal tight clusters of seeds resembling the fruitlets of a blackberry, hence their other common name. *Zones 8–11.*

BELLIS
Daisy
This genus consists of 15 species of small perennials from Europe and western

Bellis perennis

Asia. *Bellis* is from the Latin *bellus* which means 'pretty' or 'charming', while the English 'daisy' is a corruption of 'day's eye', arising from the way the flower closes up at night, opening again to greet the sunrise. The plants form rosettes with small oval to spoon-shaped leaves; each rosette produces a succession of flowerheads on individual stalks in shades of white, pink, blue or crimson.

Cultivation
While daisies are perennial in cool-temperate climates, it is usual to treat them as annuals or biennials, sowing seed in autumn. They thrive in any good garden soil in sun or part-shade. Propagate from seed or by division.

Bellis perennis
Common daisy, English daisy
This daisy has become widely natural-ized in temperate parts of the world. The flowerheads, appearing from late winter to early summer, are white with golden centers and pale purplish undersides. The garden strains mostly have double flowerheads of red, crimson, pink or white, all with a gold center. The Pomponette Series daisies are popular bedding plants and cut flowers; they have neat hemispherical flowerheads 1½ in (35 mm) wide with curled petals, on stems up to 10 in (25 cm) high, in mixed colors. *Zones 3–10.*

BERGENIA
Consisting of 6 or 7 species of rhizo-matous, semi-evergreen perennials, from near-Arctic areas to warm temperate Asia, this genus is characterized by large, paddle-shaped leaves, arising from the ground on short stalks to form loose clumps. Large clusters of flowers — mostly pale pink, but also white and dark pink — are borne on short, stout stems in winter and spring.

Cultivation

Bergenias make excellent ground cover and rock garden plants, thriving in sun or shade and tolerant of exposed sites as well as moist ground. Water well in hot weather and remove spent flowerheads to prolong flowering. Propagate by division in spring after flowering.

Bergenia cordifolia
Heartleaf saxifrage

Native to Siberia's Altai Mountains, this tough perennial has crinkly edged, more or less heart-shaped leaves up to 8 in (20 cm) wide, and produces panicles of drooping purple-pink flowers on 12–15 in (30–38 cm) stems in late winter and early spring. The plant is long flowering and the leaves remain green in winter. 'Purpurea' has magenta-pink flowers and purple tinged leaves. *Zones 3–9.*

Bergenia crassifolia

Bergenia crassifolia is one of the taller species, though the foliage is ground hugging with thick, blue-green leaves and bristly reddish margins. In early spring it produces nodding deep pink flowers in large dense clusters on stalks 12 in (30 cm) or more high. 'Aureo-

Belamcanda chinensis

Marginata', a cultivar with leaves streaked cream and dull purple, provides year-round color interest. *Zones 3–9.*

BOLTONIA
False chamomile

This is a genus of 8 species of perennial daisies, which have, in recent years, become popular as background plants for perennial borders and as cut flowers. Over winter they die back to a clump of simple, narrow leaves. In late spring, tall flowering stems begin to develop and by late summer they carry hundreds of small daisies in shades of white, pink, lilac, violet or purple.

Cultivation

They like moist, well-drained soil in any sunny position. However, they are prone to mildew from late summer. Frost hardy, they are propagated from seed or cuttings or by division.

Boltonia asteroides

This is the best known boltonia in gardens. The flowering stems may be as

Bergenia cordifolia

Boltonia asteroides

Borago officinalis

much as 8 ft (2.4 m) tall, with the flowerheads ranging in color from white through pale pink to mauve. 'Snowbank' is a white-flowered selection with stems growing up to 6 ft (1.8 m) tall. *Boltonia asteroides* var. *latisquama* differs in its larger flowerheads, which are in shades of mauve or purple. *Zones 4–9.*

BORAGO

The 3 species in this European genus of annuals and short-lived perennials are generally erect with rather coarse growth and covered with bristly hairs. They form clumps of lance-shaped basal leaves that develop in spring into branched, leafy flowering stems. By late spring the plants bear semi-pendulous, starry purple-blue or white flowers. The flowers are a rich source of nectar and are popular with beekeepers.

Cultivation

They like any light, moist, well-drained soil in full sun. Usually they are propagated from seed, which often self-sows, so plants may become invasive. Seed of the annual species can be sown in late winter for an early crop.

Borago officinalis
Borage

This annual herb has cucumber-flavored leaves and purplish blue star-shaped flowers. The plant grows to around 30 in (75 cm) high with clusters of flowers in spring and summer. Young leaves are used raw in salads and cool drinks or cooked with vegetables. The edible flowers have long been used to decorate salads. *Zones 5–10.*

BOUGAINVILLEA

Bougainvilleas are valued for their glorious, flamboyant display of blooms and their ability to cover a large area, of either ground or wall. The genus consists of 14 species from tropical and subtropical South America, but only 3 or 4 are grown as ornamentals. They are evergreen in the wet tropics, but may be deciduous in cooler climates. In more temperate climates the main flowering period is summer and fall, but in the tropics their finest display is in the dry season though they may flower on and off all year. The tubular flowers are insignificant, but the surrounding bracts are brilliantly colored. The plants produce long canes armed with strong woody thorns that aid climbing.

Cultivation

They do best in warm to hot climates in full sun; they also do well in temperate frost-free areas. Only water when needed and do not overfertilize. They

Brachycome iberidifolia 'Blue Star'

Bougainvillea 'Scarlett O'Hara'

Brachycome multifida 'Break O' Day'

need strong support for their vigorous growth, but can be controlled by pruning after flowering. Propagate from cuttings in summer.

Bougainvillea 'Scarlett O'Hara'

syns 'Hawaiian Scarlet', 'San Diego Red'
This popular free-flowering hybrid cultivar of uncertain origin is a large, vigorous grower, the new growths dark red with many thorns. The leaves are large, dark green, rather rounded, and the almost circular crimson bracts are very large, orange-tinted before they mature and often appearing before the leaves. *Zones 10–11.*

BRACHYCOME

syn. *Brachyscome*
Native to Australia, the low-growing annuals and evergreen perennials of this genus are attractive ground cover or rock garden plants. Many of the perennials are mound-forming, spreading by underground runners and having finely divided, soft, fern-like foliage. They bear a profusion of daisy-like flowerheads in shades of blue, mauve, pink and yellow.

Cultivation

They require a sunny situation and a light, well-drained garden soil. Many are moderately frost hardy and some will tolerate coastal salt spray. Do not over-water. Pinch out early shoots to encourage branching and propagate from ripe seed or stem cuttings or by division in spring or autumn.

Brachycome iberidifolia
Swan River daisy

This daisy is a weak-stemmed annual, long grown as a bedding or border plant, that grows to a height and spread of around 12 in (30 cm), sometimes taller. It has deeply dissected leaves with very narrow segments. Small, fragrant, daisy-like flowerheads, normally mauve-blue but sometimes white, pink or purple, appear in great profusion in summer and early autumn. 'Blue Star' is a cultivar with massed small, mauve to purple-blue flowers. *Zones 9–11.*

Brachycome multifida

This perennial species is a charming ground cover in warm-temperate climates, though it is not long lived. It grows about 4–6 in (10–15 cm) high and spreads to about 18 in (45 cm). The mauve-pink flowerheads bloom for weeks in late spring and summer. It likes sunshine and perfect drainage. 'Break O' Day' is a selected form with finer leaves, profuse mauve-blue flowers and a very compact habit. *Zones 9–11.*

BRACTEANTHA
syn. *Helichrysum*
Strawflower, everlasting daisy
This Australian genus consists of 7 species of annuals and perennials, until recently classified under *Helichrysum*. They differ from true helichrysums in their large, decorative flowerheads carried singly or a few together at the end of the flowering branches, each consisting of golden-yellow to white bracts of straw-like texture surrounding a disc of tiny yellow or brownish florets. The leaves are often downy on their undersides, or can be very sticky in some species.

Cultivation
Plant in moist, well-drained soil in full sun. Provided they are not waterlogged, most species will tolerate light to moderate frosts. Propagate annuals from seed and perennials from seed or tip cuttings.

Bracteantha bracteata

Bracteantha bracteata
syn. *Helichrysum bracteatum*
This annual or short-lived perennial has an erect habit and grows to a height of around 3 ft (1 m). It has weak, hollow stems, thin green leaves and from summer to early autumn bears golden-yellow blooms at the branch tips. Some more spreading, shrubby perennial plants from eastern Australia, which may be recognized as distinct species, have been named as cultivars, including the popular 'Dargan Hill Monarch', with rich yellow blooms up to 3 in (8 cm) across. *Zones 8–11.*

BRASSICA
This genus has produced a very diverse range of important vegetables. It includes about 30 wild species of annuals, biennials and subshrubs, ranging through the Mediterranean region and temperate Asia. Thousands of years ago, botanists believe, spontaneous hybrids appeared around human settlements and from one hybrid arose that major group of vegetables classified as *Brassica oleracea*. The genus in its more primitive form is characterized by its usually lobed leaves, 4-petaled yellow to white flowers and small, spindle-shaped fruiting capsules containing rows of tiny seeds.

Cultivation
Most brassicas love a lime-rich, moist, well-drained soil. Seedlings should be

Bracteantha bracteata 'Dargan Hill Monarch'

raised in seedbeds and then carefully planted out 6 to 8 weeks later in a sheltered, sunny spot. Ensure soil is kept weed-free and not too wet. Club root is a common disease, and crop rotation should be practiced.

Brassica oleracea, Acephala Group

Thought to have originated as an ancient hybrid between two or more of the wild Mediterranean species, this is one of the most versatile of all cultivated food plants. In its various forms it yields edible roots (kohlrabi), leaves (cabbage), shoots (Brussels sprouts) and flower buds (cauliflower and broccoli), as well as a few ornamentals, for example the colored-leafed kales. The kales are flat-leafed or curly-leafed cabbages that do not form a head. They are very tolerant of cold. Some forms can grow thick, knobby stems up to 6 ft (1.8 m) or more tall. In Scotland, the broth made from their leaves is a traditional Highland dish. Ornamental kales, used for bedding and also sold in pots by florists, have leaves usually lobed or dissected, and strikingly veined with purple, pink, yellow or white. *Zones 6–11.*

Brassica oleracea, Acephala Group 'Chou Palmer'

BROWALLIA
Bush violet

This genus of 6 species of bushy annuals and evergreen perennials is native to tropical South America and the West Indies. They are densely foliaged with a compact habit, soft stems and simple, strongly veined, deep green leaves. The flowers, carried singly in the leaf axils, come in shades of blue, purple or white.

Cultivation

In cool climates browallias are grown as conservatory plants or as summer annuals. In frost-free climates they grow well outdoors in moist, humus-rich, well-drained soil in a warm, part-shaded, sheltered position. Propagate the annuals from seed in spring, the perennials from seed or tip cuttings.

Browallia speciosa

This shrubby perennial Colombian species grows to around 30 in (75 cm) tall and wide with leaves up to 4 in (10 cm) long. Its flowers are purple-blue to deep purple. There are many cultivars, with flowers in all shades of blue and purple as well as white. 'Blue Troll' is a

Brunnera macrophylla

12 in (30 cm) dwarf with masses of blue flowers; 'White Troll' is similar with white flowers. *Zones 9–11.*

BRUNNERA

This is an eastern European genus of 3 species of perennials. They form clumps of heart-shaped to rather narrow basal leaves on long stalks. Leafy, branched flowering stems bear panicles of tiny 5-petaled purple or blue flowers in spring and early summer. There are forms with white flowers and variegated foliage.

Cultivation

They prefer humus-rich, moist soil with a leafy mulch and a position in dappled shade. They are cold hardy and in suitable conditions will self-sow and naturalize. Propagate from seed, by removing small rooted pieces or by taking cuttings of the soft spring shoots.

Brunnera macrophylla
Siberian bugloss

The small violet flowers of this species resemble forget-me-nots (to which they are related); they are held on slender stems 18–24 in (45–60 cm) tall above the mounds of heart-shaped leaves. When the flowers appear the new leaves grow to their full length of 4–6 in (10–15 cm). Clumps spread slowly underground but self-seed readily. *Zones 3–9.*

Browallia speciosa

C

CALADIUM

Caladiums include some of the showiest but most tender tropical foliage plants. Consisting of 7 species from tropical South America, the genus belongs to the arum family, resembling the taro genus (*Colocasia*) in growth habit with underground tubers and leaves of the 'elephant-ear' type. They are deciduous in the tropical dry season, the tubers going through a dormant stage. The flowering stems have a thin, greenish white spathe half-hidden under the leaves.

Cultivation

Caladiums can be grown outdoors only in tropical and subtropical climates. In cool climates they need a humid environment and bright light but not direct sun. Plant tubers in spring in peat moss or sphagnum, at a temperature of 70–80°F (21–27°C), transplanting when sprouted into a humus-rich potting medium. Fertilize as the leaves expand and mist-spray often in summer. Lift tubers over winter.

Caladium bicolor
syn. *Caladium × hortulanum*
Angel wings, elephant's ears, fancy-leafed caladium
Caladiums reached a height of popularity in the USA before World War II, when at least 1000 cultivars were listed.

Caladium bicolor

Their leaves are typically arrowhead-shaped but some cultivars have narrower leaves, wedge-shaped at the base. Color varies from plain green with a red or pink center to intricate combinations of green, white, pink and red, usually with dark green veining. Plants reach 12–24 in (30–60 cm) high. *Zones 10–11.*

CALENDULA
Marigold

St. Hildegard of Bingen (1098–1179) is said to have dedicated *Calendula officinalis* to the Virgin Mary and named the flowers Mary's gold, or marigold. In the Middle Ages marigolds were considered a remedy for smallpox, indigestion and 'evil humors of the head', and even today the marigold is a favorite of herbalists. The genus consists of 20-odd species of bushy annuals and evergreen perennials from the Canary Islands, Iran and the Mediterranean. They have aromatic leaves and daisy-like, orange or yellow flowers.

Cultivation

Calendulas are mostly fairly frost-hardy plants and like well-drained soil of any quality in sun or part-shade. Prolong flowering with regular deadheading. Propagate from seed, and watch for aphids and powdery mildew.

Calendula officinalis, Pacific Beauty Series

Calendula officinalis
Pot marigold, English marigold

Long valued for its medicinal qualities, this species is known in gardens only by its many cultivars and seedling strains, popular winter- and spring-flowering annuals that remain in bloom for a long time. There are tall and dwarf forms, all of bushy habit, the tall growing to a height and spread of 24 in (60 cm) and the dwarf to 12 in (30 cm). All have lance-shaped, strongly scented, pale green leaves and single or double flowerheads. The Pacific Beauty Series has double flowers in a number of different colors including bicolors. *Zones 6–10.*

CALLISTEPHUS
China aster

This genus contains just one annual species—a flower with summer blooms in shades from white to pink, blue, red and purple. The flowerheads can be either yellow-centered single daisies or fully double. The doubles can have petals that are plume-like and shaggy, more formal and straight or very short.

Cultivation

It is usually sown in spring to flower during summer, but it is usual to make successive sowings to prolong blooming

Callistephus chinensis

time. It grows in any climate, from the coolest temperate to subtropical. Give it sunshine and fertile, well-drained soil, and do not plant it in the same bed 2 years in a row—this guards against aster wilt, a soil-borne fungus.

Callistephus chinensis
syn. *Aster chinensis*

This erect, bushy, fast-growing annual from China has oval, toothed, mid-green leaves and long-stalked flowerheads. There are many seedling strains available, ranging from tall, up to 36 in (90 cm), to dwarf, about 8 in (20 cm). Stake tall cultivars and remove spent flowers regularly. *Zones 6–10.*

CALTHA

There are about 10 species of moisture-loving perennials in this genus of the ranunculus family, all occurring in cold marshlands and alpine bogs of the cool-temperate zones in both northern and southern hemispheres. They have cup-shaped, white or yellow flowers and kidney- or heart-shaped leaves, and spread by thick rhizomes. They often come into leaf and flower very early, appearing from beneath melting snow.

Cultivation

These frost-hardy plants prefer full sun

Caltha palustris 'Monstrosa'

Campanula carpatica

and rich, damp soil. Propagate by division in autumn or early spring, or from seed in fall. Watch for rust fungus, which should be treated with a fungicide.

Caltha palustris
Marsh marigold, kingcup
Occurring widely in temperate regions of the northern hemisphere, this semi-aquatic or bog plant is sometimes grown for its attractive flowers. It is deciduous or semi-evergreen with dark green, rounded leaves and glistening buttercup-like, golden-yellow flowers borne from early spring to mid-summer. It grows to a height and spread of 18 in (45 cm). The cultivars 'Monstrosa' and 'Flore Pleno' both have double flowers, while *Caltha palustris* var. *alba* has single white flowers with yellow stamens. *Zones 3–8.*

CAMPANULA
Bellflower, bluebell
This genus includes about 250 species of showy herbaceous plants, mostly perennials but a few annual or biennial, from the temperate northern hemisphere. Flowers are mostly bell-shaped but some are more tubular, urn-shaped or star-shaped, and come mainly in shades of blue and purple with some pinks and whites.

Cultivation
They are useful for rock gardens, borders and hanging baskets. All like a

Campanula glomerata 'Superba'

moderately rich, moist, well-drained soil. They grow in sun or shade, but flower color remains brightest in shady spots. Propagate from seed in spring (sow seed for alpines in autumn), by division in spring or fall, or from basal cuttings in spring. They are very frost hardy to frost tender.

Campanula carpatica
Carpathian bellflower, tussock bellflower
The slowly spreading clumps of basal leaves of this species make it well suited for use as an edging or rock garden plant. From late spring through summer, 8–12 in (20–30 cm) stems rise above the foliage, carrying upward-facing, 1–2 in (2.5 –5 cm) wide, bowl-shaped flowers in blue, lavender or white. The most

Campanula lactiflora 'Pritchard's Variety'

common cultivars available are the compact-growing 'Blue Clips' and 'White Clips', and the bright violet blue 'Wedgwood Blue'. *Zones 3–9.*

Campanula glomerata
Clustered bellflower

This variable species is found throughout Europe and temperate Asia. The violet-blue flowers are grouped in almost globular clusters on 10–15 in (25–38 cm) tall stems in early summer and again later if the spent flower stems are removed. 'Superba' grows to 24 in (60 cm); *Campanula glomerata* var. *dahurica* is a deeper violet than the species. There are also double-flowered and white versions. *Zones 3–9.*

Campanula lactiflora
Milky bellflower

Native to the Caucasus region and eastern Turkey, this popular strong-growing perennial reaches a height of 5 ft (1.5 m) and spreads into a broad clump. The strong stems bear many narrow oval leaves. In summer it produces very large and dense panicles of bell-shaped lilac-blue flowers (occasionally pink or white). If the flowering stem is cut back after flowering, side shoots may bear blooms in late autumn.

Campanula medium

'Pritchard's Variety' has deep violet-blue flowers. *Zones 5–9.*

Campanula medium
Canterbury bell

This is a slow-growing, erect, biennial plant with narrow basal leaves. In spring and early summer it has stout spires up to 4 ft (1.2 m) tall of crowded, bell-shaped, white, pink or blue flowers with recurved rims and prominent large green calyces. Dwarf cultivars grow to about 24 in (60 cm), and double forms have a colored calyx like a second petal tube. Grow as border plants in part-shade. *Zones 6–10.*

Campanula persicifolia
Peach-leafed bellflower

Native to southern and eastern Europe and temperate Asia, this well-known species has large, nodding, bowl-shaped purplish blue or white flowers borne above narrow, lance-shaped, bright green leaves in summer. It is a rosette-forming perennial spreading by rhizomes and reaching a height of 3 ft (1 m). Pinch individual flowers off upright stems as soon as they fade. 'Alba' has white flowers;

'Boule de Neige' and 'Fleur de Neige' have double white flowers. *Zones 3–9.*

Campanula portenschlagiana
syn. *Campanula muralis*
Dalmatian bellflower
Native to a small area of the Dalmatian limestone mountains of Croatia, this is a dwarf, evergreen perennial growing to a maximum height of 6 in (15 cm) with an indefinite spread. It has crowded small violet-like leaves and a profusion of small, star-shaped, violet flowers in late spring and early summer. Best suited to rockeries and wall crevices, it likes a cool, partially shaded position with good drainage. *Zones 5–10.*

Campanula rotundifolia
Harebell, Scottish bluebell
This variable species, widely distributed around the temperate northern hemisphere, has a hardy nature. Loose rosettes of rounded, long-stalked leaves arise from creeping rhizomes, followed by slender, wiry stems holding nodding lilac-blue to white bells during the summer months. *Zones 3–9.*

Campanula persicifolia

CANNA
This genus of rhizomatous perennials consists of about 9 tropical species. The apparent aboveground stems are actually tightly furled leaf bases, rising from thick knotty rhizomes. Slender flowering stems grow up through the centers of these false stems, emerging at the top with showy flowers. Most wild species have rather narrow-petaled flowers in shades of yellow, red or purple. Colors of garden cannas range from reds, oranges and yellows through to apricots, creams and pinks. Plants range in height from 18 in (45 cm) to 8 ft (2.4 m).

Cultivation
Cannas thrive outdoors in frost-free, warm climates but if grown outside in

Campanula portenschlagiana

Campanula rotundifolia

colder areas protect the roots with thick mulch in winter. They thrive in hot weather as long as water is kept up to the roots. Cut back to the ground after flowers finish. Propagate by division.

Canna × generalis

These plants are extremely variable, ranging from dwarfs less than 3 ft (1 m) to large growers that reach 6 ft (1.8 m). Foliage is also variable and may be plain green, reddish, purple or variegated. Flowers come in either in plain single colors such as the orange-red 'Brandywine', or spotted or streaked as in the yellow and red 'King Numbert'. 'Königin Charlotte' has red flowers. 'Lenape' is a dwarf hybrid cultivar with bright yellow flowers with a red throat and brownish red spots. *Zones 9–11.*

CATANANCHE
Cupid's dart

Consisting of 5 species of annuals and perennials from the Mediterranean region, the growth form of this genus of the daisy family is like a dandelion, with narrow basal leaves radiating from a root crown, and leafless flowering stems each terminating in a showy blue or yellow flowerhead. The distinctive heads have few ray florets; these are broad and flat with 5 prominent teeth at the tip of each and a darker zone at the base. The genus name is from a Greek word meaning 'love potion'.

Cultivation

Grow in full sun. Propagate from seed or root cuttings or by division.

Catananche caerulea
Common Cupid's dart

This is popular as a cottage garden plant or it can be grown among grasses in a meadow garden. A fast-growing but usually short-lived perennial, it reaches 24 in (60 cm) in height with a spread of 12 in (30 cm). The narrow leaves are gray-green and thin, forming a dense basal clump. Lavender-blue flowerheads are borne freely throughout summer on slender, weak, leafless stems. *Zones 7–10.*

Catananche caerulea

Canna × generalis

Celosia argentea, Plumosa Group

Centaurea cyanus

CELOSIA
Cockscomb, Chinese woolflower

This genus of erect annuals, perennials and shrubs in the amaranthus family contains 50 or more species, but only one (*Celosia argentea*) is widely cultivated. It has evolved in cultivation into several different forms, hardly recognizable as belonging to the one species. It has simple, soft, strongly veined leaves; the variation is almost wholly in the structure of the heads of the small flowers, which have undergone proliferation and deformation in the two major cultivated races.

Cultivation

In cool climates celosias are usually treated as conservatory plants. They are better adapted to hot climates, withstanding the fiercest summer heat. They require full sun, rich, well-drained soil and constant moisture. Propagate from seed in spring.

Celosia argentea

syns *Celosia cristata, C. pyramidalis*
This annual can reach 3 ft (1 m) or more in height. The silvery white flowers appear in summer in dense, erect, pointed spikes with a silvery sheen. There are two strikingly different cultivar groups—the Plumosa Group, with erect, plume-like heads of tiny deformed flowers in a range of hot colors, and the Cristata Group (cockscombs), with bizarre wavy crests of fused flower stalks also in many colors. Both have been developed with a range of seedling strains, differing in height as well as size and the color of the flowerheads. *Zones 10–11.*

CENTAUREA
Cornflower, knapweed

This genus of around 450 species includes annuals, biennials and perennials. Some spiny-leafed species are troublesome weeds in some parts of the world. Apart from the common annual cornflower, some perennial species are desirable garden plants; they come in colors from white through shades of blue, red, pink, purple and yellow. The flowerheads typically have an urn-shaped receptacle of fringed or spiny bracts, from the mouth of which radiate the quite large florets, each deeply divided into 5 colored petals; smaller florets occupy the center of the head, but do not form a distinct disc.

Cultivation

Cornflowers grow best in well-drained soil in a sunny position. They can be propagated from seed in spring or autumn; perennials can also be divided in spring or fall.

Centaurea macrocephala

Centaurea cyanus
Blue-bottle, bachelor's button, cornflower
One of the best known wildflowers of
Europe and northern Asia, this species
is also a common weed of cereal crops.
It is a weak-stemmed, erect annual,
24–36 in (60–90 cm) tall with narrow
leaves and small, untidy flowerheads
that are typically a slightly purplish
shade of blue. Garden varieties have
been developed with larger flowers in
shades of pale and deep pink, cerise,
crimson, white, purple and blue, some
of them dwarf and more compact.
Zones 5–10.

Centaurea macrocephala
Globe cornflower
With foliage resembling a dandelion, this
perennial species is from the subalpine
fields of Armenia and Turkey. In
summer stout leafy stems, up to 3 ft
(1 m) tall, carry yellow flowerheads
about 2 in (5 cm) across with a club-like
base of shiny brown bracts. *Zones 4–9.*

Centaurea montana
Perennial cornflower, mountain bluet
From the mountains of Europe, this
long-cultivated perennial species is up to
30 in (75 cm) high and has creeping
rhizomes; it may form large clumps
when conditions suit. The leaves are
usually smooth-edged and green, and the
2 in (5 cm) wide violet flowerheads,
borne in early summer, are distinctive
for their widely spaced florets, giving
them a delicate lacy effect. *Zones 5–9.*

CENTRANTHUS
Valerian
Around 10 species belong to this genus
of annual and perennial herbs, but only
Centranthus ruber is widely planted for
ornament. They make tufts of soft leaves
that may be smooth edged or less
commonly dissected, and the leafy,
branched flowering stems bear many
irregular heads of tiny tubular flowers.

Cultivation
Grow in full sun in moderately fertile,
well-drained, chalk or lime soil. Deadhead regularly. Divide every 3 years.
Propagate from seed or by division.

Centranthus ruber
Red valerian, Jupiter's beard, kiss-me-quick
This perennial often naturalizes on dry
banks and is ideal for dry rock gardens
and borders. It forms loose clumps of
somewhat fleshy leaves and grows to a
height of 24–36 in (60–90 cm). From

Centaurea montana

late spring to autumn it produces dense clusters of small, star-shaped, deep reddish pink to pale pink flowers that last for a long time. 'Albus' has white flowers. It requires sun and good drainage and will tolerate exposed positions and poor alkaline soil. *Zones 5–10.*

CERASTIUM

There are 60–100 species of low-growing annuals and perennials in this genus from northern temperate and arctic regions. The annuals include some common weeds of lawns, but some of the perennials are grown as ground covers or in rock gardens. They have weak stems from a network of thin rhizomes. The small leaves are usually clothed in whitish hairs. The flowers are white and have 5 petals.

Cultivation

Easily cultivated, some cerastiums can be invasive. All are frost hardy and like full sun and well-drained soil. Keep foliage dry in winter and in humid summer weather, as the hairs on the leaves tend to retain moisture and become mildewed. Propagate by division.

Cerastium tomentosum

Cerastium tomentosum
Snow-in-summer

A vigorous, fast-growing ground cover, this perennial suits a well-drained, hot dry bank or rock garden. It has narrow silvery gray leaves, and masses of star-shaped white flowers in late spring and summer. It grows to 6 in (15 cm) high and spreads indefinitely. *Zones 3–10.*

CHELONE
Turtlehead

This genus of 6 species of rather coarse but showy perennials from North America is related to *Penstemon*, which they resemble in growth habit and foliage. The name comes from the Greek *kelone* meaning a tortoise or turtle, and refers to the hooded, gaping flowers, borne in short terminal spikes. Leaves are toothed and shiny in most species.

Cultivation

They prefer moist conditions with rich soil in full sun or part-shade. Propagate by dividing clumps in early spring, from cuttings in summer or from seed.

Chelone obliqua
Rose turtlehead

From southeastern USA, this showy turtle-head has pairs of rich green leaves which line 3 ft (1 m) tall vertical stems topped with short spikes of rosy-purple flowers in late summer and autumn. *Zones 6–9.*

Centranthus ruber

CHRYSANTHEMUM
Chrysanthemum

As now recognized by most botanists, this once large and varied genus is a shadow of its former self, reduced to a mere 5 species of annuals from Europe and North Africa. As a common name, though, 'chrysanthemum' will always be understood by gardeners to refer to the group of showy hybrid plants derived from East Asian species now classified under *Dendranthema*.

Cultivation

True chrysanthemums are easily grown annuals, requiring little more than a moist, fertile, well-prepared soil and a sunny position. They prefer coolish summers but in warmer, drier climates can be timed to bloom in winter. Propagate from seed, sown in autumn or early spring.

Chrysanthemum carinatum
syn. *Chrysanthemum tricolor*
Painted daisy, summer chrysanthemum, tricolor chrysanthemum

This spectacular annual species is from Morocco and grows to 24 in (60 cm), spreading to 12 in (30 cm) with much-divided, rather fleshy leaves and banded,

Chrysanthemum carinatum

multicolored flowers in spring and early summer. 'Monarch Court Jesters' comes in red with yellow centers or white with red centers, and the Tricolor Series has many color combinations. *Zones 8–10.*

CIMICIFUGA
Bugbane

This genus of about 15 species of perennials is native to cooler regions of the northern hemisphere. The name means 'bug repellent', from the Latin *cimex* (bedbug) and *fugare* (to repel) reflecting an early use of one species. The flowering stems terminate in long, erect spikes of white, cream or pinkish flowers, the many stamens being the conspicuous part of each flower.

Cultivation

They prefer part-shade, a deep, rich soil and need regular watering. Plant rhizome divisions in spring or autumn, but do not disturb the root; they flower best when established.

Cimicifuga racemosa
Black cohosh, squawroot

From woodlands of eastern and central North America, this vigorous perennial

Chelone obliqua

Cimicifuga simplex

Clarkia amoena

has crowded, large, compound leaves arising from a knotted rhizome with densely massed fibrous roots. Flowering stems, leafy in the lower part, rise to a height of 5 ft (1.5 m) or more and bear spikes of cream flowers in summer and autumn. The whole plant has an unpleasant smell when bruised. The rhizomes were used by Native Americans in childbirth and for menstruation problems and are now known to contain an estrogen-like substance. *Zones 3–9.*

Cimicifuga simplex
Kamchatka bugbane
From Japan and far eastern Siberia, this species is the latest to flower of the whole genus, the flowers coming in late autumn. It is also smaller, reaching a height of about 4 ft (1.2 m). The flowers are white, carried on long arching wands, and the foliage is much divided. 'Elstead' has purplish buds opening to pure white. *Zones 3–9.*

CLARKIA
syn. *Godetia*
This genus, allied to the evening primroses (*Oenothera*) and consisting of about 36 species, was named in honor of Captain William Clark, of the Lewis and Clark expedition that crossed the American continent in 1806. They are

bushy annuals, undistinguished in foliage but spectacular in their short flowering season when they are covered in showy funnel-shaped flowers in various shades of pink, white and carmine. The flowers look a little like azaleas—in Germany they are called *Sommerazalee*, the summer azalea.

Cultivation
They are easily grown in full sun in any temperate climate. They prefer moist but well-drained, slightly acid soil. Propagate from seed.

Clarkia amoena
syn. *Clarkia grandiflora*
Farewell-to-spring
A free-flowering annual, this Californian native is fast growing to a height of 24 in (60 cm) and spread of 12 in (30 cm). It has lance-shaped, mid-green leaves, thin upright stems, and in summer bears spikes of open, cup-like, single or double flowers in shades of pink; a number of cultivars have been produced from this species. Allow it to dry out between watering and watch for signs of botrytis. *Zones 7–11.*

CLEMATIS
Virgin's bower, traveler's joy
The 200 or more species of mostly woody climbers in this genus are

Clematis integrifolia

Cleome hassleriana

scattered throughout the world's temperate regions, but most of the popular, larger-flowered plants come from Japan and China. They climb by twisting their leaf-stalk tendrils about a support and are ideal for veranda posts, arbors, bowers and trellises. Showy bell-shaped or flattish flowers with 4 to 8 petals (*sepals* really) are followed by masses of fluffy seed heads.

Cultivation

A well-drained, humus-rich, permanently cool soil with good moisture retention is needed. Prune old twiggy growth in spring and propagate from cuttings or by layering in summer.

Clematis integrifolia

This herbaceous clematis is hardly recognizable as belonging to this genus, at least until it flowers. It forms a gradually expanding clump with masses of stems arising from the base each spring, each one ending in a single, nodding flower. It is normally purple-blue, deeper in the center. The creamy white stamens are tightly packed. The flower stalks may need support. *Zones 3–9.*

CLEOME
Spider flower, spider plant

This genus of 150 species of bushy annuals and short-lived evergreen

shrubs, from subtropical and tropical zones all over the world, is characterized by its spidery flowers with 4 petals that narrow into basal stalks, and mostly long, spidery stamens and styles.

Cultivation

Marginally frost hardy, they require full sun and fertile, well-drained soil, regular water and shelter from strong winds. Encourage taller growth by removing side branches. Propagate from seed in spring or early summer.

Cleome hassleriana

syn. *Cleome spinosa* of gardens
Native to subtropical South America, this fast-growing, bushy annual has unusual spidery flowers. An erect plant, it grows to 4 ft (1.2 m) tall with a spread of 18 in (45 cm). It has large palmate leaves and the hairy, slightly prickly stems are topped in summer with heads of airy, pink and white flowers with long, protruding stamens. Several strains are available as seed, ranging in color from pure white to purple. *Zones 9–11.*

CLINTONIA

Five species of woodland lilies from North America and eastern Asia make up this genus, all rhizomatous perennials with rich green smooth foliage rather like that of *Convallaria*, and erect spikes or umbels (solitary in one species) of small, starry 6-petaled flowers.

Cultivation
All species need a cool, peaty, lime-free soil and a shaded, humid position, and so are best suited to a woodland garden. Winter mulching will protect from frost. Propagate from seed or division of rhizomes.

Clintonia umbellulata
Speckled wood-lily
From eastern USA, this is one of the prettiest species with dense umbels of fragrant white flowers, often speckled green or purplish, rising on stems up to 15 in (40 cm) tall above dense patches of luxuriant foliage. The flowers appear in late spring and early summer and are followed by black berries. *Zones 4–9.*

COLCHICUM
Autumn crocus
Colchicum consists of about 45 species, native to Europe, North Africa and west and central Asia, with the greatest concentration in Turkey and the Balkans. Despite the name 'autumn crocus', they bloom in either spring or autumn, depending on species. The flowers have a long tube and the petals spread at the top into a usually narrow funnel. The leaves usually appear after

Colchicum autumnale

the flowers and are mostly broad and fleshy. All parts of the plants are poisonous and even contact with the skin may cause irritation—the poisonous compound colchicine affects division of cell nuclei and is used in the treatment of certain forms of cancer; it is also used to create polyploids in plant breeding.

Cultivation
Frost hardy, they prefer cold winters. Some Mediterranean species like hot dry summer conditions and need a warm spot in the rock garden. Plant in late summer in well-drained soil in full sun or part-shade. Propagate from seed or by division in summer.

Colchicum autumnale
Autumn crocus, meadow saffron
The best-known species of the genus, *Colchicum autumnale* comes from Europe. The flowers rise to about 6 in (10 cm) above the ground and are about 3 in (8 cm) across. Appearing from late summer to mid-autumn, they vary a little in color but are usually a delicate shade of lilac pink. This is one of the most moisture tolerant species, and the one occurring furthest north. 'Album' has white flowers. *Zones 5–9.*

CONSOLIDA
Larkspur
These annuals were often treated as species of *Delphinium*, but the consensus

Clintonia umbellulata

now is that the 40 or so species consti-
tute a distinct genus. The name *Consolida*
was bestowed in the Middle Ages
because of the plants' use in the healing
of wounds; they were believed to help
the clotting (consolidating) of blood.
Garden larkspurs are mostly derived
from *Consolida ajacis*, and include many
strains, mostly grown as mixed colors.
They have finely divided, feather-like
leaves and poisonous seeds.

Cultivation
They succeed in any temperate or even
mildly subtropical climate and like full
sun and rich, well-drained soil. Tall
cultivars need to be staked. Propagate
from seed and watch for powdery
mildew.

Consolida ambigua
syns *Consolida ajacis, Delphinium consolida*
The name larkspur comes from the
nectar spur at the back of the flowers,
hidden in the open blooms but clearly
visible on unopened buds. This Mediterranean species originally had blue
flowers. Present-day garden larkspurs
are the result of hybridizing this species

Consolida ambigua

Convallaria majalis

with *Consolida orientalis* to give the
'rocket larkspurs', or may be derived
from *C. regalis* in the case of the 'forking
larkspurs'. Blooms may be pink, white
or purple and are usually double, borne
mainly in summer. *Zones 7–11*.

CONVALLARIA
Lily-of-the-valley
This plant spreads over the forest floor
by slender underground rhizomes which
at intervals send up pointed oval leaves
and slender flowering stems adorned
with little white bells. The red berries
that follow have their uses in medicine,
but they are poisonous.

Cultivation
The rhizomes should be planted in
autumn in a part-shaded spot. Grow in
fertile, humus-rich, moist soil. Propagate
from seed or by division.

Convallaria majalis
Renowned for its glorious perfume, this
beautiful plant does best in cool climates.
It is low growing, 8–12 in (20–30 cm)
high but of indefinite spread, with dark
green leaves. The dainty white bell-
shaped flowers appear in spring. Pink-
flowered variants are known, collectively referred to as *Convallaria majalis*
var. *rosea*, and there are several cultivars
with variegated or gold foliage.
Zones 3–9.

Convolvulus tricolor

Coreopsis grandiflora

CONVOLVULUS

Found in many temperate regions of the world, this genus of some 250 species consists mainly of slender, twining creepers (the bindweeds) and small herbaceous plants. Only a few species are shrubby, and even these are soft stemmed and renewed by shooting from the base. They have simple, thin-textured, usually narrow leaves and the flowers are like morning glories, with a strongly flared tube that opens by unfurling 'pleats'.

Cultivation

They adapt to most soils and exposed as well as sheltered positions, but always prefer full sun. Propagate from cuttings.

Convolvulus tricolor

syn. *Convolvulus minor*
This bedding annual from the Mediter-ranean bears profuse deep purple-blue or white flowers with banded yellow and white throats. The small leaves are lance-shaped and mid-green. A slender, few-branched plant, it grows to a height of 8–12 in (20–30 cm) and blooms continuously from late spring to early autumn but individual flowers last only one day. 'Blue Ensign' has very deep blue flowers with pale yellow centers. *Zones 8–11.*

COREOPSIS

Around 80 species of annuals and perennials from cooler or drier regions of the Americas make up this genus of the daisy family. The flowerheads, borne on slender stems mainly in summer, are mostly shades of gold or yellow, some bicolored. Leaves vary from simple and narrow, usually toothed, to deeply divided, and may be basal or scattered up the stems.

Cultivation

Both annuals and perennials prefer full sun and a fertile, well-drained soil. Propagate perennials by division of old clumps in winter or spring, or by spring cuttings. Propagate annuals from seed in spring or autumn.

Coreopsis grandiflora
Tickseed

Among the easiest of perennials, this cheerful, bright golden-yellow daisy provides color from late spring to mid-summer. Somewhat hairy leaves and stems form a loose mound to 12–24 in (30–60 cm) tall and wide, the flower stems rising to nearly 24 in (60 cm) or usually flopping on their neighbors. Tickseed can be treated as an annual and self-seeds freely. Cultivars of more compact habit such as 'Badengold', 'Sunray' or 'Early Sunrise' are the best choices for the well-maintained border. *Zones 6–10.*

Coreopsis verticillata 'Moonbeam'

Coreopsis lanceolata

This is a tufted perennial with long-stalked, lance-shaped basal leaves and bright golden-yellow flowerheads on leafy stems up to about 24 in (60 cm) high. It is extremely floriferous and when mass planted can make sheets of gold in spring and early summer. Short lived, it is very free-seeding, and has become an environmental weed in some parts of the world. Double forms are sometimes grown. 'Baby Sun' is a compact long blooming cultivar about 12 in (30 cm) high. *Zones 3–11.*

Coreopsis verticillata

This perennial species produces crowded erect stems to 30 in (75 cm) tall from a tangled mass of thin rhizomes; the leaves, in whorls of 3, are divided into very narrow segments. The abundant bright yellow flowerheads are borne from late spring until autumn. It does best in light soil of low fertility. 'Moonbeam' is slightly lower and more compact with lemon-yellow blooms. *Zones 6–10.*

CORYDALIS

The 300 or so species that make up this genus, allied to the fumitories (*Fumaria*), occur widely as natives in temperate regions of the northern hemisphere, with a great concentration in the mountains

Coreopsis lanceolata 'Baby Sun'

of East Asia. The genus includes some annuals but species are mostly perennials, with basal tufts of ferny, deeply dissected leaves springing from fleshy rhizomes or tubers. The smallish tubular flowers have a short backward-pointing spur that may be curved; they are usually grouped in short spikes or clusters and come in mostly creams, yellows, pinks and purples but a few have clear blue flowers.

Cultivation

Soil should be well drained but moisture-retentive, rich in humus for the woodland species. Several species, such as *Corydalis lutea*, self-seed freely. Propagate from seed or by division.

Corydalis lutea
Yellow corydalis

The most easily cultivated species, this native of Europe's southern Alps region is widely naturalized in temperate climates around the world. A rhizomatous perennial, it makes broad clumps or mounds of fresh green foliage, to about 12 in (30 cm) high, and is dotted from spring to autumn with short sprays of soft yellow flowers. It often self-seeds in wall crevices or moist chinks in rock gardens. In a woodland garden it makes an attractive ground cover. *Zones 6–10.*

COSMOS
Mexican aster

This genus of annuals and perennials contains 25 species native to warmer parts of the Americas but mostly to Mexico. They have erect but weak, leafy stems and the leaves are variously lobed or deeply and finely dissected. The flowerheads, on slender stalks terminating branches, are daisy-like with showy, broad ray-florets surrounding a small disc; they range in color from white through pinks, yellows, oranges, reds and purples to deep maroon.

Cultivation

They are moderately frost hardy and in cold climates need protection in winter. They need a sunny spot with protection from strong winds, and well-drained soil that is not over-rich. Mulch with compost and water well in hot weather. Propagate annuals from seed in spring or autumn, perennials from basal cuttings in spring.

Cosmos atrosanguineus
Black cosmos, chocolate cosmos

A tuberous-rooted, clump-forming perennial growing to 24 in (60 cm) in height and spread, the unusual black cosmos has long-stalked, very dark maroon flowerheads that have a chocolate scent, most noticeable on warm days. It flowers from summer to autumn. The leaves are rather few-lobed and tinged dull purplish. It normally dies back in fall and requires fairly dry soil if the rootstock is not to rot; alternatively the roots can be lifted and stored for the winter like dahlias. *Zones 8–10.*

Cosmos bipinnatus
Common cosmos, Mexican aster

This feathery-leafed annual reaches 5–6 ft (1.5–1.8 m) in height with showy daisy-like flowerheads in summer and autumn, in shades of pink, red, purple or white. Taller plants may need staking. Newer strains are usually more compact and can have double flowers and striped petals. 'Sea Shells' has usually pink, sometimes crimson or white flowerheads with edges of ray-florets curled into a tube. *Zones 8–11.*

CROCOSMIA
syns *Antholyza, Curtonus*
Montbretia

These 7 species of South African cormous perennials have narrow, bayonet-shaped, pleated leaves. These fan out from the base of the plant, similar to a gladiolus. A branched spike

Corydalis lutea

Cosmos atrosanguineus

of attractive, brightly colored flowers appears in summer.

Cultivation

Plant the corms in winter in rich soil with adequate drainage in a position that receives morning sun. Water well through summer. They will multiply freely and should not be divided unless overcrowded; this should be done in spring if necessary.

Crocosmia × crocosmiiflora

Growing to 36 in (90 cm), the stem of this hybrid bears a branching spike of up to 40 orange-red, gladiolus-like flowers about 1 in (25 mm) wide. This species is frost hardy, but needs full sun in cold climates. In cold-winter areas, lift the corms for the winter and replant in spring. Recently, larger flowered hybrids in a wider range of colors (yellow to red) have been raised in England. 'Bressingham Blaze' has bright orange-red flowers; 'Lucifer' has bright red flowers. Both are a little hardier than the species. *Zones 7–11.*

CROCUS

There are about 80 species, and numerous garden forms and hybrids, in this genus of cormous perennials from Europe, North Africa and temperate Asia. The goblet-shaped flowers taper at the base into a long tube that originates below the soil surface. Color varies greatly, though lilac-blue, mauve, yellow and white are usual. They can be divided into spring-flowering, the flowers appearing with or before the new leaves, and autumn-flowering, blooming in full leaf. The foliage is grass-like, usually with a central silver-white stripe.

Cultivation

Very frost-hardy plants, they do best in cool to cold areas. Plant corms in early fall in moist, well-drained soil in full sun or part-shade. Water well until the foliage begins to die. Plant seeds in autumn. These will usually not flower for 3 years.

Crocus chrysanthus

syns *Crocus cannulatus* var. *chrysanthus,* *C. croceus*

This species from Turkey and the Balkan Peninsula has bright orange flowers feathered with bronze, and orange anthers; they appear in late winter or early spring. Leaves are up to 10 in (25 cm) long and appear at the same time as the flowers. There are a number of hybrid cultivars, including 'Cream Beauty', with creamy yellow flowers; and 'E. A. Bowles', with deep butter-yellow flowers with bronze feathering mainly at the base of the petals. *Zones 4–9.*

Cosmos bipinnatus 'Sea Shells'

Crocosmia × *crocosmiiflora*

Crocus chrysanthus

Cynoglossum amabile

Crocus sativus

Crocus vernus

Crocus sativus
Saffron crocus

This small species is famous for the saffron, obtained from its reddish orange stigmas, which is used as a dye and to flavor food. *Crocus sativus* grows to 2 in (5 cm) high, and has lilac or purple flowers in autumn. It does not set seed. *Zones 6–9.*

Crocus vernus
Dutch crocus

There are many spring-flowering hybrid crocuses derived from *C. vernus* and known as Dutch crocuses. The species itself, a native of eastern and central Europe, grows to 4 in (10 cm) high and bears solitary white, pink or purple flowers from spring to early summer. The Dutch hybrids are vigorous plants with large flowers up to 6 in (15 cm) long, in a varied color range—white to yellow, purple or bluish; there are also some striped varieties. *Zones 4–9.*

CYNOGLOSSUM

This genus of 55 species of annuals, biennials and perennials occurs in most temperate regions of the world. All are frost hardy and have a long flowering period. They are related to the common forget-me-not, which many resemble.

Cultivation

All species need a fertile but not too rich soil; if over-nourished the plants tend to flop over. Propagate from seed sown in fall or spring, or by division.

Cynoglossum amabile
Chinese forget-me-not

This upright annual or biennial, growing to a height of about 20 in (50 cm) has dull green hairy lanceolate leaves and flowers in racemes, generally blue although white and pink forms can occur. Flowers are produced in spring and early summer. It self-seeds readily. 'Firmament' has pendulous sky-blue flowers. *Zones 5–9.*

D

Dahlia × *hortensis* 'Bishop of Llandaff'

Dahlia, Waterlily or nymphaea-flowered (Group 4) 'Gerrie Hoek'

Dahlia, Semi-cactus (Group 9) 'Brandaris'

DAHLIA

This genus of about 30 species, native from Mexico to Colombia, has had a big impact on gardens. Of this number only 2 or 3 species were used to create the thousands of named varieties available. So many different flower forms have been developed that the hybrids are classified into about 10 different groups, determined by the size and type of their flowerheads.

Cultivation

Dahlias are not frost resistant, so in cold climates lift the tubers each year and store in a frost-free place to be split and replanted in spring. Most prefer a sunny,

sheltered position in well-fertilized, well-drained soil. Feed monthly and water well when in flower. Propagate bedding forms from seed, others from seed, cuttings from tubers or by division.

Dahlia × *hortensis* 'Bishop of Llandaff'

Peony-flowered dahlias, which are kept as a separate group in some countries, usually have one or two rows of flat petals with a center which can be open or partly covered by small twisted petals, such as 'Bishop of Llandaff' with its brilliant scarlet blooms above its beautiful deep burgundy leaves. *Zones 8–10.*

Dahlia, Waterlily or nymphaea-flowered (Group 4)

These fully double-flowered dahlias have slightly cupped petals that have a more than passing resemblance to their namesakes, the waterlilies. The overall effect is of a flattish flower. 'Cameo' has white flowers with a cream base; 'Gerrie Hoek' has pink waterlily flowers on strong stems and is popular as a cut flower. *Zones 8–10.*

Dahlia, Semi-cactus (Group 9)

This group of fully double-flowered dahlias have long, narrow rolled petals giving the flowers a spidery look. 'So Dainty' is a miniature with golden

Delphinium, Belladonna Group

Delosperma nubigenum

bronze and apricot flowers; 'Brandaris' is a medium form with soft orange and golden yellow flowers; 'Hayley Jane' has purplish pink flowers and white bases; and 'Salmon Keene' has large salmon pink to golden flowers. *Zones 8–10.*

DELOSPERMA

Belonging to the large mesembryanthemum alliance, this is a genus of over 150 species of mainly shrubby succulents native to South and East Africa as well as Madagascar. Although these plants are usually quite drought-tolerant and ideal for desert gardens, some are moderately frost-tolerant as well. The leaves are borne in opposite pairs and can be triangular or circular in cross section. The flowers, which are usually produced in summer, are somewhat daisy-like and often brightly colored.

Cultivation

An aspect in full sun with good drainage and little frost will suit most species. Propagate from seed or cuttings.

Delosp erma nubigenum

This very prostrate trailing species makes a lovely ground cover or trailer. Its blooms are comparatively small but they are a bright yellow to orange-red. *Zones 8–11.*

DELPHINIUM

This genus of 250 or so species ranges from self-seeding annuals or dwarf alpine plants up to statuesque perennials that exceed 8 ft (2.4 m) in height. Nearly all start as a tuft of long-stalked basal leaves, their blades divided into 3 to 7 radiating lobes or segments. The tufts elongate into erect, sometimes branched flowering stems bearing flowers with a backward-pointing nectar spur. Recognized groups include the Belladonna, Elatum and Pacific hybrids.

Cultivation

Very frost hardy, most like a cool to cold winter. They prefer full sun with shelter from strong winds, and well-drained, fertile soil. Apply a liquid fertilizer at 2–3 week intervals. Propagate from cuttings or by division.

Delphinium, Belladonna Group

These frost-hardy perennials (*Delphinium elatum* × *D. grandiflorum*) have an upright, loosely branching form. Their widely spaced blue or white flowers are single or sometimes semi-double and borne on loose spikes ranging in height up to 4 ft (1.2 m). They bloom in early and late summer. Propagate by division or from basal cuttings in spring. *Zones 3–9.*

Delphinium grandiflorum
syn. *Delphinium chinense*
Butterfly delphinium, Chinese delphinium
Native to China, Siberia, Japan and
Mongolia, this tufted perennial grows to
a height of 18 in (45 cm) and a spread of
12 in (30 cm). The leaf segments are
divided into narrow lobes. It bears large
bright blue flowers over a long period in
summer. It is fully frost hardy. 'Azure
Fairy' is a pale blue-flowering form;
'Blue Butterfly' has bright blue flowers.
Zones 3–9.

Delphinium, Pacific Hybrid 'Black Knight'

Delphinium grandiflorum 'Blue Butterfly'

Delphinium, Pacific Hybrids
These short-lived perennials are usually
grown as biennials. They are stately
plants to 5 ft (1.5 m) or more in height
with star-like single, semi-double or
double flowers of mostly blue, purple or
white, clustered on erect rigid spikes.
Cultivars include 'Astolat', a perennial
with lavender-mauve flowers with dark
eyes; 'Black Knight', with deep rich
purple flowers with black eyes;
'Guinevere' with pale purple flowers
with a pinkish tinge and white eyes; and
'Summer Skies' with pale sky-blue
flowers. *Zones 7–9.*

DENDRANTHEMA
This genus of about 20 species of upright
perennials was previously included in
the genus *Chrysanthemum*. It has a
distribution from Europe to central and
eastern Asia. They are very popular
temperate region flowers. With continuous hybridization the flowerheads have
diversified in size, shape and disposition
of the florets in the blooms. There are 10
main groups of classification based largely
upon floral characteristics. All but a few
flower in mid- to late autumn.

Cultivation
Dendranthemas are generally frost
hardy, though some forms may be
somewhat frost tender. Grow in a sunny
position in a well-drained slightly acidic
soil, improved with compost and well-
rotted manure. Propagate from seed, by
division or cuttings.

Dendranthema × grandiflorum
syns *Chrysanthemum indicum, C.
morifolium*
Florists' chrysanthemum
This hybrid is the parent of hundreds of
cultivars. It is a vigorous subshrub to
5 ft (1.5 m) tall with thick, strongly
aromatic lobed leaves to 3 in (8 cm) in

length with a gray felted underside. The single blooms have yellow centers and spreading ray florets in white, yellow, bronze, pink, red or purple. There are numerous cultivars of various shapes and sizes and new ones are being raised annually. 'Elizabeth Shoesmith' bears large deep pink to purple flowers; 'Flame Symbol' has burnt orange double flowers; 'Yellow Symbol' has bright golden yellow blooms. *Zones 4–10*.

DESCHAMPSIA
Hair grass
This genus of mainly evergreen perennial grasses has a wide distribution in temperate zones. There are about 50 species although few are grown as garden plants. Those that are make attractive clumps with airy, graceful flowerheads in summer that are often still attractive, albeit dead, into winter. They can be used fresh or dried for floral indoor arrangements. Like many other grasses, much selection of superior garden forms has been carried out in recent years so that new named varieties become available regularly. Plant in groups for a delicate, airy mass of blooms in the garden.

Cultivation
These adaptable grasses usually do best in compost-enriched, moist soil in part-shade. Species can be raised from seed.

Deschampsia caespitosa

Deschampsia caespitosa
Tufted hair grass
This mound-forming, evergreen perennial reaches 24–36 in (60–90 cm) in height with a 24 in (60 cm) spread. The flowers are borne in open panicles which rise above the coarse, arching foliage; colors range from pale greenish yellow to gold (in the cultivar 'Goldgehänge'), to silver and bronze ('Bronzeschleier'). Other cultivars of tufted hair grass include 'Goldschleier' ('Gold Veil'), which has silver-tinged golden yellow flower panicles; and 'Goldtau' ('Golden Dew'), with reddish brown flowers that age to golden yellow. *Zones 4–10*.

DIANTHUS
Carnation, pink
This large genus consists of some 300 species. Much hybridizing has created several different groups of pinks and carnations bred for specific purposes. Border carnations are annual or perennial plants up to 24 in (60 cm). Perpetual-flowering carnations are often disbudded leaving only the top bud to develop. American Spray carnations are treated like perpetuals except that no disbudding is carried out. Malmaison Carnations are thought to resemble the Bourbon rose 'Souvenir de la Malmaison'. Other groups are the Modern Pinks, the Old-fashioned Pinks and the Alpine or Rock Pinks.

Dendranthema × grandiflorum

Dianthus chinensis 'Strawberry Parfait'

Dianthus, Modern Pink 'Doris'

Dianthus barbatus

Cultivation

Dianthus species like a sunny position, protection from strong winds, and well-drained, slightly alkaline soil. Propagate perennials by layering or from cuttings in summer; annuals and biennials from seed in autumn or early spring. Watch for aphids, thrips and caterpillars, rust and virus infections.

Dianthus barbatus
Sweet William

A slow-growing, frost-hardy perennial usually treated as a biennial, sweet William self-sows readily and grows to a height of 18 in (45 cm) and spread of 6 in (15 cm). The crowded, flattened heads of fragrant flowers range from white through pinks to carmine and crimson-purple and are often zoned in

two tones. They flower in late spring and early summer and are ideal for massed planting. The dwarf cultivars, about 4 in (10 cm) tall, are usually treated as annuals. *Zones 4–10*.

Dianthus chinensis
Chinese pink, Indian pink

This Chinese annual has a short, tufted growth habit, and gray-green, lance-shaped leaves. In late spring and summer it bears masses of single or double, sweetly scented flowers in shades of pink, red, lavender and white. It is slow growing to a height and spread of 6–12 in (15–30 cm), and is fully frost hardy. 'Strawberry Parfait' has single pink flowers, lightly fringed with deep red centers. *Zones 7–10*.

Dianthus, Modern Pinks

These are densely leafed, mound-forming perennials derived from crosses between cultivars of *Dianthus plumarius* and *D. caryophyllus*. They have gray-green foliage and many erect flowering stems, each carrying 4 to 6 fragrant, single to fully double flowers in shades of white, pink or crimson, often with dark centers and with plain or fringed petals. Most are 12–18 in (30–45 cm) tall with a spread of 18 in (45 cm) and flower from late spring until early

Dianthus, Old-fashioned Pink 'Pink Mrs. Sinkins'

Dianthus superbus 'Rainbow Loveliness'

Dicentra formosa

autumn; some are clove-scented. 'Doris' is a scented, pale pink double with deep pink center. *Zones 5–10.*

Dianthus, **Old-fashioned Pinks**

These are tuft-forming perennials that grow to 18 in (45 cm) high. In late spring and early summer they bear single to fully double, clove-scented flowers in colors varying from white, through pale pink and magenta to red, often fringed and with contrasting centers. 'Mrs. Sinkins' has pure white shaggy flowers prone to split at the calyx; it is highly perfumed. 'Pink Mrs. Sinkins' is a pale pink form of 'Mrs. Sinkins'. *Zones 5–9.*

Dianthus superbus

This species is a loosely tufted perennial sometimes as much as 3 ft (1 m) high.

The rich purple-pink fragrant flowers, produced singly or in pairs through summer, have petals deeply divided giving flowers a loosely fringed appearance. It has been used in producing garden hybrids and is better known as a parent of the Loveliness Strain which includes 'Rainbow Loveliness', with deeply fringed single flowers of mauve and pink shades carried on slender stems in spring. *Zones 4–10.*

DICENTRA
Bleeding heart

This genus consists of about 20 species of annuals and perennials admired for their feathery leaves and the graceful carriage of their flowers, although they do not grow or flower well without a period of winter chill. The flowers, pendent and heart-shaped, come in red, pink, white, purple and yellow. They flower from mid-spring into early summer. From Asia and North America, they are usually found in woodland and mountainous areas.

Cultivation

Mostly quite frost hardy, dicentras love humus-rich, moist but well-drained soil and some light shade. They can be propagated from seed in autumn or by division in late winter.

Dicentra formosa
syn. *Dicentra eximia*
Western bleeding heart
This spreading plant grows to about 18 in (45 cm) high with a spread of 12 in (30 cm). Dainty pink and red flowers appear on slender arching stems throughout spring and summer. *Zones 3–9.*

Dicentra spectabilis
Bleeding heart
This popular garden perennial grows 24–36 in (60–90 cm) tall with a spread of 18–24 in (45–60 cm). Pink and white heart-shaped flowers on long arching stems appear in late spring and summer. After flowering, the foliage usually dies down to the ground. 'Alba' is a pure white form with green-yellow markings and pale green leaves. *Zones 2–9.*

DICTAMNUS
Burning bush
The Book of Exodus tells how God spoke to Moses on Mount Sinai from a bush that burned yet was not consumed by the fire. Gardeners insist that it must

have been *Dictamnus albus*, the only species in its genus and indigenous to the Mediterranean and temperate Asia. In still, warm conditions so much aromatic oil evaporates from the leaves that if you strike a match near it the vapor ignites and the bush is engulfed in flame, but so briefly that it is not damaged.

Cultivation
This perennial needs full sun and fertile, well-drained soil. It resents disturbance. Propagate from fresh seed in summer.

Dictamnus albus
syn. *Dictamnus fraxinella*
Burning bush, dittany, gas plant
This herbaceous, woody-stemmed perennial bears early summer spikes of fragrant, star-shaped, white, pink or lilac flowers with long stamens. It grows to 3 ft (1 m) tall with a similar spread and has glossy light green leaves. It is quite frost hardy. *Dictamnus albus* var. *purpureus* (syn. *D. a.* var. *rubra*) bears purple-pink flowers. *Zones 3–9.*

DIGITALIS
Foxglove
These 22 species of biennials and perennials, some of them evergreen, bear

Dicentra spectabilis 'Alba'

Dictamnus albus

Digitalis purpurea

tall, majestic spikes of tubular, 2-lipped flowers which come in many colors including magenta, purple, white, cream, yellow, pink and lavender. The medicinal properties of digitalis have been well-known since ancient times, and the plant is still used in the treatment of heart ailments.

Cultivation
Marginally to fully frost hardy, they grow in most sheltered conditions, preferring cool climates in part-shade and humus-rich, well-drained soil. Cut flowering stems down to the ground after spring flowering to encourage secondary spikes. Propagate from seed in autumn or by division.

Digitalis × mertonensis
A hybrid of *Digitalis grandiflora* and *D. purpurea*, this frost-hardy perennial forms a clump about 36 in (90 cm) tall and 12 in (30 cm) wide. Summer flowering, it bears spikes of tubular, pink to salmon flowers above a rosette of soft, hairy, oval leaves. Divide after flowering. *Zones 4–9*.

Digitalis purpurea
The common foxglove is a short-lived, frost-hardy perennial with an upright habit, a height of 3–5 ft (1–1.5 m) and a spread of 24 in (60 cm). The flowers are purple, pink, rosy magenta, white or pale yellow, above a rosette of rough, oval leaves. All parts of the plant are poisonous. Many seedling strains are available, grown as bedding annuals, the Excelsior Hybrids in mixed colors being very popular. *Digitalis purpurea* f. *albiflora* has pure white flowers sometimes lightly spotted brown inside. *Zones 5–10*.

DIMORPHOTHECA
African daisy, Cape marigold
These 7 species of annuals, perennials and evergreen subshrubs from South Africa have colorful, daisy-like flowers from late winter. Related to the genus *Osteospermum*, they are useful for rock gardens and borders.

Cultivation
They need an open sunny situation and fertile, well-drained soil; they are salt tolerant. The flowers only open in sunshine. Deadheading prolongs

Digitalis × mertonensis

Disporum flavens

Dimorphotheca pluvialis

DISPORUM
Fairy bells

Disporum is a genus of between 10 and 20 species of elegant and attractive woodland plants related to and similar to Solomon's seal (*Polygonatum*). Species are native to the USA, eastern Asia and the Himalayas. They have creeping rhizomes that can travel some distance but they are not invasive. The arching stems are often slightly branched and clothed with attractive alternating leaves. The flowers are bell-shaped and hang under the stems. They can be white to green-yellow.

Cultivation

As these are woodland plants, give them a cool part-shaded position with ample organic material like leafmold. They are definitely not for tropical or arid zones. Propagation is usually from seed or by division.

flowering. Propagate annuals from seed in spring and perennials from cuttings in summer. Watch for fungal diseases in summer rainfall areas.

Dimorphotheca pluvialis
syn. *Dimorphotheca annua*
Rain daisy

This bedding annual produces small flowerheads in late winter and spring that are snow white above, purple beneath, with brownish purple centers. Low growing, it reaches 8–12 in (20–30 cm) in height with a similar spread. *Zones 8–10.*

Disporum flavens

This Korean woodland perennial grows in neat clumps to 30 in (75 cm) high by 12 in (30 cm) across. It has attractive lance-shaped leaves and in early spring will produce up to 3 drooping soft yellow flowers per stem. These are followed in autumn by small black berries. *Zones 5–9.*

Dodecatheon meadia

Doronicum columnae 'Miss Mason'

DODECATHEON
Shooting star

The shooting stars (about 14 species) are western North America's equivalent to Europe's cyclamens and, like them, they are perennials and related to the primrose. Most are rosette-forming and grow to about 15 in (38 cm) high, with pink or white flowers. They have swept-back petals and protruding stamens.

Cultivation

Fully frost hardy, shooting stars prefer part-shade in moist, well-drained acidic soil. Most require a dry dormant summer period after flowering. Propagation is from seed in autumn or by division in winter.

Dodecatheon meadia

This is the best-known species, bearing white, rose pink or cyclamen pink, nodding flowers. It has primula-like, clumped rosettes of pale green leaves, and ranges from 6–18 in (15–45 cm) high with a spread of 18 in (45 cm). It was named for English scientist Richard Mead (1673–1754), a patron of American botanical studies. *Zones 3–9.*

DORONICUM
Leopard's bane

The 35 species of herbaceous perennials that make up this genus extend from Europe through western Asia to Siberia. Species have attractive, bright yellow daisy-like flowers which are produced in spring and summer above fresh bright green foliage. Most species make attractive border plants of restrained habit and are also good as cut flowers.

Cultivation

Doronicums will cope with a range of habitats, but prefer a moisture-retentive but not wet soil, high in humus; part-shade or morning sun is preferred but never heavy dark shade. Propagate from seed or by division.

Doronicum columnae 'Miss Mason'

This is a large-flowered selection with blooms about 3 in (8 cm) across in mid- to late spring. Its bright yellow daisies are held well above its heart-shaped leaves on stems up to 24 in (60 cm) tall. *Zones 5–9.*

Doronicum pardalianches

Dorotheanthus bellidiformis

Doronicum pardalianches
syn. *Doronicum cordatum*
Leopard's bane
Doronicum pardalianches is a spreading, clump-forming perennial to 3 ft (1 m) tall and wide. The oval basal leaves, to 5 in (12 cm) long, have heart-shaped bases. Bright yellow daisy-like flowers are borne on slender, branching stems from late spring to mid-summer. *Zones 5–9*.

DOROTHEANTHUS
Ice plant, Livingstone daisy
A genus of about 10 species of succulent annuals from South Africa, these mat-forming plants bear masses of daisy-like flowers in bright shades of red, pink, white or bicolored with dark centers in summer. They are ideal for borders and massed displays.

Cultivation
Marginally frost hardy, they like well-drained soil in a sunny position. Dead-head to prolong flowering. In frost-prone areas plant out after the likelihood of frost has passed. Propagate from seed.

Dorotheanthus bellidiformis
Ice plant, Livingstone daisy, Bokbaai vygie
This small succulent annual has daisy-like flowerheads in dazzling shades of yellow, white, red or pink in summer sun; flowers close in dull weather. It grows to 6 in (15 cm) tall and spreads to 12 in (30 cm) and has fleshy light green leaves to 3 in (7cm) long with glistening surface cells. *Zones 9–11*.

DRYAS
Mountain avens
A genus of 3 species from alpine and Arctic regions of the northern hemisphere, *Dryas* species make dense mats of evergreen foliage somewhat like tiny oak leaves; these often turn dark bronze in winter. Although the foliage and stems

Dryopteris erythrosora

hug the ground, the showy flowers and seed heads sit up well above them.

Cultivation
Completely cold tolerant, they may be less than satisfactory in warm climates. They make good rock garden or ground cover plants and are also useful between paving slabs. Grow in full sun or part-shade in a well-drained, humus-rich soil. Propagate from seed or cuttings.

Dryas octopetala
Mountain avens
This lovely alpine plant can make evergreen mats up to 4 in (10 cm) tall in flower with a spread exceeding 3 ft (1 m). The pure white flowers, 1½ in (4 cm) across and with a boss of golden stamens in the center, are produced in late spring and early summer and followed by equally ornamental fluffy silver seed heads. *Zones 2–9.*

DRYOPTERIS
Shield fern, wood fern
This genus of about 200 species of deciduous or semi-evergreen terrestrial ferns is found mainly in the northern hemisphere woodlands by streams and

Dryas octopetala

lakes. Most cultivated species have elongated fronds that are pinnately divided. Many make excellent garden ferns and handsome potted plants.

Cultivation
They require part-shade and moist, humus-rich soil. Remove fading fronds regularly. Protect from wind damage and do not overwater established plants. Propagate from spores in summer or by division in autumn or in winter.

Dryopteris erythrosora
Autumn fern, Japanese shield fern
Native to eastern Asia, this fern produces new fronds that range from

Dryopteris filix-mas 'Depauperata'

copper to very bright red. As the fronds age they become glossy green. Bright red spore-masses dot the undersides of the pinnules. A mature fern reaches 18 in (45 cm), spreading to 12 in (30 cm). *Zones 5–9.*

Dryopteris filix-mas
Male fern

Common to Europe, Asia and North America, this deciduous or semi-evergreen fern has lanceolate, pinnate, elegantly arching fronds that arise from crowns of large, upright rhizomes. It grows up to 4 ft (1.2 m) high and 3 ft (1 m) wide. 'Grandiceps Wills', the

crested male fern, has a lovely form with a crested top almost as wide as the frond as well as finely crested leaflets. 'Depauperata' grows to 15 in (38 cm) high and has rich green fronds that blend together at the top. *Zones 2–9.*

Dryopteris marginalis
Marginal shield fern, leather wood fern

This attractive fern from North America has stiffly upright, slightly arching, olive green bipinnate fronds arising from a tight, central crown to a height of some 12–24 in (30–60 cm). The spore-masses are borne along the margins of the leaflets. *Zones 4–8.*

E

Echinacea purpurea

Echinops ritro

ECHINACEA
Coneflower
The 9 coneflower species, all native to the USA, share their common name with their cousins the rudbeckias. They are clump-forming plants with thick edible roots. The daisy-like flowerheads are usually mauve-pink or purple, with darker and paler garden forms available. The dried root and rhizome of *Echinacea angustifolia* and *E. purpurea* are used in herbal medicine and allegedly increase the body's resistance to infection.

Cultivation
Very frost hardy, they like full sun and fertile soil. Divide them only to increase stock, otherwise leave them alone and mulch each spring. Deadhead regularly. Propagate by division or from root cuttings from winter to early spring.

Echinacea purpurea
syn. *Rudbeckia purpurea*
Purple coneflower
This showy, summer-flowering perennial has dark green, lance-shaped leaves and large, daisy-like, rosy purple flowers with high, orange-brown central cones. The flowerheads are borne singly on strong stems. Of upright habit, it grows to 4 ft (1.2 m) tall and spreads to about 18 in (45 cm). 'Robert Bloom' has dark pink flowers with orange-brown centers; 'White Swan' has large, pure white flowers with orange-brown centers. *Zones 3–10.*

ECHINOPS
Globe thistle
This genus, related to thistles, contains some 120 species of erect perennials, biennials and annuals, found in Europe, Asia and tropical Africa. The cultivated species make bold additions to mixed or herbaceous borders and many are used in dried flower arrangements. The foliage is usually gray-green and thistle-like. The ball-shaped flowerheads can be blue, blue-gray or white, and up to 2 in (5 cm) in diameter. Most cultivated species grow to about 4 ft (1.2 m).

Cultivation
They are usually fully frost hardy and heat tolerant, requiring a sunny aspect with a well-drained soil of any quality. Cut them to the ground in autumn or early winter. Propagate by division or from seed.

Echinops ritro
This perennial is a useful plant for the herbaceous border, and its globe-like, spiky flowers can be cut and dried for winter decoration. It has large, deeply cut, prickly leaves with downy under-

Epilobium angustifolium

Echium vulgare

sides, silvery white stems and round, thistle-like, purplish blue flowerheads in summer. Of upright habit, it grows 30 in (75 cm) tall and wide. *Zones 3–10.*

ECHIUM

Indigenous to the Mediterranean, Canary Islands, western Europe and Madeira, the 40 or so species of annuals, perennials and shrubs in this genus have spectacular bright blue, purple or pink flowers in late spring and summer. The hairy leaves form rosettes at the bases of the flowering stems. Ingestion of the plants can cause stomach upsets.

Cultivation

Very frost hardy to frost tender, they require a dry climate, full sun and a light to medium, well-drained soil. Prune gently after flowering. Propagate from seed or cuttings in spring or summer. In mild climates they self-seed readily.

Echium vulgare
Viper's bugloss

This spectacular European biennial to 3 ft (1 m) tall has erect leafy stems. The funnel-shaped flowers, borne in spikes or panicles, are usually a rich violet,

although white and pink forms exist. A dwarf form is available with white, blue, pink or purple flowers. *Zones 7–10.*

EPILOBIUM

syn. *Chamaenerion*
Willow herb

This is a large genus of about 200 species of annuals, biennials, perennials and subshrubs in the evening primrose family, widely distributed throughout the temperate and cold zones of both hemispheres. Most species are invasive, but some are valued for their pretty deep pink or white flowers, which are produced over a long period from summer to autumn.

Cultivation

Plant in sun or shade in moist, well-drained soil. They are mostly quite frost hardy. Remove spent flowers to prevent seeding. Propagate from seed in spring or autumn, or from cuttings.

Epilobium angustifolium
syn. *Chamaenerion angustifolium*
Fireweed, Rose Bay willow herb

This is a tall, vigorous perennial to 5 ft (1.5 m) found throughout the northern and mountainous parts of Eurasia and North America, most widespread in areas that have been recently burned or logged. Drifts of rose-pink flowering spikes are produced in late summer. It will spread indefinitely unless confined by pruning or containing the root system and self-seeds freely. *Zones 2–9.*

Epilobium canum subsp. *canum*
syn. *Zauschneria californica*
Californian fuchsia
The common name refers both to the species' Californian origin and to its flowers, which are indeed like the related fuchsias. These are bright red, appearing in terminal spikes on erect, slender stems in late summer and early autumn. This evergreen shrub is highly variable and grows 12–24 in (30–60 cm) tall and 3–6 ft (1–1.8 m) wide. It needs only occasional water and is hardy to around 15°F (–9°C). *Zones 8–10.*

EPIMEDIUM
Barrenwort
This genus of about 40 species comes mainly from temperate Asia with a few species extending to the Mediterranean. A useful low-growing perennial for

Epilobium canum subsp. *canum*

shady situations, the barrenworts produce delightful sprays of delicate, often spurred flowers in late spring or early summer just above the foliage. Slowly spreading to form a broad mound or mat, they serve well as ground covers or in rock gardens.

Cultivation
Frost hardy, most tolerate dry conditions. All prefer woodland conditions and well-drained soil. Propagate from seed or by division in autumn.

Epimedium × *rubrum*
Red barrenwort
This hybrid can be variable, but generally has spiny leaves that are strikingly veined in red. Low mounds are topped by 12 in (30 cm) stems with crimson and white, 1 in (25 mm) wide flowers in spring. It can be used as a ground cover. *Zones 4–9.*

Epimedium × *rubrum*

Epimedium × versicolor

This hybrid of *Epimedium grandiflorum* and *E. pinnatum* is a carpeting perennial to 12 in (30 cm) high and wide. The green, heart-shaped leaves are tinted reddish when young. Clusters of pendent pink and yellow flowers with red spurs are produced in spring. 'Sulphureum' has sulfur-yellow flowers and reddish bronze-tinted young foliage. As summer advances it turns green, then russet again in autumn. *Zones 5–9.*

ERANTHIS
Winter aconite

From Europe and temperate Asia, these 7 species of clump-forming perennials have the ability to naturalize under deciduous trees. They flower in late winter and early spring. The short-stemmed, yellow, buttercup-like flowers are surrounded by a ruff of green leaves.

Cultivation

Very frost hardy, they like full sun or part-shade. Slightly damp conditions during the summer dormancy and an alkaline, well-drained soil are conducive to good growth and plentiful flowers. Propagate from seed or by division.

Eranthis hyemalis

Native to Europe, this ground-hugging perennial with knobbly tubers grows to a height of 3 in (8 cm). The yellow, cup-shaped flowers are borne above a ruff of lobed leaves. *Zones 5–9.*

EREMURUS
Foxtail lily, desert candle

There are 50 or so species in this Asian genus. Their dramatic flower spikes, each of which can contain hundreds of flowers in pale shades of white, yellow or pink, rise to well over head height. Foliage is luxuriant but low, so the flower stems rise almost naked, which makes them all the more imposing.

Cultivation

In the wild these cool- to cold-climate plants are protected from the winter cold by a thick blanket of snow; in milder climates they need a winter mulch to ensure the soil does not freeze. They also need sun and a well-drained soil. Propagate from fresh seed or by division.

Eranthis hyemalis

Epimedium × versicolor 'Sulphureum'

Erigeron foliosus

Eremurus × *isabellinus*, Shelford Hybrid

Eremurus × isabellinus, Shelford Hybrids

These frost-hardy perennials have lofty spikes of close-packed flowers. They produce rosettes of strap-like leaves and in mid-summer each crown yields spikes of blooms with strong stems and hundreds of shallow cup-shaped flowers in a wide range of colors including white, pink, salmon, yellow, apricot and coppery tones. 'Shelford Desert Candle' is a pure white form. They grow to about 4 ft (1.2 m) in height with a spread of 24 in (60 cm). *Zones 5–9.*

ERIGERON
Fleabane

This large genus of about 200 species of annuals, biennials and perennials, some evergreen, occurs throughout the world's temperate regions, but predominantly in North America. Some species were believed to repel fleas. The mainly erect stems are capped by masses of pink, white or blue, daisy-like flowers and suit borders or rock gardens. They flower between late spring and mid-summer.

Cultivation

Frost hardy, they prefer a sunny position sheltered from strong winds and moderately fertile, well-drained soil. Do not allow to dry out during the growing season. Cut back immediately after flowering to encourage compact growth and prevent unwanted self-seeding. Some erigerons can become invasive. Propagate from seed or by division in spring.

Erigeron 'Foersters Liebling'

Bearing its semi-double, dark pink flowers in summer, this clump-forming perennial reaches a height of 24 in (60 cm) and spread of 18 in (45 cm). The lance-shaped leaves are grayish green. *Zones 5–9.*

Erigeron foliosus

This clump-forming species grows to about 8 in (20 cm) in flower and comes from western North America. Its leaves are narrow-oblong and reduce in size up the stem. The flowers are usually blue with a yellow center. *Zones 5–9.*

Erigeron karvinskianus

Erigeron karvinskianus
syn. *Erigeron mucronatus*
Mexican daisy, Santa Barbara daisy, fleabane daisy
This scrambling or mound-forming perennial from Mexico and Central America makes an informal ground cover and in mild climates will bloom profusely throughout the year. The small flowers open white, fading to various shades of pink and wine red. It grows to about 15 in (38 cm) tall with an indefinite spread, and has lax stems and narrow, often lobed, hairy leaves. It can be quite invasive in mild climates. *Zones 7–11.*

ERYNGIUM
Sea holly
Mostly native to South America and Europe, these 230 species of biennials and perennials are members of the same family as the carrot, and have spiny collared flowerheads that usually have a bluish metallic sheen. They flower over a long period in summer and may be cut before they fully open, and dried for winter decoration. The spiny margins of the strongly colored, thistle-like bracts that surround the central flower give rise to the common name 'holly'.

Eryngium bourgatii

Cultivation
Mostly frost hardy, they need sun, good drainage and sandy soil. Propagate species from fresh seed; selected forms by root cuttings in winter or by division in spring.

Eryngium bourgatii
This striking herbaceous perennial from the eastern Mediterranean has basal leaves that are leathery, gray-green and silver veined. Its flower spikes rise up to 30 in (75 cm) tall and support numerous blue or gray-green flowers surrounded by silvery spiny bracts. 'Othello' is a compact form that produces shorter flowers on strong, thick stems. *Zones 5–9.*

Eryngium giganteum
Miss Willmott's ghost
This short-lived, clump-forming perennial grows to a height of about 3–4 ft (1–1.2 m) and spreads about 30 in (75 cm). The leaves are heart-shaped and mid-green,

and it bears large, rounded, blue or pale green thistle heads surrounded by silvery bracts. It dies after its late summer flowering, but if conditions are good its seeds will thrive. *Zones 6–9*.

ERYSIMUM
syn. *Cheiranthus*
Wallflower
Some of the 80 species of annuals and perennials in this genus are suitable for rock gardens, such as 'Orange Flame'; others fit nicely into the border. Short-lived species are best grown as biennials. Some are fine winter–spring-flowering plants, while some flower all winter or all year in very mild regions. The older types are sweetly scented, while the newer cultivars have no fragrance but bloom well over a long season.

Cultivation
Mostly frost hardy, they like a well-drained, fertile soil in an open, sunny position. Cut back perennials after flowering so only a few leaves remain on each stem. Propagate from seed in spring or cuttings in summer.

Erysimum × allionii
syn. *Cheiranthus × allionii*
Siberian wallflower
This slow-growing but short-lived hybrid is a bushy evergreen suitable for rock gardens, banks and borders. It has toothed, mid-green leaves and bears bright yellow or orange flowers in spring, putting on a dazzling display for a long period. It reaches a height and spread of 12–18 in (30–45 cm). *Zones 3–10*.

Erysimum 'Golden Bedder'
syn. *Cheiranthus* 'Golden Bedder'
This is one of the color forms of the Bedder Series, bred for compact shape and available in shades from cream through yellow to orange and red. They can flower for months, often starting in winter in mild climates. *Zones 8–10*.

Erysimum linifolium
Native to Spain and Portugal, this narrow-leafed, mat-forming perennial

Erysimum 'Golden Bedder'

Eryngium giganteum

Erysimum × allionii

grows to about 30 in (75 cm) tall and has long spikes of comparatively small, deep mauve flowers almost all year round in mild climates. Several forms exist including 'Bicolor', with pink-mauve as well as white flowers, and 'Variegatum', with mauve flowers and white-edged leaves. *Zones 6–10.*

ERYTHRONIUM
Dog's tooth violet, trout lily, fawn lily

Native to temperate Eurasia and North America, these little perennial lilies bear delicate, reflexed, star-shaped flowers in spring. They come in shades of yellow or pink, and there are some very pretty hybrids available. The dark green foliage is often attractively mottled. The common name of dog's tooth violet refers to the shape of the corm.

Cultivation

Frost hardy, they do best in cooler areas. Plant the tubers in autumn in part-shade in well-drained, humus-rich soil, and keep moist. They multiply easily and should be left undisturbed until over-crowding occurs. Propagate from offsets in summer or from seed in fall.

Erythronium californicum
Californian fawn lily

This is a native of northern California, where it grows on the coastal ranges in pine and evergreen woods. The flowers, shaped like Turks' caps, have pale bright white petals and appear in mid-spring. The leaves are variable but in some strains are deeply and decoratively marked in purple. It reaches 8–12 in (20–30 cm) in height. 'White Beauty' is a robust form with white flowers zoned in reddish brown markings. *Zones 5–9.*

Erythronium revolutum
Pink trout lily

This variable species grows in the wild in lightly wooded country and on the edges of streams in northeastern North America. The leaves are mottled and the stalks are often, but not always, suffused with a pinkish glow. The petal color can

Eschscholzia caespitosa

Erysimum linifolium

Erythronium californicum

Eschscholzia californica

Erythronium revolutum

vary between pink, purple and white with yellow central bands and yellow anthers. This species reaches about 12 in (30 cm) in height. 'Pagoda' has marbled green foliage and nodding, deep yellow flowers. *Zones 5–9.*

ESCHSCHOLZIA
California poppy

This genus from western North America was named by botanist/poet Adalbert von Chamisso (1781–1838) in honor of his friend, Johan Friedrich Eschscholz. It is a genus of 8 to 10 annuals and perennials with deeply dissected leaves. They bear yellow to orange poppy-like flowers that close up in dull weather, and capsular fruits.

Cultivation

Species thrive in warm, dry climates but will tolerate quite severe frosts. They do not like transplanting so should be sown directly where they are to grow. Grow in poor, well-drained soil. Propagate from seed sown in spring.

Eschscholzia caespitosa

This fast-growing, slender, erect annual bears cup-shaped, solitary yellow flowers 1 in (25 mm) wide in summer and early autumn. It has bluish green leaves and reaches a height of 6 in (15 cm). *Zones 7–10.*

Eschscholzia californica

This short-lived perennial, the official floral emblem of California, has cup-shaped flowers that open out from gray-green feathery foliage into vivid shades of orange, though cultivated strains have extended the color range to bronze, yellow, cream, scarlet, mauve and rose. It flowers in spring with intermittent blooms in summer and autumn; the flowers close on cloudy days. It grows to 12 in (30 cm) high. *Zones 6–11.*

EUCOMIS
Pineapple lily

The 15 species of pineapple lily, all deciduous and native to southern Africa, bear spikes of small, star-shaped flowers with crowning tufts of leaves resembling a pineapple. They grow from enlarged bulbs, and the basal rosette of glossy foliage is rather bulky—these are substantial border plants in their own right. The Xhosa people use the bulbs, boiled into a poultice, as a cure for rheumatism.

Eucomis comosa

Eupatorium fistulosum

Cultivation

Marginally frost hardy, they prefer warm-temperate climates in full sun in moist, well-drained soil; they dislike water during the dormant winter months. Where frost may reach the bulbs, winter indoors in pots. Propagate from seed or by division.

Eucomis comosa

syn. *Eucomis punctata*

This species grows to about 30 in (75 cm) in height. Dark green, crinkly, strap-like leaves surround the tall, purple-spotted scapes. The hundreds of flowers, white to green and sometimes spotted with purple, are borne in late summer and autumn. Water well through the growing season. It makes an excellent, long-lasting cut flower. *Zones 8–10.*

EUPATORIUM

This genus contains about 40 species of perennials and subshrubs, mainly from the Americas but a few from Asia and Europe. Only a few are cultivated for their large terminal panicles of small flowerheads, which come in white or shades of purple, mauve or pink.

Cultivation

Mostly quite frost hardy, they need full sun or part-shade and moist but well-drained soil. Prune lightly in spring or after flowering. Propagate from seed in spring, from cuttings in summer or by division in early spring or autumn.

Eupatorium coelestinum

syn. *Conoclinium coelestinum*

Mist flower, hardy ageratum

Native to the eastern USA, this is a robust herbaceous perennial with large heads of clear blue fluffy flowers in late summer. It is suited to naturalizing in damp places near water. *Zones 5–9.*

Eupatorium fistulosum

Joe pye weed

Native to the southeastern states of the USA, this variable perennial grows 3–10 ft (1–3 m) tall and about as wide. It enjoys constantly moist, humus-rich soil and will tolerate periods of wetness. It produces heads of rosy-mauve flowers from mid-summer to early autumn. It can be invasive, but is easily controlled by division every second year. *Zones 7–10.*

EUPHORBIA

Milkweed, spurge

This genus has close to 2,000 species, among them annuals, herbaceous perennials, shrubs and numerous succulent species. The flowers of all species consist of only a stigma and a stamen, always green, and usually carried in small clusters. Many species have showy bracts. Mainly tropical and subtropical, the genus also includes many temperate species. All euphorbias have milky sap which is corrosive to sensitive areas of the skin.

Cultivation

They like sun or part-shade in moist, well-drained soil. Cold tolerance varies depending on the species; the more highly succulent species are generally frost tender. Propagate from cuttings in spring or summer, allowing succulent species to dry and callus before placing in barely damp sand, by division or from seed.

Euphorbia characias

This is a sun-loving, frost-hardy sub-shrub usually up to 3 ft (1 m) or so. It likes a sunny, well-drained site and where happy, will self-seed. It has deep brown nectaries giving a brown spot in the center of each yellow-green bract. *Euphorbia characias* subsp. *wulfenii* (syn.

Euphorbia characias

E. wulfenii) has blue-green leaves densely clothing the erect stems, which in spring are topped by dome-like chartreuse flowerheads. *Zones 8–10.*

Euphorbia griffithii

This perennial from the eastern Himalayas, which grows to a height of 3 ft (1 m), produces small, yellow flowers surrounded by brilliant orange bracts in summer. The lanceolate, green leaves have prominent pinkish midribs and turn red and yellow in autumn. 'Fireglow' produces orange-red floral bracts in early summer. *Zones 6–9.*

Euphorbia marginata
Snow on the mountain, ghostweed

Native to central areas of North America, this bushy annual makes an excellent foil for brighter flowers. It has pointed oval, bright green leaves, sharply margined with white, and broad, petal-like white bracts surrounding small flowers in summer. It is fairly fast growing to about 24 in (60 cm) tall with a spread of about 12 in (30 cm), and will endure cold conditions. *Zones 4–10.*

Euphorbia griffithii 'Fireglow'

Euphorbia myrsinites

This trailing species is only 6–8 in (15–20 cm) tall but spreads to over 24 in (60 cm) wide. Blue-green, oval leaves spiral around the stems, each stem ending in a rounded flowerhead of soft chartreuse in spring. It is excellent in a rock garden or at the top of a low wall. It ranges in the wild from southern Europe to central Asia. It self-seeds readily and will tolerate frost, poor soil, heat and dry conditions. *Zones 5–10*.

Euphorbia polychroma

syn. *Euphorbia epithymoides*
Cushion spurge

Native to central and southern Europe, this frost-hardy, clump-forming perennial is grown for its heads of bright chrome-yellow flowers produced from spring to summer. It has softly hairy, deep green leaves and a rounded, bushy habit, reaching a height and spread of about 18 in (45 cm). 'Major' has yellowish green flowers in loose clusters. *Zones 6–9*.

EUSTOMA

syn. *Lisianthus*
Belonging to the gentian family, this genus consists of 3 species of annuals, biennials and perennials. Japanese plant breeders extended the pastel color range to white, pale blue and pink as well as the original violet, and also developed double-flowered strains. Any unopened buds on the spray develop beautifully in water, so these give pleasure for an extended period.

Cultivation

Usually regarded as frost tender, they like any warm-temperate climate. Give them sun, perfect drainage and fertile soil; they rarely perform well after their first year. Propagate from seed in spring or from cuttings in late spring or summer.

Euphorbia myrsinites

Euphorbia marginata

Euphorbia polychroma

Eustoma grandiflorum

Eustoma grandiflorum
syn. *Lisianthus russellianus*
Prairie gentian, Texas bluebell, lisianthus
Native to America's Midwest from
Nebraska to Texas, this biennial's
flowers last up to 3 weeks in water after
cutting. It has gray-green leaves and 2 in
(5 cm) wide, flared, tulip-like flowers in
colors of rich purple, pink, blue or white.
Of an upright habit, the plant is slow
growing to a height of 24 in (60 cm) and
spread of 12 in (30 cm). *Zones 9–11.*

EXACUM
This genus also belongs to the gentian
family; it consists of about 25 species of
annuals, biennials or perennials, with
mostly yellow, white, blue or purple
flowers that are often broadly cup-shaped
or flat. Only one species, *Exacum affine*,
has become widely cultivated, a miniature from the hot dry island of Socotra
just off the horn of Africa at the mouth
of the Red Sea; it is grown as an indoor
plant, and has a neat shrub-like growth
habit and long succession of flowers.

Cultivation
They can only be grown outdoors in
warm, frost-free climates, where they do
best in a sunny position in rich, moist

Exacum affine

but well-drained soil. Indoors they like
diffused sun and a night temperature not
below 50°F (10°C). Propagate from seed
in early spring.

Exacum affine
Persian violet, German violet
This showy miniature has shiny, oval
leaves and bears a profusion of small,
5-petaled, saucer-shaped, usually purple-
blue flowers with yellow stamens
throughout summer. A biennial usually
treated as an annual, it grows to a height
and spread of 8–12 in (20–30 cm). 'Blue
Midget' grows to only half as big and
has lavender-blue flowers, while 'White
Midget' has white flowers. *Zones 10–11.*

F, G

Felicia amelloides

FELICIA
Blue daisy
This genus, which ranges from southern Africa to Arabia, consists of 80 species of annuals, perennials and evergreen subshrubs. They are sprawling plants with aromatic foliage; in mild climates they flower on and off almost all year. The daisy-like, usually blue flowerheads are borne in masses.

Cultivation
These fully frost hardy to frost tender plants need full sun and well-drained, humus-rich, gravelly soil; they do not like wet conditions. Frost-tender perennial species need protection in winter with open-ended cloches. Propagate from cuttings taken in late summer or autumn or from seed in spring.

Felicia amelloides
Blue marguerite
This bushy, evergreen subshrub has a spreading habit, growing to 24 in (60 cm) in height and twice as wide. It has roundish, bright green leaves and sky blue flowerheads with bright yellow centers borne on long stalks from late spring to autumn. Frost tender, it is fast growing in temperate climates and is suitable for seaside gardens. It is often grown as an annual in cool areas. 'Santa Anita' has extra large blue flowers and 'Alba' is a white form. *Zones 9–11*.

Festuca glauca

Festuca ovina

FESTUCA
Fescue
Native to temperate zones worldwide, this genus consists of about 300 to 400 species of tuft-forming perennial grasses with evergreen linear leaves. The panicles of flowerheads composed of generally small and flattened spikelets are produced from spring to summer. Several fescues are grown as fine lawns; others are grown for their ornamental gray-blue foliage.

Cultivation
Grow in any well-drained soil. They do best in full sun but will tolerate semi-shade and withstand dry conditions and the severest frosts. Propagate from seed in spring or autumn or by division in spring.

Festuca glauca
syn. *Festuca ovina* var. *glauca*
Blue fescue, gray fescue
This clump-forming European grass reaches a height and spread of 12 in

(30 cm). The narrow leaves range in color from silvery white to blue-gray, and insignificant flowers bloom in summer. It is suitable as an edging or ground cover. Cultivars include 'Blausilber' ('Blue Silver') with intensely silver-blue leaves; 'Elijah Blue' with paler silver-blue leaves; 'Seeigel' ('Sea Urchin'), which forms a tight, compact tuft of soft, silver-blue leaves; and 'Golden Toupee', with rounded tufts of bright green and yellow leaves. *Zones 5–10.*

Festuca ovina
Sheep's fescue

Native to cooler temperate regions of the world, this clump-forming grass to 12 in (30 cm) high may form dense tussocks. It has stiff, very narrow green to gray-green leaves. In mid- to late summer it bears narrow open panicles with purple-tinged spikelets of 4 to 5 flowers. It is cultivated mainly as a forage and meadow grass. The New Zealand native *Festuca ovina* var. *novae-zelandiae* (syn. *F. novae-zelandiae*) has very narrow leaves to 18 in (45 cm) long and spikelets of 5 to 7 flowers. *Zones 5–10.*

FILIPENDULA

This is a genus of 10 species of herbaceous perennials from northern temperate regions. All except *Filipendula vulgaris* occur naturally in moist waterside habitats. They have alternate pinnate leaves and erect stems bearing large panicle-like clusters of tiny, 5-petaled flowers with fluffy stamens. They do well at the back of large perennial borders and in waterside positions.

Cultivation

Fully frost-hardy, they like full sun or part-shade in any moisture-retentive but well-drained soil. Propagate from seed or by division in spring or autumn. Check for powdery mildew.

Filipendula ulmaria
syn. *Spiraea ulmaria*
Meadowsweet, queen-of-the-meadow

Native to Europe and western Asia, this clump-forming perennial grows to 6 ft (1.8 m) high. It has pinnate leaves with sharply toothed ovate leaflets. The creamy white flowers are borne in dense heads to 10 in (25 cm) across in summer. 'Aurea' has golden-green leaves that are yellow when young; the leaves of 'Variegata' are striped and mostly blotched yellow. *Zones 2–9.*

FRAGARIA
Strawberry

The 12 or so species in this genus from northern temperate zones and Chile are low-growing, creeping or tufted perennials. The palmate leaves have 3 toothed leaflets, and the white or pink, 5-petalled flowers appear in cymes. The strawberry is a false fruit consisting of tiny pips on a fleshy receptacle. Strawberry plants can produce fruit for 6 months, or all year round in a warm climate.

Cultivation

Grow these frost-hardy plants in beds or containers lined with straw, in free-draining, acidic soil. They need full sun or light shade. Propagate from seed or by runners and replant with fresh stock every few years. Botrytis can be a problem in high rainfall areas.

Filipendula ulmaria 'Variegata'

Fragaria 'Pink Panda'

Fritillaria imperialis 'Aurora'

Fritillaria meleagris

Fragaria 'Pink Panda'

This spreading, ground cover perennial to 6 in (15 cm) high with an indefinite spread is grown for its pretty bright pink flowers to 1 in (2.5 cm) across, which appear from late spring to autumn. It rarely bears fruit. *Zones 4–10.*

FRITILLARIA
Fritillary

There are about 100 species in this genus of bulbs, relatives of the lily and the tulip, native to temperate regions of the northern hemisphere. Christian tradition has it that the fritillaries refused to bow their heads at the crucifixion but, in shame, have bowed them ever since. Their pretty, nodding, bell- or goblet-shaped flowers are borne mainly in spring.

Cultivation
Mostly quite frost hardy, they do best in areas with cold winters. Plant in early autumn in part-shade in rich, organic, well-drained soil. Water well through the growing season but dry out after flowering. In areas with high summer rainfall, lift bulbs and keep them out of the ground for as short a time as possible. Propagate from offsets in summer, but do not disturb clumps for a few years. Seed can be sown in fall but will take 4 to 5 years to bloom.

Fritillaria imperialis
Crown imperial

Native to Turkey, Iran, Afghanistan and Kashmir, this is the tallest of the species and the easiest to grow. The leafy stems up to 5 ft (1.5 m) high bear whorls of lance-shaped pale green leaves. Pendent clusters of up to 8 yellow, orange or red bell-shaped flowers appear in late spring and early summer. The flowers have an unpleasant odor. 'Aurora' bears apricot flowers. *Zones 4–9.*

Fritillaria meleagris
Snake's head fritillary, checkered lily

In spring this European species produces slender stems reaching 12 in (30 cm), each bearing one nodding, goblet-shaped

Fuchsia Hybrid 'Display'

Fuchsia magellanica

bloom that is maroon, green or white, 1 in (25 mm) long, and blotched or checkered. A few slender leaves grow along the stem. *Zones 4–9.*

FUCHSIA

This genus consists of about 100 species and many hybrids and cultivars developed for their pendulous flowers, which come in a variety of forms (usually with a long or short perianth tube, spreading sepals and 4 broad petals) and a range of colors in shades of red, white, pink and purple. They are mostly evergreen trees, shrubs or perennials. The genus is confined to South and Central America except for 4 species in New Zealand and one in Tahiti. Most of the larger-flowered American species inhabit areas of very high rainfall; they are pollinated by hummingbirds.

Cultivation

Moderately frost hardy to frost tender, they require moist but well-drained, fertile soil in sun or partial shade and shelter from hot winds and afternoon sun. Propagate from seed or cuttings, and check for white fly, spider mite, rust and gray mold.

Fuchsia Hybrids
syn. *Fuchsia × hybrida*
This useful gardener's name covers the thousands of modern large-flowered

hybrid cultivars derived mainly from *Fuchsia magellanica* and *F. fulgens*. *Fuchsia* 'Display' is a strong, upright, branching shrub that grows to 30 in (75 cm) high. It bears medium-sized, single saucer-shaped flowers in shades of pink. *Fuchsia* 'Swingtime' is a vigorous shrub bearing medium to large double flowers with red tubes and sepals, and creamy white, red-veined petals. It has a spreading habit and grows to 24 in (60 cm) in height. *Zones 9–11.*

Fuchsia magellanica
Ladies' eardrops, hardy fuchsia
From Chile and Argentina, this vigorous erect shrub grows up to 10 ft (3 m) tall. It has lance-shaped to ovate leaves usually held in whorls of three. The pendulous red tubular flowers with red sepals and purple petals are produced over a long period in summer; black fruit follow. Prune it back to maintain its shape. 'Alba' can grow to a considerable size and bears white flowers. *Zones 7–10.*

GAILLARDIA
Blanket flower
This genus of around 30 species of annuals, perennials and biennials is native to the USA, with 2 from South America. The perennials are better suited to cool-temperate climates. All bloom for a long season from summer until the first frosts. The common name

arose because the colors of the flowers resemble the bright yellows, oranges and reds of the blankets traditionally worn by Native Americans.

Cultivation

These hardy garden flowers tolerate extreme heat, cold, dryness, strong winds and poor soils. Plant in full sun in well-drained soil and stake if necessary. Propagate from seed in spring or early summer. Divide perennials in spring.

Gaillardia × *grandiflora*

These hybrids of *Gaillardia aristata* and *G. pulchella* are the most commonly grown of the blanket flowers. The plants form mounds up to 3 ft (1 m) high and wide and have narrow, slightly lobed hairy leaves. The flowerheads, 3–4 in (8–10 cm) in diameter, come in red, yellow, orange and burgundy. They are propagated by division or from cuttings to provide named cultivars. 'Kobold' ('Goblin') has compact growth to 12 in (30 cm) high and rich red flowers with yellow tips. *Zones 5–10.*

GALANTHUS
Snowdrop

This genus of about 19 species of small bulbs is native to Europe and western Asia. Small, white, nodding, sometimes perfumed flowers appear above leaves like those of daffodils but much shorter. The 3 inner petals, much shorter than the outer 3 and usually with green markings, are the feature by which this genus is recognized. Snowdrops suit lightly shaded woodland areas and rock gardens. They flower in late winter and herald the coming of spring.

Cultivation

Very frost hardy, they do best in cooler climates. Grow in rich, moist, but well-drained soil in part-shade. Water adequately during the growing period. Propagate from fresh ripe seed or divide clumps as soon as the flowers fade and while still in leaf.

Galanthus elwesii
Giant snowdrop

This species from Turkey and the Balkans multiplies well in temperate climates and has distinctive gray-blue leaves folded one inside the other at the base. It bears nodding white flowers with the inner petals marked by 2 green spots (these spots sometimes join to form a single V-shaped mark). They flower in late winter and spring and grow to 10 in (25 cm) tall. *Zones 6–9.*

Gaillardia × *grandiflora* 'Kobold'

Galanthus nivalis

Galanthus nivalis
Common snowdrop

This most commonly grown species reaches 6 in (15 cm) tall. The erect leaves are bluish green. Each stem bears a nodding, bell-shaped, 1 in (25 mm) wide scented flower in late winter. The outer petals are white, and the inner petals have a green marking at the tip. There are many very attractive cultivars. *Zones 4–9.*

GAURA

Related to the evening primrose *(Oenothera)*, this genus of about 20 species of annuals, biennials, perennials and subshrubs from North America are apt to be weedy, despite their showy flowers and the genus name that translates as 'gorgeous'. They have simple, narrow leaves and either racemes or panicles of flat, star-shaped, pink or white flowers.

Cultivation

They prefer full sun and light, well-drained soil. Cut ruthlessly to the ground when flowering has finished. Propagate from seed in autumn or spring, or from cuttings in summer.

Gaura lindheimeri

Native to the USA–Mexico border region, this clump-forming, long-flowering perennial is useful for backgrounds and mixed flower borders. It has loosely branched stems covered with tiny hairs, and from spring to autumn produces long sprays of lovely flowers which open white from pink buds. It grows to 4 ft (1.2 m) in height with a spread of 3 ft (1 m). *Zones 5–10.*

GAZANIA

This African genus, named in honor of the medieval scholar Theodore of Gaza (1398–1478), consists of about 16

Gaura lindheimeri

species of low-growing annuals and perennials. The leaves are long and narrow, often dark green on top and white- or silver gray-felted beneath, or in some species silvery haired on both sides. The flowerheads, borne singly on short stalks, range from cream to yellow, gold, pink, red, buff, brown and intermediate shades, usually with contrasting bands or spots at the petal bases. They appear from early spring until summer. They are useful for bedding, rock gardens, pots and tubs and for binding soil on slopes.

Cultivation

Grow these plants in full sun in sandy, fairly dry, well-drained soil. Mulch with compost and water during dry periods. Propagate by division or from cuttings in autumn, or from seed in late winter to early spring.

Gazania rigens

This perennial grows to a height of 12 in (30 cm) with a similar spread. It is a mat-forming plant with crowded rosettes of mostly unlobed leaves that are green above and whitish beneath, and orange flowerheads with a black eye spot at petal bases. The leaves of *Gazania rigens* var. *leucolaena* are silvery green on both sides and the flowers are yellow; *G. r.*

Gazania rigens var. leucolaena

Gazania, Sunshine Hybrid

Geranium 'Johnson's Blue'

var. *uniflora* has flowers that are smaller and short stalked. *Zones 9–11.*

Gazania, Sunshine Hybrids

These mat-forming perennials may be grown as annuals. The height and spread is around 8 in (20 cm) and solitary flowers, borne in summer, range in color with the disc-florets usually ringed in a darker color. *Zones 9–11.*

GERANIUM
Cranesbill

Over 300 species of annual, biennial and perennial geraniums, some evergreen, grow all over the world mainly in cool-temperate regions. They make small, showy clumps with pink to blue or purple and white, 5-petaled flowers. The true geraniums or cranesbills, so-called for the shape of their small, dry fruitlets, are often confused with species of the genus *Pelargonium*, also commonly known as 'geraniums'. Symmetrical flowers are their chief point of distinction from pelargoniums, which produce irregularly shaped or marked flowers. They are useful for rock gardens, ground covers and borders. Compact species and hybrids are also good for containers.

Cultivation

Mostly quite frost hardy, they prefer a sunny situation and damp, well-drained soil. Transplant during winter. Propagate from cuttings in summer or seed in spring, or by division in autumn.

Geranium endressii

From the Pyrenees, this rhizomatous perennial forms clumps to 18 in (45 cm) high and 24 in (60 cm) across. The leaves are deeply lobed and toothed and pale pink flowers, becoming darker with age, are produced from early summer to early autumn. *Zones 5–9.*

Geranium 'Johnson's Blue'

This rhizomatous perennial may be merely a form of *Geranium himalayense.* It

Geranium himalayense

Geranium maculatum

has deeply divided leaves and bears cup-shaped lavender-blue flowers with pale centers throughout summer. It has a spreading habit, reaching 18 in (45 cm) tall and 30 in (75 cm) wide. *Zones 5–9*.

Geranium himalayense

syn. *Geranium grandiflorum*

This clump-forming perennial has cushions of neatly cut leaves and grows to 18 in (45 cm) high and 24 in (60 cm) wide. In summer large, cup-shaped violet-blue flowers with white centers appear on long stalks. 'Gravetye' (syn. *Geranium grandiflorum* var. *alpinum*) has lilac-blue flowers with reddish centers and leaves that turn russet before dying down in autumn. 'Plenum' (syn. 'Birch Double') has double, purplish pink flowers with darker veins. *Zones 4–9*.

Geranium macrorrhizum

The sticky, deeply lobed leaves of this clump-forming perennial are aromatic, often turning red or bronze in autumn. The flowers appear on 12 in (30 cm) stems above the foliage in spring and early summer. Flower color varies from pink or purplish to pure white. It makes an excellent ground cover for a dry, shady site. 'Album' has white petals with reddish calyces; 'Ingwersen's Variety'

Geranium macrorrhizum 'Ingwersen's Variety'

has pale pink flowers and smoother glossy leaves. *Zones 4–9*.

Geranium maculatum

Native to eastern American woodlands, this species is best used in woodland gardens as it is less showy and more open in habit than others. It is an erect, clump-forming perennial to 30 in (75 cm) tall with deeply lobed, glossy leaves and bears saucer-shaped, lilac-pink flowers with white centers in late spring to mid-summer. *Zones 6–9*.

Geranium sanguineum
Bloody cranesbill

This European species is a low-growing perennial of around 8 in (20 cm) tall spreading by rhizomes. The dark green leaves are deeply cut into toothed lobes. Abundant cup-shaped bright magenta flowers with notched petals are produced during summer. 'Vision' bears deep pink flowers. *Zones 5–9.*

Geranium sylvaticum
Wood cranesbill

Another well-known European species, this upright, clump-forming perennial to 30 in (75 cm) tall has deeply divided basal leaves from which arise branching stems carrying bluish purple, cup-shaped flowers with white centers from late spring to summer. 'Album' has white flowers; 'Mayflower' has rich violet-blue flowers with white centers. *Zones 4–9.*

Geranium sylvaticum 'Album'

Gerbera jamesonii cultivar

GERBERA

This genus of around 40 perennial species is from Africa, Madagascar and Asia. The showy flowerheads, in almost every color except blue and purple, are carried on bare stems 18 in (45 cm) long. They are ideal rock garden plants in frost-free climates.

Cultivation

They need full sun to part-shade in hot areas and fertile, composted, well-drained soil. Water well during summer. In the greenhouse, they require good light and regular feeding during the growing season. Propagate from seed in fall or early spring, from cuttings in summer or by division.

Gerbera jamesonii
Barberton daisy, Transvaal daisy

This decorative daisy is an excellent cut flower. From a basal rosette of deeply lobed, lance-shaped leaves, white, pink, yellow, orange or red flowerheads, up to 3 in (8 cm) wide, are borne singly on long stems in spring and summer. Florists' gerberas derive from crosses between *Gerbera jamesonii* and the tropical African *G. viridifolia*. Some have flowerheads as much as 12 in (30 cm) across, in a wide range of colors, as well as double, for example 'Brigadoon Red', and quilled forms. *Zones 8–11.*

Geranium sanguineum 'Vision'

Geum chiloense 'Mrs. Bradshaw'

Geum chiloense 'Lady Stratheden'

summer. 'Lady Stratheden' (syn. 'Goldball') has semi-double, golden-yellow flowers. 'Mrs. Bradshaw' bears rounded semi-double scarlet flowers. *Zones 5–9.*

GEUM
Avens

This genus of 50 or so herbaceous perennials is from the temperate and colder zones of both northern and southern hemispheres. Species form basal rosettes of hairy, lobed leaves and bear masses of red, orange and yellow flowers with prominent stamens from late spring until early autumn, and almost all year in frost-free areas. They suit mixed herbaceous borders and rock gardens, but may require a lot of room.

Cultivation

Frost hardy, they prefer a sunny, open position and moist, well-drained soil. Propagate from seed in fall or by division in fall or spring.

Geum chiloense

syns *Geum coccineum* of gardens, *G. quellyon*
Scarlet avens

This Chilean native reaches a height of 24 in (60 cm) with a spread of 12 in (30 cm). It forms a basal rosette of deep green, pinnate leaves to 12 in (30 cm) long. The vivid scarlet, cup-shaped flowers appear in terminal panicles in

GLADIOLUS

syns *Acidanthera, Homoglossum*
This is a genus of about 180 species of cormous perennials with sword-shaped leaves in fanlike tufts native to Africa, Europe and the Middle East, though the species with the most conspicuous and colorful flowers are nearly all come from South Africa. The cultivated gladioli are mainly large-flowered hybrids, with showy, funnel-shaped flowers. Plants vary from the very small and sometimes fragrant species to the spectacular, colorful spike of the florists' gladiolus. The 3 main hybrid groups are the Grandiflorus (or Large-flowered) Group, the Primulinus Group and the Nanus (or Butterfly) Group.

Cultivation

Plant corms about 4 in (10 cm) deep in well-drained, sandy soil in a sunny position. In cool areas plant in early spring; in warm areas plant from autumn. Water well in summer. Tall stems may need staking. Lift corms over winter in cold climates; lift large-flowered corms in all areas, especially those with high winter rainfall; store

Gladiolus × colvillei 'The Bride'

Gladiolus communis

when perfectly dry. Propagate from seed or cormlets in spring.

Gladiolus × colvillei
Baby gladiolus

This dainty plant was the earliest known gladiolus hybrid, originating in England in 1823 as a cross between *G. cardinalis* and the cream *G. tristis*. It bears up to 10 elegant, 3 in (8 cm) dark pink, yellow or white blooms on an 18 in (45 cm) spike, usually in late spring. 'The Bride' has white flowers. There is now a range of similar hybrids, all about 15 in (38 cm) tall, with similarly blotched flowers in shades of white and pink. *Zones 8–10.*

Gladiolus communis

From spring to summer this vigorous species from southern Europe produces spikes of pink flowers streaked or blotched with white or red. It grows to a height of 3 ft (1 m) and has very narrow, tough leaves. *Gladiolus communis* subsp. *byzantinus* (syn. *G. byzantinus*) bears up to 15 pink to magenta blooms from late spring to early summer. All forms of the species are hardier than any of the South African gladioli. *Zones 6–10.*

Gladiolus, Grandiflorus Group

Gladiolus, Grandiflorus Group

These very large-flowering hybrids produce long, densely packed spikes of broadly funnel-shaped flowers in summer. The sometimes ruffled flowers are arranged in alternating fashion mostly on one side of a 3–5 ft (1–1.5 m) stem. They are regarded as too demanding for normal garden use, in terms of pest and disease control, as well as requiring support to keep upright, so are grown mainly for exhibition or as commercial cut flowers. 'Red Majesty' has lightly ruffled red flowers. *Zones 9–11.*

GLAUCIUM
Horned poppy, sea poppy
This is one of the most distinctive genera of poppy relatives, consisting of 25 species of annuals, biennials and perennials from temperate Asia and the Mediterranean region (with one extending to Atlantic coasts). Their characteristic feature is the up to 12 in (30 cm) long, narrow seed capsule that rapidly elongates after the petals fall from the flowers. Showy flowers terminate the leafy branches and may be yellow, red or white, usually with a darker blotch at the base of each petal.

Cultivation
Fairly frost hardy, they prefer a sunny position and sandy, well-drained soil. Propagate from seed in spring or fall.

Glaucium flavum
Yellow horned poppy
This native of western and southern Europe and northern Africa occurs

Glaucium flavum

naturally in coastal areas and is widely naturalized elsewhere. It is a slightly hairy, short-lived perennial with a basal rosette of pinnately lobed, glaucous gray-green leaves. The golden-yellow or orange flowers, to 3 in (8 cm) across, are produced in summer. *Zones 7–10.*

GOODENIA
This genus of about 170 species of perennials or shrubs is mostly found in Australia with 3 species extending to Papua New Guinea and Indonesia. Growth habit is variable but most are dwarf evergreen perennials or subshrubs, some with a basal rosette of leaves and well-displayed, mostly bright yellow flowers, their 5 petals spreading like fingers. Some bear flowers in various shades of pink, mauve or blue.

Cultivation
Frost tender to moderately frost hardy, they require good drainage and a sunny or part-shaded position. Prune back after flowering. Propagate from seed or cuttings.

Goodenia macmillanii
Pinnate goodenia
This small shrub with a suckering habit may reach up to 3 ft (1 m) high. It has

Goodenia macmillanii

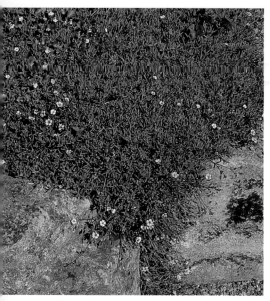

Gypsophila repens 'Rosea'

Gypsophila paniculata

pinnate basal leaves to 3 in (8 cm) and small lobed leaves on the stems. The fragrant flowers, borne in spring and summer, are pink with purple streaks and about 1 in (25 mm) across. *Zones 9–11.*

GYPSOPHILA

Native to Europe, Asia and North Africa, there are over 100 species of these annuals and perennials, some of which are semi-evergreen. They have masses of small, dainty, white or pink flowers, often used by florists as a foil for bolder flowers or foliage. The narrow leaves are borne in opposite pairs.

Cultivation

Plant in full sun with shelter from strong winds. Fully frost hardy, they tolerate most soils but prefer deep, well-drained soil lightened with compost or peat. Cut back after flowering. Transplant when dormant during winter. Propagate from cuttings in summer or from seed in spring or autumn.

Gypsophila paniculata
Baby's breath

This short-lived perennial, mostly treated as an annual, has small, dark green leaves and sprays of tiny white spring flowers. It reaches a height and spread of 3 ft (1 m) or more. 'Bristol Fairy' has double white flowers. 'Compact Plena' has double white or soft pink flowers. *Gypsophila paniculata* makes an excellent cut flower, as it is quite long-lasting. *Zones 4–10.*

Gypsophila repens

This prostrate perennial has stems forming low mounds up to 8 in (20 cm) high and 18 in (45 cm) wide. It has narrow, bluish green leaves and bears panicles of star-shaped white, lilac or pale purple flowers in summer. It is an ideal plant for trailing over rocks, and is also suitable for a container. 'Dorothy Teacher' has abundant pale pink flowers ageing to deep pink. 'Rosea' has deep pink flowers. *Zones 4–9.*

H

Hakonechloa macra 'Aureola'

HAKONECHLOA

This tufted perennial grass genus occurs in Japan and has only one species. It grows to a height of 12–18 in (30–45 cm) and has bright green leaves that turn orange-bronze in autumn in cooler climates. There are a number of very attractive variegated forms that tend to be more compact and look best in light shade.

Cultivation

This frost-hardy grass prefers full sun or part-shade and fertile, humus-rich, moist but well-drained soil. Propagate the species from seed, the cultivars by division.

Hakonechloa macra 'Aureola'
Golden variegated hakonechloa

This slowly spreading, perennial grass from the mountains of Japan provides a striking accent to the garden. The narrow, 8 in (20 cm) long, bright yellow leaves are lined with fine green stripes with a pink-red tint in autumn. It can be used as a specimen or planted in drifts. Reaching heights of 24 in (60 cm), it is very good in a pot. Zones 5–11.

HELENIUM
Sneezeweed, Helen's flower

This genus found in the Americas consists of about 40 species of annual, biennial or perennial herbs. The mid-green leaves, which are alternate on erect stems, are oval to lance-shaped. Daisy-like flowerheads appear in summer and have yellow, red-brown or orange ray florets and yellow, yellow-green, red or brown disc florets.

Cultivation

Frost hardy, heleniums grow in any temperate climate as long as they get sun. The soil should be moist and well drained. Remove spent flowers regularly to prolong the flowering period. Propagate by division of old clumps in winter or from seed in spring or autumn.

Helenium 'Moerheim Beauty'

Helenium 'Moerheim Beauty'

This upright perennial has sprays of daisy-like, rich orange-red flowerheads with prominent, chocolate-brown central discs. They are borne in summer and early autumn above mid-green foliage. Easily grown, it gives color to borders and is useful for cut flowers. Slow growing to 3 ft (1 m) high and 24 in (60 cm) wide, it enjoys hot summers. *Zones 5–9.*

HELIANTHEMUM
Rock rose, sun rose

Helianthemum means flower of sunshine, an appropriate name for flowers that only open in bright sunlight. The genus contains over 100 species found on rocky and scrubby ground in temperate zones of the northern hemisphere. They are sturdy, short-lived, evergreen or semi-evergreen shrubs or subshrubs. The foliage ranges in color from silver through mid-green. Wild plants have flowers resembling 1 in (25 mm) wide

Helianthemum nummularium

wild roses, but garden forms can be anything from white through yellow and salmon-pink to red and orange, and some have double flowers.

Cultivation

Plant in full sun in freely draining, coarse soil with a little peat or compost added during dry periods. Propagate from seed or cuttings.

Helianthemum nummularium

A variable species from Europe and Turkey, *Helianthemum nummularium* has a neat, prostrate habit and grayish foliage. Its small but profuse flowers vary in color from yellow or cream to pink and orange. Most of the cultivars traditionally listed under this name are in fact of hybrid origin. *Zones 5–10.*

HELIANTHUS

This genus of the daisy family includes one of the world's most important oilseed plants, also used for livestock fodder, as well as the Jerusalem artichoke with edible tubers, and many ornamentals. Consisting of around 70 species of annuals and perennials, native to the Americas, they have large daisy-like, usually golden-yellow flowerheads, which are on prolonged display from summer to autumn. They have hairy, often sticky leaves and tall, rough stems.

Cultivation

Frost hardy, they prefer full sun, well-drained soil and protection from wind. Fertilize in spring. Cut perennials down to the base after flowering. Propagate from seed or by division in fall or early spring.

Helianthus annuus
Common sunflower

This fast-growing, upright annual can reach a height of 10 ft (3 m) or more. Large daisy-like, 12 in (30 cm) wide yellow flowerheads with brown centers are borne in summer. This species produces one of the world's most important oilseeds. Newer varieties have been developed that grow to about 6 ft

Helictotrichon sempervirens

(1.8 m), including 'Autumn Beauty' with medium-sized flowers usually brownish red, deep red, light yellow or golden yellow; and 'Teddy Bear', a compact grower with double, dark yellow flowers. *Zones 4–11.*

Helianthus × multiflorus

Helianthus × multiflorus is a clump-forming perennial to 6 ft (1.8 m) in height and 3 ft (1 m) in spread. The domed flowers can be up to 6 in (15 cm) across and appear in late summer to mid-fall. Popular cultivars include 'Capenoch Star', 'Loddon Gold', 'Soleil d'Or' and 'Triomphe de Gand'. *Zones 5–9.*

HELICTOTRICHON
Oatgrass

This is a genus of about 50 species of tussocky grasses from temperate Europe, North America and western Asia, some growing over 3 ft (1 m) tall. The long, narrow leaves may be flat or creased. The flowers, which appear in summer, may be either upright or arching.

Cultivation

Grow in very well-drained, sandy or

Helianthus annuus

Heliopsis helianthoides 'Light of Loddon'

Helianthus × multiflorus 'Triomphe de Gand'

gravelly soil in full sun. In very cold climates plants should be sheared to the ground in late autumn and covered with a thick layer of straw or bracken. In warmer areas, shear to the ground in late winter to make room for new growth. Propagate by division of established clumps or by sowing seed in spring.

Helictotrichon sempervirens
syns *Avena candida, A. sempervirens*
Blue oatgrass
This evergreen, perennial grass from central and southwest Europe is the most commonly grown and should be given prominence in a garden planting. It has arching blue-gray leaves that grow to about 3 ft (1 m). The oat-like summer flowers are produced in drooping panicles on stems that can reach a height of 4 ft (1.2 m). This frost-hardy grass looks good when contrasted with purple and pink low-growing plants. *Zones 4–9.*

HELIOPSIS
Orange sunflower, ox eye
The name *Heliopsis* means resembling a sunflower, and these perennials from the North American prairies do look like

sunflowers, though on a rather reduced and more manageable scale. There are about 12 species, with stiff, branching stems and toothed, mid to dark green leaves. The solitary, usually yellow flowers are up to 3 in (8 cm) wide and make good cut flowers.

Cultivation
These plants are easily grown, and for a while even tolerate poor conditions; however they thrive in fertile, moist but well-drained soil and a sunny position. They are all very frost hardy. Deadhead regularly and cut back to ground level after flowering finishes. Propagate from seed or cuttings in spring, or by division in spring or autumn.

Heliopsis helianthoides
This species grows to 5 ft (1.5 m) tall and 3 ft (1 m) in spread. It has coarse, hairy leaves and golden-yellow flowers in summer. 'Light of Loddon' has rough, hairy leaves and strong stems that carry dahlia-like, bright yellow, double flowers in late summer; it grows to a height of 3 ft (1 m) and a spread of 24 in (60 cm). 'Patula' has semi-double orange flowers. *Zones 4–9.*

Helleborus orientalis

Helleborus foetidus

HELLEBORUS
Hellebore

Native to areas of Europe and western Asia, these 15 perennial or evergreen species are useful winter- and spring-flowering plants for cooler climates. They bear beautiful, open flowers in white or shades of green, red and purple and are effective planted in drifts or massed in the shade of deciduous trees. All are poisonous.

Cultivation

Grow in part-shade and moist, well-drained, humus-rich soil; do not dry out in summer. Cut off old leaves from deciduous species just as the buds start to appear. Remove flowerheads after seeds drop. A top-dressing of compost or manure after flowering is beneficial. Propagate from seed or by division in autumn or early spring. Check for aphids.

Helleborus foetidus
Stinking hellebore

This clump-forming European perennial has attractive, dark green, divided leaves. In winter or early spring the clusters of pale green, bell-shaped flowers, delicately edged with red, are borne on short stems. Established plants will often self-seed readily. *Zones 6–10.*

Helleborus orientalis
Lenten rose

The most widely grown of the genus, this evergreen, clump-forming species from Greece, Turkey and the Caucasus grows to 24 in (60 cm) high and wide. The large nodding flowers come in a great variety of colors from white, green, pink and rose to purple, sometimes with dark spots. Very frost hardy, it flowers in winter or early spring. The dense foliage fades and can be trimmed back before flowering. *Zones 6–10.*

HEMEROCALLIS
Daylily

These east Asian perennials have showy flowers which come in a range of vibrant

Hemerocallis Hybrid 'Stella d'Oro'

colors. Individual blooms last only for a day, but are borne in great numbers on strong stems above tall, grassy foliage and continue flowering from early summer to autumn. Flower size varies from 3 in (8 cm) to 6 in (15 cm) or more, single or double; plant height ranges from about 24 in (60 cm) to about 3 ft (1 m).

Cultivation
Position carefully when planting as the flowers turn their heads towards the sun and the equator. Most are fully hardy. Propagate by division in fall or spring and divide every 3 or 4 years. Check for snails, aphids and spider mite.

Hemerocallis 'Apricot Queen'
Raised in the 1940s, 'Apricot Queen' remains popular, producing a prolific supply of buds and holding each opened flower for about 16 hours. The petals display blended shades of red and orange. It is clump-forming and grows to a height of about 3 ft (1 m). The mid-green leaves are reed-like. Being fully deciduous it is well suited to cold winter climates. A sunny position is recommended. *Zones 4–9.*

Hemerocallis Hybrids
Almost all the cultivated species of *Hemerocallis* have played their part in

Hemerocallis 'Apricot Queen'

Hemerocallis lilioasphodelus

producing the vast range of modern daylily hybrids. A recent development is a range of miniatures, in many colors and with either broad or narrow petals: one of the most popular is 'Stella d'Oro' with clear golden-yellow flowers of almost circular outline. *Zones 5–11.*

Hemerocallis lilioasphodelus
syn. *Hemerocallis flava*
Pale daylily, lemon daylily
This is one of the first daylilies used for breeding and is found across China. It

forms large spreading clumps with leaves up to 30 in (75 cm) long. The lemon-yellow flowers are sweetly scented and borne in a cluster of 3 to 9 blooms. It has a range of uses in Chinese herbal medicine: some parts may be eaten, while others may be hallucinogenic. *Zones 4–9.*

HEPATICA
Liverleaf

Hepatica is closely related to *Anemone*, as the flower shape suggests. There are 10 species from North America, Europe and temperate Asia. They are all small, hairy, spring-flowering perennial herbs. The supposed resemblance of their leaves to a liver gave them their common and botanical names: *hepar* is Latin for liver. They have medicinal uses in liver and respiratory complaints, as well as for indigestion. There are a number of garden varieties with white, blue or purple flowers, sometimes double.

Cultivation

They occur naturally in woodlands so prefer part-shade and rich, moist but well-drained soil. Propagate from seed or by division, especially for the double varieties.

Hepatica nobilis

syns *Anemone hepatica, Hepatica triloba*
An inhabitant of mountain woods across much of Europe, this small perennial has solitary blue, pink or white ½–1¼ in (12–30 mm) flowers on long stalks. It has evergreen leaves with 3 broad, rounded lobes, usually purplish beneath. Although the plant is poisonous, it has been used as a herbal remedy for coughs and chest complaints. *Zones 5–9.*

HESPERIS

From the Mediterranean and temperate Asia, this genus consists of 60 species of biennials and herbaceous perennials allied to stocks (*Matthiola*). They have narrow, usually undivided leaves that may be toothed or toothless, and showy pink, purple or white flowers in long racemes. Some have fragrant flowers.

Cultivation

Species are readily grown in temperate areas and will naturalize, but cultivars are sometimes more difficult. Frost hardy, they prefer full sun and moist but well-drained, neutral to alkaline, not too fertile soil. Propagate from seed or cuttings. Check regularly for mildew and watch for slugs and snails.

Hepatica nobilis

Hesperis matronalis

Hesperis matronalis
Dame's rocket, sweet rocket

Ranging from Europe to central Asia, the flowers of *Hesperis matronalis* become very fragrant on humid evenings. It has smooth, narrowly oval leaves and branching flowerheads with white to lilac flowers borne in summer. There is also a purple form. Upright in habit, it grows 12–36 in (30–90 cm) high with a spread of about 24 in (60 cm). Plants lose their vigor after a time and are best renewed every 2 to 3 years. *Zones 3–9.*

HEUCHERA
Alum root, coral bells

There are about 55 species of these evergreen and semi-evergreen perennials, native to North America and Mexico. They form neat clumps of scalloped leaves, often tinted bronze or purple, from which arise stems bearing masses of dainty, nodding, white, crimson or pink bell flowers often over a long flowering season. They are good as ground covers, in rock gardens or as edging plants.

Cultivation

Mostly frost hardy, these plants like either full sun or semi-shade and well-drained, coarse, moisture-retentive soil. Propagate species from seed or by division; cultivars by division in fall or early spring. Remove spent flower stems and divide established clumps every 3 or 4 years.

Heuchera micrantha var. *diversifolia* 'Palace Purple'

This cultivar is grown for its striking, purple, palmate leaves and panicles of tiny white flowers in summer. It is clump forming, with a height and spread of about 18 in (45 cm). The leaves last well as indoor decoration. *Zones 5–10.*

Heuchera sanguinea
Coral bells

This, the most commonly grown species, occurs naturally from Arizona to New Mexico. It grows to 18 in (45 cm) and has sprays of scarlet or coral red flowers above toothed, deeply lobed leaves. British and American gardeners have developed strains with a wider color range—from pale pink to deep red—and slightly larger flowers. Bressingham hybrids are typical. *Zones 6–10.*

× HEUCHERELLA

This hybrid genus is the result of a cross between *Heuchera* and *Tiarella*, both members of the saxifrage family. Plants are evergreen, clumping or ground-covering perennials with tall, airy stems

Heuchera sanguinea

Heuchera micrantha var. diversifolia 'Palace Purple'

× *Heucherella tiarelloides*

Hibiscus coccineus

of dainty pink or white flowers. These are produced over a long season from late spring. Leaves are rounded, lobed and have distinct veins. When young they are bronze-red, turning green during summer then reddish in autumn.

Cultivation
They enjoy leafy, rich, moist but well-drained soil. Where summers are mild, full sun is best, but in hotter areas dappled or part-shade suits. Propagate by division in autumn or winter in mild areas, spring in cooler places.

× *Heucherella tiarelloides*
Growing about 12 in (30 cm) tall with flower stems rising a further 12–15 in (30–38 cm), this fully hardy perennial spreads by creeping stolons. The leaves are lobed and toothed and form a dense, rounded mound. Small pink flowers appear on red stems. In the cultivar 'Bridget Bloom' the flowers are a soft, pastel pink and very freely produced. *Zones 5–9.*

HIBISCUS
While the genus name conjures up the innumerable cultivars of *Hibiscus rosa-sinensis*, the genus of around 220 species is quite diverse, including hot-climate evergreen shrubs and small trees, some deciduous, temperate-zone shrubs and some annuals and perennials. The leaves are mostly toothed or lobed and the flowers are of characteristic shape with a funnel of 5 overlapping petals and a central column of fused stamens.

Cultivation
The shrubby species thrive in sun and slightly acid, well-drained soil. Water regularly and feed during the flowering period. Trim after flowering to maintain shape. Propagate from seed or cuttings or by division, depending on the species. Check for aphids, mealybugs and whitefly.

Hibiscus coccineus
This tall perennial species from the marshes of Georgia and Florida has distinctively shaped petals, each petal narrowing at the base to a slender basal stalk. The elegant flower, up to 8 in (20 cm) wide, also has the long column of stamens typical of many hibiscus, which dusts the head and back of birds with pollen. *Zones 7–11.*

Hosta fortunei 'Albomarginata'

Hibiscus moscheutos
Common rose mallow, swamp rose mallow

Native to North America, this herbaceous perennial grows to 8 ft (2.4 m) high and 3–5 ft (1–1.5 m) wide. Single, hollyhock-like flowers 4–8 in (10–20 cm) wide are carried on robust, unbranched stems in late summer and autumn. Colors vary from white to pink, some with deeper throat markings. The leaves are large, toothed and softly hairy beneath. A range of lower-growing cultivars with dramatic large flowers has been bred from this species, including 'Southern Belle' with rose-pink blooms up to 10 in (25 cm) across. *Zones 5–9.*

HOSTA
Plantain lily

The 40 species in this genus of frost-hardy perennials are from Japan, China and Korea. They produce wide leaves, some marbled or marked with white and others a bluish green. All-yellow foliage forms are also available. They do well in large pots, and are excellent for ground cover, or on the margins of lily ponds or bog gardens. Tall stems to about 18 in (45 cm) of nodding white, pink or shades of purple and blue, bell- or trumpet-shaped flowers appear in warmer weather.

Hibiscus moscheutos 'Southern Belle'

Cultivation
They grow well in shade and rich, moist, neutral, well-drained soil. Feed regularly during the growing season. Propagate by division in early spring, and guard against snails and slugs.

Hosta fortunei
This strong-growing perennial has given rise to many hybrids. It has ovate or broad lanceolate, pleated and pointed leaves. In summer tall flower stems are produced from which hang lavender flowers. Plants grow at least 18 in (45 cm) tall but spread nearly twice as wide. 'Albomarginata' has gray-green leaves with creamy yellow to white margins; 'Albopicta' has leaves marbled or

irregularly marked in 2 shades of green; and 'Aurea' is a luminous golden green. *Zones 6–10.*

Hosta 'Krossa Regal'

This hybrid has beautiful powdery gray-green leaves that are upward folded, wavy edged and distinctly pleated. *Zones 6–10.*

Hosta plantaginea
August lily, fragrant plantain lily

Popular for its pure white, fragrant flowers on 30 in (75 cm) stems, this Chinese species has mid-green leaves forming a mound 3 ft (1 m) across. It flowers in late summer. *Zones 3–10.*

Hosta sieboldiana

This robust, clump-forming plant from Japan grows to 3 ft (1 m) high and 5 ft (1.5 m) wide. It has puckered, heart-

Hosta plantaginea

shaped, bluish gray leaves and bears racemes of mauve buds opening to trumpet-shaped white flowers in early summer. 'Frances Williams' has heart-shaped, puckered blue-green leaves with yellowish green margins. *Hosta sieboldiana* var. *elegans* also has heart-shaped, puckered leaves. *Zones 6–10.*

Hosta undulata
Wavy leafed plantain lily

Hosta undulata has creamy white, wavy or twisted leaves that are splashed or streaked green along their edges. Mauve flowers on tall stems in summer complete this attractive and desirable specimen. *Zones 6–10.*

Hosta fortunei 'Aurea'

Hosta 'Krossa Regal'

HOUTTUYNIA

There is one species in this genus, a wide-spreading herbaceous perennial from moist or wet, part- or fully shaded parts of eastern Asia. It is a good ground cover in moist gardens, beside ponds and in boggy ground. In summer it bears spikes of tiny yellowish flowers with 4 pure white bracts at the base of each spike.

Cultivation

This frost-hardy plant likes moist, leafy rich soil. In cooler climates it tolerates sun so long as the ground is moist, but in hotter places some shade is desirable. Where winters are always cold, reduce water in winter or cover the roots with a thick layer of straw. Propagate from ripe seed or from cuttings, or by division.

Houttuynia cordata

Ranging from the Himalayas to Japan, this water-loving deciduous perennial makes a good ground cover but may

Hosta sieboldiana

Hosta undulata

Hypericum 'Hidcote'

Hypericum olympicum

Houttuynia cordata

become invasive. It is a vigorous plant, growing to 12 in (30 cm) high with an indefinite spread. It grows from underground runners which send up bright red branched stems bearing aromatic green leaves. However, the most popular form, 'Chameleon' (syns 'Tricolor', 'Variegata') is strikingly variegated in red, cream, pink and green. *Zones 5–11.*

HYPERICUM
St. John's wort

This is a varied genus of 400 species of annuals, perennials, shrubs and a few small trees, some evergreen but mostly deciduous, with showy flowers in shades of yellow with a central mass of prominent golden stamens. It has a cosmopolitan distribution. Species range in size from diminutive perennials for the rock garden to over 10 ft (3 m) tall.

Cultivation

Mostly cool-climate plants, they prefer full sun but will tolerate some shade. They like fertile, well-drained soil, with plentiful water in late spring and summer. Remove seed capsules after flowering and prune in winter. Propagate cultivars from cuttings in summer, and species from seed in autumn or from cuttings in summer.

Hypericum 'Hidcote'

This dense bushy shrub reaches 4 ft (1.2 m) in height and has a spread of 5 ft (1.5 m). It bears large, cup-shaped, 2½ in (6 cm) golden-yellow flowers from midsummer to early autumn and has lance-shaped, dark green leaves. *Zones 7–10.*

Hypericum olympicum

This low, spreading deciduous shrub to 12 in (30 cm) tall is native to Greece and Turkey and has many erect, outward arching or near horizontal branches. The leaves are about 1 in (25 mm) long, oblong and gray-green. The flowers are quite large and showy and very generously produced in summer. *Zones 6–10.*

I, J, K

Iberis sempervirens

IBERIS

This genus of around 50 species of annuals, perennials and evergreen subshrubs are mainly from southern Europe, northern Africa and western Asia. Highly regarded as decorative plants they are excellent for rock gardens, bedding and borders. Showy flowers are borne in either flattish heads in colors of white, red and purple, or in erect racemes of pure white flowers.

Cultivation
Fully to marginally frost hardy, they require a warm, sunny position and a well-drained, light soil, preferably with added lime or dolomite. Propagate from seed in spring or autumn—they may self-sow, but are unlikely to become invasive—or from cuttings in summer.

Iberis sempervirens
Candytuft, evergreen candytuft
A low, spreading, evergreen subshrub, this species from southern Europe is ideal for rock gardens. It has narrow, dark green leaves and dense, rounded heads of unscented white flowers in spring and early summer. It is frost hardy, and grows 6–12 in (15–30 cm)

high with a spread of about 18–24 in (45–60 cm). The cultivar 'Snowflake' has glossy dark green leaves and semi-spherical heads of white flowers. Lightly trim after flowering. *Zones 4–11.*

Iberis umbellata
Globe candytuft
Native to the Mediterranean region, this upright, bushy annual has lance-shaped, mid-green leaves. Flattish heads of small, mauve, lilac, pink, purple, carmine or white flowers are produced in late spring and summer. This frost hardy plant grows to a height of 6–12 in (15–30 cm) and a spread of 8 in (20 cm). The Fairy Series has flowers in shades of pink, red, purple or white which appear in spring. Lightly trim after flowering. *Zones 7–11.*

IMPATIENS

This genus of around 850 species of succulent-stemmed annuals, evergreen perennials and subshrubs is widely distributed, especially in the subtropics and tropics of Asia and Africa. Many hybrid strains are perennial in mild climates, but in colder climates are usually grown as annuals. Their botanical name, *Impatiens*, refers to the impatience with which they grow and multiply.

Cultivation
Frost hardy to frost tender, they grow in sun or part-shade. They prefer a moist but freely drained soil, and need protection from strong winds. Tip prune to encourage shrubby growth and more abundant flowers. Propagate from seed or stem cuttings in spring or summer.

Impatiens, New Guinea Hybrids
These fast-growing perennials are also grown as annuals in cool climates. They are frost tender and grow to a height and

Impatiens, New Guinea Hybrid cultivar

Impatiens walleriana

spread of 12–18 in (30–45 cm). The leaves are oval, pointed and bronze green, or may be variegated with cream, white or yellow. The flat, spurred flowers are pink, orange, red or cerise, sometimes with white markings. Culti-vars include 'Concerto', with crimson-centered deep pink flowers; 'Tango', with deep orange flowers and bronze leaves; and 'Red Magic', with scarlet flowers and bronze-red leaves. They like brightly lit positions indoors in cooler climates, or on enclosed verandas or patios in warmer areas. *Zones 10–11.*

Impatiens usambarensis

This tropical African species gets its name from the Usambara Mountains on the borders of Kenya and Tanzania, where it was first discovered. It is related to the better known *Impatiens walleriana* and has been used in the breeding of the many colorful 'busy Lizzie' hybrids in this group. *I. u × walleriana* displays just one of the many possible color outcomes in such crosses. *Zones 10–11.*

Impatiens walleriana

syn. *Impatiens sultanii*
Busy Lizzie

From tropical East Africa, this succu-lent, evergreen perennial has soft, fleshy stems with reddish stripes and oval,

Impatiens usambarensis × walleriana

fresh green leaves. Flattish spurred flowers ranging through crimson, ruby red, pink, orange, lavender and white, some variegated, are produced from late spring to late autumn. There are many cultivars, and all are easy to grow. It is marginally frost hardy, fast growing and bushy, and grows to a height and spread of about 12–24 in (30–60 cm); water well. *Zones 9–11.*

IMPERATA

This grass genus consists of a single species, a moderately frost-hardy perennial with creeping underground rhizomes. The wild forms are usually of little horticultural merit; however, the colored-leaf types are uniquely attractive plants. *Imperata* ranges widely through eastern and southern Asia and south-ward to Australia.

Cultivation

They prefer full sun or dappled shade and humus-rich, moist but well-drained soil. Propagation is usually by division for colored-leaf forms or from seed for wild types.

Imperata cylindrica

This plant has slender leaf tufts to 30 in (75 cm) in height and in late summer produces 2 in (5 cm) long panicles of silver-white feathery spikelets. 'Rubra' (syn. 'Red Baron'), the Japanese blood grass, has erect, mid-green leaves; in mid- to late summer their ends turn the color of blood, hence the common name. By autumn the whole plant has turned this vibrant color. This is an excellent plant for providing color contrast. *Zones 8–12.*

IPOMOEA

syns *Calonyction, Mina, Pharbitis, Quamoclit*
Morning glory

This genus of some 300 mostly climbing, evergreen shrubs, perennials and annuals is widespread throughout the tropics and warm-temperate regions of the world. It includes sweet potato and some of the loveliest of the tropical flowering vines. Most have a twining habit and masses of funnel-shaped,

Imperata cylindrica 'Rubra'

flowers which in many species wither by midday. The flowers are usually short lived, lasting only one day (or night), but blooming prolifically and in succession.

Cultivation

Marginally frost hardy to frost tender, they are best suited to warm coastal districts or tropical areas. They prefer moderately fertile, well-drained soil and a sunny position. Some can become extremely invasive in warm districts. Propagate in spring from seed which has been gently filed and pre-soaked to aid germination, or from cuttings in summer (for perennial species).

Ipomoea tricolor

syns *Ipomoea rubrocaerulea, I. violacea, Pharbitis tricolor*
This Mexican perennial is more often grown as an annual. It can reach a height of 10 ft (3 m) with a spread of 5 ft (1.5 m), and has cord-like, twining stems and heart-shaped, light green leaves. From summer to early autumn, it bears large blue to mauve, funnel-shaped flowers which open in the morning and gradually fade during the day. Widening to a trumpet as they open, they can reach 6 in (15 cm) across. The cultivar 'Heavenly Blue' is particularly admired for its color. *Zones 8–12.*

Ipomoea tricolor 'Heavenly Blue'

IRESINE

Belonging to the amaranthus family, these tropical perennials from the Americas and Australia—some 80 species—are sometimes treated as annuals. They vary in habit from upright to ground-hugging. The flowers are insignificant, but their leaves are often brilliantly colored.

Cultivation

These frost-tender plants only make permanent garden plants in tropical to warm temperate climates. In cooler areas they can be grown in greenhouses. They prefer good loamy, well-drained soil and must be kept moist during the growth period. They need bright light, with some sun, to retain the brilliant color in their leaves. Pinch out tips in the growing season. Propagate from cuttings.

Iresine herbstii
syn. *Iresine reticulata*
Beefsteak plant, bloodleaf

Native to Brazil, this species makes an attractive tropical bedding or potted plant. Although perennial, it is often treated as an annual that is overwintered as struck cuttings in a greenhouse in cold areas. It grows to 24 in (60 cm) tall with a spread of 18 in (45 cm), but usually much less if grown as an annual. It has red stems and rounded purple-red leaves up to 4 in (10 cm) long, with notches at the tips and yellowish red veins. *Zones 10–12.*

IRIS

This wide-ranging genus of more than 200 species is named for the Greek goddess of the rainbow. Each flower has 6 petals: 3 outer petals, called 'falls', which droop away from the center and alternate with the inner petals, called 'standards'. Irises are divided into 2 main groups, rhizomatous and bulbous. Rhizomatous irises have sword-shaped leaves, are sometimes evergreen, and are subdivided into 3 groups: bearded (or flag) irises, with a tuft of hairs (the 'beard') on the 3 lower petals; beardless irises, without the tuft; crested or Evansia irises, with a raised crest in lieu of a beard.

The bulbous irises are divided into 3 groups, the Juno, Reticulata and Xiphium irises, the first 2 consisting of beautiful but mostly difficult bulbs from west and central Asia. The Xiphium irises are more easily grown; they have given rise to a group of bulbous hybrids including the so-called English, Spanish and Dutch irises; it is the latter that are commonly seen in florist shops.

Cultivation

Growing conditions vary greatly; however, as a rule rhizomatous irises, with the exception of the crested or Evansia irises, are frost hardy and prefer a sunny position. Bulbous irises are frost hardy, and prefer a sunny position with ample moisture during growth, but very little during their summer dormancy. Bulbous irises are prone to virus infection and need to be kept free of aphids, which will spread the infection. Propagate by division in late summer after flowering or from seed in fall; named cultivars by division only.

Iresine herbstii

Iris cristata

Iris, Tall Bearded, 'Blue Shimmer'

Iris, Intermediate Bearded, 'Sunny Dawn'

Iris, Bearded Hybrids

The bearded irises have fat creeping rhizomes, sword-shaped, grayish foliage and stems bearing several large flowers. They come in an enormous range of colors—everything but true red—with many varieties featuring blended colors, contrasting standards and falls, or a broad band of color around basically white flowers (this pattern is called 'plicata').

All prefer a temperate climate, sun and mildly alkaline, well-drained soil. Do not over-water in summer. Bearded irises are subdivided into 3 groups: Dwarf Bearded, which grow about 6–15 in (15–40 cm) tall and flower earlier than the others; Intermediate Bearded, which grow to about 24 in (60 cm) tall. 'Sunny Dawn' is typical, with yellow flowers

with red beards. Tall Bearded irises are the last to bloom and grow to 3 ft (1 m) tall or higher. 'Blue Shimmer' has white flowers with liac-blue stitching. *Zones 5–10*.

Iris cristata
Crested iris

A woodland crested or Evansia iris, this creeper grows 4–9 in (10–22.5 cm) high. Native to northeastern USA, it bears faintly fragrant, pale blue to lavender or purple flowers held just above the foliage in spring; each fall has a white patch with an orange crest. It prefers moist soil in part-shade, making it suitable as a ground cover in shaded gardens; it spreads slowly by rhizomes. 'Alba' is a vigorous cultivar with white flowers. *Zones 6–9*.

Iris ensata
syn. *Iris kaempferi*
Japanese flag, higo iris

This beardless iris grows to 3 ft (1 m) tall. It has purple flowers with yellow blotches on each fall, which appear from late spring to early summer; the leaves have a prominent midrib. The many named varieties bear huge flowers, up to 10 in (25 cm) wide, in shades of white,

Iris japonica

Iris ensata

Iris, Louisiana Hybrid 'Art World'

lavender, blue and purple, often blending 2 shades and some with double flowers. They prefer part-shade in hot areas, rich, acid soil and plenty of moisture. 'Exception' has particularly large falls and deep purple flowers; 'Mystic Buddha' has purple-blue flowers with red edging. *Zones 4–10.*

Iris japonica
syn. *Iris fimbriata*
Crested iris
This is the best known of the crested or Evansia species. Native to Japan and China, it grows to 18–32 in (45–80 cm) in height, forming large clumps of almost evergreen, glossy mid-green leaves. In late winter and spring, it bears sprays of ruffled, pale blue or white flowers; each fall has a violet patch around an orange crest. It prefers an acidic soil, a lightly shaded position, and a mild climate. Keep shaded from afternoon sun. A variety with white-striped leaves, it is rather shy flowering. *Zones 8–11.*

Iris, Louisiana Hybrids
This colorful group of rhizomatous, beardless hybrid irises are evergreen with fine strap-like foliage and can build into substantial clumps; divide after 2 to 3 years. They are not fully frost hardy in very cold climates, but are becoming increasingly popular in southern USA. Although basically swamp or water irises, they will grow in the garden if kept well watered. They like a sunny position with average to damp, humus-rich soil. They rarely exceed 3 ft (1 m) high. Hybrids include 'Art World', with mauve-pink duo-toned flowers; 'Dural Dreamtime', with its fine white flower with green veins; 'Insider', a new Australian hybrid which has yellow-edged reddish brown standards and falls of reddish brown with yellow spray patterning; and 'Vermilion Treasure', with a red-violet flower with lighter spray patterning. *Zones 7–10.*

Iris pallida
Dalmatian iris

This bearded iris has fragrant, pale blue flowers with yellow beards, which are borne on 4 ft (1.2 m) high stems in late spring. It is often grown as a source of orris, a volatile substance that develops in the dried and aged rhizomes and is used in perfumes, dental preparations and breath fresheners. 'Variegata' (syn.

Iris pallida 'Variegata'

'Aurea Variegata') has handsome leaves striped in gray-green and cream. *Zones 5–10.*

Iris pseudacorus
Water flag, yellow flag

A robust beardless iris from Europe, the water flag has handsome, mid-green leaves and profuse bright yellow flowers on 3 ft (1 m) stems which are borne in

Iris sibirica

Iris pseudacorus

early spring. The flowers usually have brown or violet veining, with a darker yellow patch on the falls. It prefers to grow in shallow water and rich soil; plant in autumn in a box of rich earth and place in a sunny position in the garden pond. The cultivar 'Variegata' has yellow- and green-striped foliage during the spring months, often turning green in summer; it is less vigorous than the species. *Zones 5–9.*

Iris sibirica
Siberian flag

This beardless iris makes strongly vertical clumps of slender bright green leaves 2–4 ft (0.6–1.2 m) high. In late spring or early summer, flowering stems rise above the foliage with narrow-petaled, blue, purple or white flowers, often veined in a deeper color. It prefers full sun to light shade (particularly in hot areas), a moderately moist, rich soil that may be slightly acid and water during the hottest periods. It does best in cold winter climates. Cultivars include 'Perry's Blue', with rich lilac-blue flowers with yellow markings; and 'Vi Luihn', with flowers in a rich violet shade. *Zones 4–9.*

Iris, Spuria Hybrids

Iris spuria (from northern Africa and southern France), *I. sibirica* (from eastern Europe) and allied species have been much hybridized. The more common hybrids bear numerous 4 in (10 cm) wide flowers on 4 ft (1.2 m) long stems in early summer. Colors are in the white to blue range, with some yellow and white forms. All prefer sun, rich soil and lavish watering while they are growing and flowering. *Zones 4–9.*

KALANCHOE

This genus, native to subtropical and tropical Africa and Madagascar, with

Kalanchoe blossfeldiana

some species in Asia, consists of 150 species of perennial succulents, climbers or shrubs. These vary from small, leafy succulents to tree-like shrubs. Plants grow from 6 in (15 cm) to 12 ft (3.5 m) high and bear white, yellow or orange to brown, red or purple, tubular or bell-shaped flowers in early spring, followed by seed-bearing capsules.

Cultivation

They need full sun or part-shade and well-drained soil, and only light watering in the colder months; they range from marginally frost hardy to frost tender. Propagate from stem or leaf cuttings in late spring to summer, seed at the end of spring.

Kalanchoe blossfeldiana
Flaming Katy

This small, shrubby African species reaches 12 in (30 cm) high and wide. Its multiple, upstretched branches are covered with round to rectangular, deep green leaves with red margins and notched tips. Thick racemes of small, deep red, cylindrical flowers appear from winter to early summer; cultivated strains may be pink, yellow and also orange. Frost tender, it requires part-shade, and is a popular potted plant. *Zones 10–11.*

KNIPHOFIA
Red-hot poker, torch lily, tritoma

There are 68 species in this southern African genus of perennials, some of which are evergreen. Upright, tufted plants with long leaves, in summer they carry showy, brightly colored, tubular flowers in dense spikes on tall bare stems. Originally the flowers were mostly flame colored, but now they can also be pink, orange or yellow. They range from head-high to miniatures growing to 24 in (60 cm) or less.

Cultivation
Frost hardy to somewhat frost tender, they like full sun, well-drained soil and plenty of water in summer. Where winter temperatures are below 5°F (−15°C) lift and store indoors to be planted again in spring, or mulch heavily. Propagate species from seed or by division; cultivars by division.

Kniphofia ensifolia
Winter poker

This moderately frost-hardy evergreen perennial forms a dense clump, growing to 5 ft (1.5 m) tall. It has slender, sword-shaped, mid-green leaves and bears torches of prolific, lemon-yellow flowers in late autumn and winter. *Zones 8–10.*

Kniphofia 'Little Maid'

'Little Maid' is a dwarf form that reaches a height of 24 in (60 cm). It has buff-tinted soft-yellow flowers opening from pale green buds. *Zones 7–10.*

Kniphofia 'Winter Cheer'

syn. *Kniphofia* 'Zululandiae'
This evergreen, upright perennial reaches 5 ft (1.5 m) in height with a spread of 3 ft (1 m). It is fairly frost hardy and bears large torches of orange-yellow flowers in winter that gradually turn yellow. *Zones 7–10.*

Kniphofia 'Winter Cheer'

Kniphofia 'Little Maid'

Kniphofia ensifolia

L

Lamium album

Lamium galeobdolon 'Hermann's Pride'

LAMIUM
syns *Galeobdolon, Lamiastrum*
Deadnettle
This Eurasian genus of over 50 species
of annuals and rhizomatous perennials
belongs, in fact, to the mint family. Some
have been used in folk medicine; some
are an important source of nectar for
bees. Leaves have toothed margins,
arranged in opposite pairs and sometimes splashed with paler gray-green or
white, and short spikes or axillary
whorls of white, yellow, pink or purple
2-lipped flowers, the upper lip curved
over in a helmet-like shape.

Cultivation
These frost hardy plants grow in most
soils. Flower color determines planting

season: plant white- and purple-flowered
species in spring in full sun; plant
yellow-flowered species in autumn in
shade. Propagate from seed or by
division in early spring.

Lamium album
White deadnettle, archangel
Ranging across Europe and northern
Asia, this species has foliage that
superficially resembles that of the
common nettle *(Urtica urens)*. An erect
perennial of 12–24 in (30–60 cm) high, it
produces whorls of pure white flowers
from late spring to early autumn. It
became known as archangel because it
flowers around the 8th of May, the feast
day of the Archangel Michael in the old
calendar. It sometimes flowers in mid-
winter. *Zones 4–10.*

Lamium galeobdolon
syns *Galeobdolon luteum, G. argentatum,
Lamiastrum galeobdolon*
Yellow archangel
This perennial species from Europe and
western Asia spreads both by rhizomes
and surface runners to form extensive,
loose mats of foliage usually about 12 in
(30 cm) deep, spreading over moist,
shady areas beneath trees. Its leaves are
variably splashed with silvery gray and
in summer it bears leafy spikes of bright
yellow flowers. 'Hermann's Pride' is
densely mat forming and has narrow
leaves streaked and spotted with silver.
Zones 6–10.

Lamium maculatum
Spotted deadnettle
Its wild forms often regarded almost as
weeds, this variable species may have
erect stems to 24 in (60 cm) tall, or have
a lower, more spreading habit. The
strongly toothed leaves have a central
blotch or stripe of pale silvery green, and
leafy whorled spikes of pale pink to deep

Lathyrus odoratus

Lamium maculatum 'Roseum'

Lathyrus latifolius

rose flowers appear in spring and summer. The cultivars mostly have a compact mat-forming habit and do not grow more than 6 in (15 cm) high. 'Roseum' has silver-striped foliage and pinkish lilac flowers. *Zones 4–10.*

LATHYRUS

This genus consists of 150 or so species of annuals and perennials, and is widespread in temperate areas, except Australasia. The uppermost pair of leaflets is usually modified into tendrils. Pea-shaped flowers come in a range of colors, from red, mauve and white to blue and yellow. *Lathyrus odoratus*, the sweet pea, has a proud place in scientific history—it was one of the plants used by Gregor Mendel (1822–84) in his hybridizing experiments which laid the foundations of genetic science.

Cultivation

These frost-hardy plants like fertile, well-drained soil in full sun. Deadhead regularly. Propagate annuals from seed; perennials from seed or by division.

Lathyrus latifolius
Perennial pea, everlasting pea

This perennial tendril climber from Chile grows to about 6 ft (1.8 m) in height, with many stems and densely massed foliage. It bears dense heads of pink, rose or white, scentless pea-flowers in spring and summer. The dull green leaves have narrow leaflets. Feed and water regularly when the buds are forming. *Zones 5–10.*

Lathyrus odoratus
Sweet pea

This vigorous, climbing annual has abundant, sweetly scented flowers in white, cream, pink, blue, mauve, lavender, maroon and scarlet. They bloom several to the stem from late winter to early summer. It grows to 6 ft' (1.8 m) high or more, although there are dwarf, non-climbing cultivars available. The climbers need good support, and are ideal for covering walls or fences. *Zones 4–10.*

LAVANDULA
Lavender

These fragrant, evergreen, aromatic shrubs of the mint or labiate family occur naturally from the Mediterranean region through the Middle East to India. There are around 25 species, several of which are cultivated for the perfume industry. Most species grow 24–36 in (60–90 cm) high and a similar width. The small mauve-purple or bluish purple flowers emerge from between bracts in erect, short spikes held on stalks above the foliage, mostly in spring. There are oil glands at the flower bases that produce the pungent oil of lavender.

Cultivation

They prefer full sun and fertile, well-drained soil. Hardiness varies with the species, although most are moderately frost hardy if the growth is well ripened by warm autumn weather. Propagate from seed or cuttings in summer.

Lavandula angustifolia
syns *Lavandula officinalis, L. spica, L. vera*
Lavender

This dense, bushy subshrub comes from the Mediterranean region of southern Europe. It grows to about 3 ft (1 m) tall though usually lower, with narrow, furry gray leaves. It is grown mainly for the long-stemmed heads of purple, scented flowers that appear in summer and through the warm months; these are easily dried for lavender sachets, potpourri and the like. *Lavandula angustifolia* makes an attractive low hedge and can be trimmed after flowering. There are a number of selected cultivars, of which 'Munstead' and the dwarf 'Hidcote' are outstanding. *Zones 6–10.*

Lavandula × intermedia
English lavender, lavendin

These naturally occurring and cultivated hybrids between *Lavandula angustifolia* and *L. latifolia* show considerable variation in plant size and flower form. Few exceed 3 ft (1 m) tall but they are otherwise something of a catch-all group. 'Provence' has green foliage and small-bracted spikes of mauve-pink flowers. *Zones 6–10.*

Lavandula latifolia
Spike lavender

This subshrubby species is very similar to *Lavandula angustifolia*, differing in its slightly wider leaves but narrower floral bracts. A rounded clump rarely reaching 3 ft (1 m) high and wide, its gray stems and foliage are downy and fragrant. The heavily scented, light purple flowers

Lavandula angustifolia 'Munstead'

Lavandula × intermedia 'Provence'

appear in spikes in summer. Its compact form makes it ideal for containers and dwarf hedges. *Zones 7–10.*

Lavandula stoechas
Spanish lavender, French lavender

Native to the western Mediterranean, this marginally frost-hardy species is the most striking in flower of all lavenders, at least in some of its varied forms. A small neat shrub 20–30 in (50–75 cm) high, it has pine-scented, narrow silvery green leaves with inward-curling edges. In late spring and summer it is covered with spikes of deep purple flowers. Several bracts at the apex of each spike are elongated into pinkish purple 'rabbit ears' of varying size. *Zones 7–10.*

Lavandula latifolia

Lavatera 'Barnsley'

LAVATERA

Closely related to the mallows and hollyhocks, this genus of 25 species of annuals, biennials, perennials and softwooded shrubs has a scattered distribution around temperate regions of the world, mostly in Mediterranean or similar climates. A few species have colorful mallow flowers, generally produced over a long season. The plants are upright in habit with simple to palmately lobed leaves. The shrubs and perennials are not very long-lived.

Cultivation

Moderately to very frost-hardy, they prefer a sunny site and well-drained soil. Prune after flowering. Propagate annuals, biennials and perennials from seed sown *in situ* (cuttings do not strike well), and shrubs from cuttings.

Lavatera 'Barnsley'

This semi-evergreen soft shrub grows to 6 ft (1.8 m) and bears sprays of pale pink flowers with deep pink centers throughout summer. It is very frost hardy. *Zones 6–10.*

Lavatera trimestris
Annual mallow

This shrubby Mediterranean annual is grown mainly for its silken, trumpet-

Lavandula stoechas

shaped, brilliant white or pink flowers which appear from summer to early fall. They are short lived but are borne in profusion. It has an erect, branching habit and grows to a height of 24 in (60 cm) and a spread of 18 in (45 cm). 'Mont Blanc' (syn. *Lavatera* 'Mont Blanc') has pure white flowers. *Zones 8–11.*

LEUCANTHEMUM

There are about 25 species of annuals or perennials in this genus from Europe and northern Asia. They are clump-forming plants with variably toothed or lobed leaves that are unlike those of other chrysanthemum relatives. Long-stalked daisy-like flowerheads arise from leafy stems, with white or yellow ray florets and yellow disc florets.

Cultivation

They are largely undemanding, growing well in a border or garden bed in full sun or morning shade in moderately fertile, moist but well-drained soil. Propagate from seed or cuttings, or by division.

Leucanthemum × superbum

syns *Chrysanthemum maximum* of gardens, *C. × superbum*

Shasta daisy

Growing to a height and spread of 2–3 ft (60–90 cm), this robust, popular peren-nial has large, daisy-like white flowerheads with pale golden centers in summer and early autumn. They were once thought to be *Leucanthemum maximum*, but are now believed to be hybrids between that species and *L. lacustre*; they naturalized on Mount Shasta in Washington State and attracted the attention of the famous plant breeder Luther Burbank. There are many cultivars, always white-flowered, but including doubles as well as singles, some with fringed petals. *Zones 5–10.*

LEUCOJUM
Snowflake

This genus consists of 10 species of bulbous perennials, resembling the snowdrop, which bear delightful flowers that bloom in spring and autumn. They are native to North Africa and the southern Mediterranean. The pendent, bell-shaped flowers consist of 6 petals, borne singly or in twos and threes at the top of a thin stem growing up to 24 in (60 cm). The mid-green to deep green leaves are narrow and strap-like.

Cultivation

Some species prefer part-shade in moist soil, while others thrive in sunny positions with well-drained soil; they are moderately to fully frost hardy. Plant

Lavatera trimestris 'Mont Blanc'

Leucanthemum × superbum

Leucojum aestivum var. pulchellum

Leucojum autumnale

bulbs in late summer or early fall; only lift for dividing when they produce few flowers and many leaves. Propagate from offsets in spring or early fall or from seed sown in fall.

Leucojum aestivum
Summer snowflake, giant snowflake

This dainty, spring flowering bulb is native to Europe and western Asia. The fragrant flowers are white with a green spot near the tip of each petal and are borne in clusters atop 18 in (45 cm) stems. The blue-green leaves are long and slender. Frost hardy, the small bulbs are best planted under a deciduous tree. *Leucojum aestivum* var. *pulchellum* is found in the wild near or in water in the southern parts of Europe and western Asia. Growing to a height of 24 in (60 cm), it naturalizes freely in similar situations and climates and grows in sun or shade. *Zones 4–10.*

Leucojum autumnale
Autumn snowflake

This species has delicate white flowers flushed with pink that appear singly or in twos and threes at the top of a thin, 10 in (25 cm) high stem. Its erect, very fine basal leaves, which usually follow the flowers, add to the plant's dainty air. As both common and scientific names imply, the flowers appear in late summer or early autumn. The bulbs should be planted 2 in (5 cm) deep in well-drained soil in a sunny position. *Zones 5–10.*

Leucojum vernum
Spring snowflake

A native of central Europe that blooms in late winter and early spring, this species grows to a height of 18 in (45 cm). The plant naturalizes freely in damp conditions, in sun or shade, and survives dry summers in style. The leaves are strap-like and the bell-shaped flowers, 2 to a stalk, carry white petals of equal length that are marked with either a green or yellow spot. *Zones 5–10.*

LEWISIA
Bitter root

This genus honors the explorer Meriwether Lewis (1774–1838), and contains about 20 species of small perennials with deep tap roots, leathery leaves and starry flowers, native to the Rocky Mountains. The roots have wonderful powers of survival: some 5

Lewisia cotyledon

Liatris spicata

years after Lewis returned to civilization in 1806, a botanist in London, studying his dried plant specimens found one trying to grow. He planted it and the following summer it flowered.

Cultivation
They like a cool climate, full sun or part-shade and excellent drainage, to avoid winter-wet rotting the roots. Propagate herbaceous species from seed, and evergreen species from seed or offsets.

Lewisia cotyledon
This evergreen, which hybridizes readily, has rosettes of fleshy, toothed leaves and bears clusters of white to yellow, apricot and pink to purple flowers on upright stems. It grows to a height of 12 in (30 cm). *Lewisia cotyledon* var. *howellii* spreads to 6 in (15 cm). 'Pinkie', with pink flowers, grows 1 in (25 mm) tall and 2 in (5 cm) wide. *Zones 6–10.*

LIATRIS
Blazing star
These 40 species of perennials come from central and eastern North America.

In summer they shoot up tall, cylindrical spikes of fluffy flowers from a knobby rootstock. They belong to the daisy family but their spike-like inflorescences, with crowded small flowerheads opening from the top downward, are quite unlike those of other daisies.

Cultivation
They grow in most soils and conditions including damp places such as stream banks and ditches, although they prefer climates with low humidity. They thrive with minimum care, making excellent border plants. Propagate from seed or by division of old clumps in winter.

Liatris spicata
syn. *Liatris callilepis* of gardens
Gay feather, spike gay feather
This low-growing species has lilac purple flowers, although they can occur in pink and white. They are produced in crowded, fluffy spikes in late summer, opening from the top downwards, the opposite of most flowering spikes. It grows to some 24 in (60 cm) high, with thickened, corm-like rootstocks and basal tufts of grassy foliage. 'Floristan' is a seedling strain growing to 5 ft (1.5 m) tall; it is available in 2 colors: deep violet ('Floristan Violett') and white ('Floristan Weiss'). *Zones 3–10.*

Ligularia dentata

LIGULARIA

There are at least 150 species of perennials in this genus which is found mainly
in temperate eastern Asia. Many are
large-leafed, clump-forming plants that
produce tall spires of daisy-like
flowerheads, mostly in shades of yellow
or orange. They are stately plants and
vigorous growers, adapted to moist,
sheltered sites such as stream banks and
woodland glades and flowering mainly
in summer and early autumn.

Cultivation

Quite frost hardy, they prefer moist,
well-drained soil and grow in either sun
or part-shade. Propagate by division in
spring or from seed in spring or fall.
Watch for slugs and snails.

Ligularia dentata

syns *Ligularia clivorum, Senecio clivorum*
This compact species, native to China
and Japan, has showy flowerheads. It
grows to a height of 4 ft (1.2 m) and a
spread of 3 ft (1 m). It has kidney-
shaped, long-stalked, leathery, brownish

green leaves and bears clusters of large,
orange-yellow flowerheads on long
branching stems in summer.
'Desdemona', has green leaves heavily
overlaid with bronze and maroon.
'Gregynog Gold' has round green leaves
and orange flowers. *Zones 4–9*

LILIUM
Lily, lilium

Many plants are referred to as 'lilies',
usually signifying that they belong to the
lily family or one of its allied families,
but in the narrowest sense this word
means a member of the bulbous genus
Lilium; this consists of around 100
species, native in temperate Eurasia
(extending to high mountains of the
Philippines) and North America, with
the largest number found in China and
the Himalayas. All species grow from
buried bulbs consisting of overlapping
fleshy scales which do not encircle one
another as in the classical onion-type
bulb. The stems are elongated with
spirally arranged or whorled leaves that
vary from narrow and grass-like to very
short and broad. One to many 6-petaled
flowers are borne in terminal sprays, the
blooms erect, nodding or pendent and
often with strongly recurved petals.
Lilies have been cultivated for centuries
and have acquired many religious and
mystical associations. *Lilium candidum*,
for example, was the flower of the Virgin
Mary and so became a symbol of purity.
In the Middle Ages the lily was the
symbol of peace.

Cultivation

The most important requirement for
lilies is good drainage. Place about 4 in
(10 cm) of soil over the bulb. Liliums
can be propagated by means of offsets
from the main bulb, from bulb scales or
seed or, in some species, from bulbils
which form in the leaf axils up the stem.

Lilium, American Hybrids

These are derived from various American species and include the popular Bellingham Hybrids—all have Turk's cap-shaped flowers. 'Shuksan' is a very fine variety with tangerine-gold flowers, 4–6 in (10–15 cm) across, spotted with a darker hue and with crimson tips to the petals. *Zones 5–10.*

Lilium, Asiatic Hybrids

These have been bred from various central and west Asian species and form by far the largest hybrid group. They include most of the varieties grown commercially as cut flowers or potted plants as well as the widely grown Mid-Century hybrids. Most, however, lack fragrance. There are 3 sub-groups:

Lilium candidum

Lilium, Asiatic Hybrid

Upward-facing: These have an upright habit to 30 in (75 cm) and normally flower in early summer. 'Golden Pixie' has deep golden-yellow flowers; 'Red Carpet' is a strong-growing variety with deep red flowers.

Outward-facing: This group is also early flowering and with an upright habit. 'Connecticut Lemon Glow' is a popular cut-flower variety with bright yellow unspotted flowers and quite short stems, usually only 18 in (45 cm) tall.

Downward-facing: Normally a little later to flower than the others, this group includes 'Citronella', a strain rather than a single variety with flowers ranging from pale lemon to yellow, spotted with purple-black and slightly recurving petals; and 'Rosemary North', one of a range of Asiatics bred by Dr. North at the Scottish Crop Research Institute producing dull buff-orange flowers. *Zones 5–10.*

Lilium candidum
Madonna lily

This beautifully scented species from southern Europe is probably the oldest species in cultivation. It grows to 6 ft (1.8 m) high and bears up to 20 trumpet-shaped blooms in summer. The pure white flowers can be 6 in (15 cm) long and are slightly reflexed, held close to

Lilium lancifolium

the stem. The bulb produces basal leaves and a few leaves are scattered along the length of the stem; the basal leaves normally persist over winter. This is one lily that should not be planted deeply; in fact, the nose of the bulb should be almost at ground level. It prefers an alkaline soil. *Zones 6–10.*

Lilium lancifolium
syn. *Lilium tigrinum*
Tiger lily
This species from Japan, Korea and eastern China grows to a height of 4 ft (1.2 m) and produces numerous bright orange pendulous flowers, spotted with purple on the lower parts of the petals, in mid- to late summer. The stems are black and large quantities of dark purple bulbils are produced in the leaf axils. This vigorous lily will thrive even in poor soils. The bulbs and flower buds of tiger lily are food items in Japan and China. *Zones 4–10.*

Lilium regale
Regal lily, Christmas lily
This species from western China is one of the best of the trumpet-flowered species. Growing to 6 ft (1.8 m) in height, it bears up to 30 blooms. The heavily scented flowers are white on the inside with a yellow base, flushed with carmine on the outside; each is about 6 in (15 cm) long and they are normally crowded together. The leaves are dark green and lanceolate. This species is stem rooting and produces a number of stem bulblets. *Zones 5–10.*

LIMONIUM
Statice, sea lavender
Statice is an obsolete botanical name of this genus of around 150 species, scattered around the world's temperate regions mostly in saline coastal and

Lilium regale

Limonium latifolium

desert environments. They include evergreen and deciduous subshrubs, perennials, biennials and annuals, some of the latter popular for their many-colored heads of small papery flowers which can be cut and dried for decoration. The tapering, almost stalkless leaves appear in basal rosettes.

Cultivation
Statices like full sun and well-drained, sandy soil. They benefit from light fertilizing in spring. Propagate by division in spring, from seed in early spring or autumn or from root cuttings in late winter.

Limonium latifolium
syn. *Limonium platyphyllum*
From eastern Europe, this tall-stemmed perennial bears clusters of lavender-blue

or white flowers over summer. Clump forming and large leafed, it grows 24 in (60 cm) tall and spreads 18 in (45 cm). The dried flower stems have a delicate appearance. *Zones 5–10.*

Limonium sinuatum

syn. *Statice sinuata*

This bushy, upright Mediterranean perennial is usually grown as an annual. It produces dense rosettes of oblong, deeply waved leaves and masses of tiny papery flowers on winged stems. It flowers in summer and early autumn and is fairly slow growing, reaching a height of 18 in (45 cm) with a spread of 12 in (30 cm). The Petite Bouquet Series are dwarf plants to 12 in (30 cm) in height

Limonium sinuatum

Linaria purpurea

and with golden- or lemon-yellow, white, cream, salmon-pink, purple or blue spikelets. *Zones 9–10.*

LINARIA
Eggs and bacon, toadflax

Native mainly in the Mediterranean region and western Europe, these 100 species of adaptable annuals, biennials and perennials are related to snapdragons and have naturalized in many places. They grow to 18 in (45 cm) with masses of tiny snapdragon-like blooms in many colors. The erect stems have stalkless, usually gray-green leaves.

Cultivation

They require rich, well-drained, preferably sandy soil, moderate water and full sun. Seed sown directly in autumn or very early spring will germinate in 2 weeks. Seedlings need to be thinned to a 6 in (15 cm) spacing.

Linaria purpurea
Purple toadflax

This perennial from Europe is naturalized in some areas and grows to 3 ft (1 m). It bears violet-tinged purple flowers in summer. 'Canon J. Went' has tiny pale pink flowers. *Zones 6–10.*

LINUM
Flax

This genus contains 200 species of annuals, biennials, perennials, subshrubs and shrubs, some evergreen, distributed widely in temperate regions. It includes the commercial flax, *Linum usitatissimum*, grown for fiber and oilseed. Several ornamental species have profusely blooming, 5-petaled flowers, which can be yellow, white, blue, red or pink.

Cultivation

They are mostly quite frost hardy. Grow in sun in humus-rich, well-drained, peaty soil. After perennial species flower, prune hard. Propagate annuals, biennials and perennials from seed and perennials by division. Most self-sow readily.

Linum narbonense

A perennial native of the Mediterranean region, this most handsome of all the blue flaxes has violet, funnel-shaped flowers borne on slender stems. The flowers last for many weeks in summer. It has soft, green leaves and forms clumps 18 in (45 cm) high and wide. *Zones 5–10.*

Linum perenne

syn. *Linum sibiricum*
Of wide occurrence in Europe and temperate Asia, this is a vigorous, upright perennial that forms a shapely, bushy plant 24 in (60 cm) high with a spread of 12 in (30 cm). It has slender stems with grass-like leaves, and clusters of open, funnel-shaped, light blue flowers are borne throughout summer. *Zones 5–10.*

LIRIOPE

This genus contains 5 species of clump-forming, rhizomatous, evergreen perennials native to Vietnam, China, Taiwan and Japan. Some cultivars are so dark in leaf they are practically black. They do not creep, and for ground cover

have to be planted 6 in (15 cm) apart. Color ranges from white to pale purple.

Cultivation

Grow in full sun or part-shade in well-drained soil. In early spring cut back shabby leaves, just before the new ones appear. Propagate from seed in autumn or by division in early spring.

Liriope muscari

syns *Liriope platyphylla, L. graminifolia*
This clumping, evergreen perennial is a useful ground cover. It bears erect spikes of rounded, bell-shaped, violet flowers in late summer. It grows to 12–24 in (30–60 cm) high with a spread of 18 in (45 cm). Flower spikes are held just above the foliage. 'Lilac Beauty' is a larger example of the species. *Zones 6–10.*

Linum narbononse

Linum perenne

Liriope muscari

Lobelia erinus

Lobelia cardinalis

Lobelia erinus 'Cambridge Blue'

LOBELIA

Widespread in temperate and tropical areas, the growth habits of this genus of 370 species of annuals, perennials and shrubs vary from low bedding plants to tall herbaceous perennials or shrubs. They all have ornamental flowers and suit flower boxes, hanging baskets and rock gardens.

Cultivation

These frost-hardy to frost-tender plants prefer well-drained, moist, light loam enriched with compost. Most grow in sun or part-shade but resent wet winter conditions. Prune after flowering, fertilize weekly with a liquid manure during the season. Propagate annuals from seed, perennial species from seed or by division and perennial cultivars by division only.

Lobelia cardinalis
Cardinal flower

This clump-forming perennial from eastern North America is useful for growing in wet places and beside streams and ponds. From late summer to mid-autumn it produces spikes of brilliant, scarlet-red flowers on branching stems above green or deep bronze-purple foliage. It grows to a height of 3 ft (1 m) and a spread of 12 in (30 cm). *Zones 3–10.*

Lobelia erinus
Edging lobelia

This slow-growing, compact annual is native to South Africa and grows to a

Lobelia siphilitica

Lobularia maritima 'Violet Queen'

height of 4–8 in (10–20 cm) and spread of 4–6 in (10–15 cm). It has a tufted, often semi-trailing habit, with dense oval to lance-shaped leaves tapering at the base. It bears small, 2-lipped pinkish purple flowers continuously from spring to early autumn. 'Color Cascade' bears a mass of blue to violet to pink and white flowers. *Zones 7–11.*

Lobelia siphilitica
Blue cardinal flower, big blue lobelia
This frost-hardy perennial from eastern USA bears racemes of 2-lipped violet-blue flowers in late summer and autumn. It reaches a height of 2–3 ft (60–90 cm) and does well in moist, heavy soil. Along with other North American lobelias this was formerly employed as a powerful drug, allegedly effective in the treatment of syphilis among other diseases, but they are all quite toxic. *Zones 5–9.*

LOBULARIA
This genus consists of 5 species of frost-hardy, dwarf plants from the Mediterranean and the Canary Islands; they are useful for rock gardens, window boxes and borders. Although there are both annual and perennial forms, the annuals are most commonly grown. They bear tiny, fragrant flowers in compact, terminal racemes in summer and early fall.

Cultivation
Grow in full sun in fertile, well-drained soil. Deadhead regularly. Propagate from seed in spring or, if used outdoors, from late spring to fall.

Lobularia maritima
syn. *Alyssum maritimum*
Sweet alyssum, sweet Alice
This fast-growing, spreading annual is a popular edging, rock garden or window box plant. It produces masses of tiny, honey-scented, 4-petaled white flowers over a long season, from spring to early autumn. Lilac, pink and violet shades are also available. It has a low, rounded, compact habit, and grows to a height of 3–12 in (8–30 cm) and a spread of 8–12 in (20–30 cm). 'Violet Queen' is the darkest of the garden varieties of sweet Alice. *Zones 7–10.*

LUNARIA
Honesty
The origin of the common name for this genus, allied to stocks *(Matthiola)*, of

3 species of annuals, biennials and perennials is uncertain, although it could be from the way the silver lining of the seed pods is concealed in the brown husk somewhat like a silver coin, the reward of virtue that does not flaunt itself. Sprays of honesty have been

Lunaria rediviva

Lunaria annua

popular as dried flower arrangements since the 18th century.

Cultivation
Plant in full sun or part-shade in fertile, moist but well-drained soil. Propagate perennials from seed or by division in autumn or spring, biennials from seed. They self-seed quite readily.

Lunaria annua
syn. *Lunaria biennis*
A fast-growing biennial native to southern Europe and the Mediterranean coast, this plant has attractive flowers and curious fruit. It has pointed, oval, serrated, bright green leaves and bears heads of scented, 4-petaled, rosy magenta, white or violet-purple flowers in spring and early summer. These are followed by seed pods with a silvery, translucent membrane. Erect in habit, it grows to 30 in (75 cm) high with a spread of 12 in (30 cm). *Zones 8–10.*

Lunaria rediviva
Perennial honesty
This perennial grows to 3 ft (1 m) high with a spread of 12 in (30 cm). It has hairy stems, heart-shaped leaves and pale violet flowers; the fruit are silver pods. *Zones 8–10.*

LUPINUS
Lupin, lupine
This legume genus of 200 species of annuals, perennials and semi-evergreen and evergreen shrubs and subshrubs have long, erect spikes of showy pea-flowers in a range of colors including blue, purple, pink, white, yellow, orange and red. They are used as ornamentals, as animal fodder, and as a 'green manure' crop (because of their nitrogen-fixing capacity). The leaves are distinct among legumes in being palmate, with 5 or more leaflets radiating from a

Lupinus, Russell Hybrids

common stalk. They are widespread in northern temperate zones except Asia.

Cultivation

Most prefer climates with cool wet winters and long dry summers. They like full sun and well-drained, moderately fertile, slightly acidic, sandy soil. Propagate species from seed and Russell lupin cultivars from cuttings or by division.

Lupinus, Russell Hybrids

This fine strain of strong-growing lupins bear long spikes of large, strongly colored flowers in cream, pink, orange, blue or violet, some varieties bicolored, in late spring and summer. They produce a magnificent clump of deeply divided, mid-green leaves, growing to 3 ft (1 m) high. 'Noble Maiden', from the Band of Nobles series, has cream flowers; 'Polar Princess' has white flowers; and the blooms of 'Troop the Colour' are bright red. There are also dwarf strains, such as the popular 'Lulu', which grows to 24 in (60 cm) high. *Zones 3–9.*

Lupinus texensis
Texas blue bonnet

A bushy annual to 12 in (30 cm) high, this species has bright green leaves

Lychnis chalcedonica

Lupinus texensis

divided into 5 small leaflets that are hairy on the undersides, and bears dark blue and white flowers in late spring. Easily grown, it thrives in poor soil and is quick to flower from seed. This is the state flower of Texas, beyond which it does not occur wild. *Zones 8–10.*

LYCHNIS
Campion, catchfly
Native to temperate regions of the northern hemisphere, these 15 to 20 species of biennials and perennials have summer flowers that range in color from white through pinks and oranges to deep red. All have flat 5-petaled flowers, but in many species the petals are notched or deeply forked or sometimes divided into narrow teeth.

Cultivation
These plants are frost hardy and easily grown in cool climates, preferably in sunny sites, and any well-drained soil. Higher mountain species do best in soil that is protected from excessive solar warmth. Remove spent stems after flowering and deadhead frequently to prolong the flowering period. Propagation is normally by division or from seed in autumn or early spring. Some species self-seed readily.

Lychnis chalcedonica
Maltese cross
This perennial species from far eastern Europe and western Russia has been popular with gardeners since the 17th century. Its color is such a dazzling orange-red that its garden companions should be chosen with care. It flowers for a short season in early summer, grows about 4 ft (1.2 m) tall, and takes its common name from the shape of the flower. White and pink varieties and one with double flowers exist, but these are fairly rare. *Zones 4–10.*

Lychnis coronaria

Lychnis coronaria
Rose campion, dusty miller, mullein pink
A clump-forming European perennial
sometimes grown as a biennial, this
striking plant grows to a height of 30 in
(75 cm) and a spread of 18 in (45 cm). It
forms a dense clump of silvery white
downy leaves, and many-branched gray
stems carry large, deep rose-pink to
scarlet flowers throughout summer.
'Alba' is a white-flowered cultivar. In
ancient times the flowers were used for
garlands and crowns. It is drought
tolerant and often self-seeds. *Zones 4–10.*

Lychnis flos-jovis
Flower of Jove, flower of Jupiter
This perennial species from the Alps
grows to a height of 18 in (45 cm). It has
tufts of ground-hugging leaves, from the
center of which the flower stems arise to
carry the flowers in clusters in summer.
The leaves are gray and downy and the
flowers are bright pink. *Zones 5–9.*

Lychnis viscaria 'Splendens Plena'

Lychnis viscaria
German catchfly
This perennial is widely distributed
through Europe and western Asia.
Growing to 18 in (45 cm) tall and with a
similar spread, it is a densely clumping

plant with bronze stems and narrow dark green leaves with sticky hairs. It produces spike-like panicles of mauve to magenta flowers in early summer. 'Splendens Plena' (syn. 'Flore Pleno') has larger, bright magenta double flowers. *Zones 4–9*.

LYSIMACHIA
Loosestrife
Ranging through temperate and sub-tropical regions of the northern hemisphere, this genus of mainly evergreen

Lysimachia clethroides

perennials and shrubs of the primula family consists of around 150 species. Growth habit varies from low, creeping plants to clumps with tall, spike-like racemes of crowded flowers. The 5-petaled flowers are mostly yellow or white, sometimes pink or purple. The botanical name is Latinized Greek for 'ending strife' though why they deserve this name is unclear.

Cultivation
They prefer slightly acidic soil with a good mix of organic matter and medium to moist conditions in sun or part-shade. Some grow best at the edge of a pond or stream. Propagate from seed or cuttings, or by division.

Lysimachia clethroides
Japanese loosestrife
This somewhat hairy perennial grows to 3 ft (1 m) high making a broad, leafy clump of erect stems. In summer it produces tapering terminal spikes, gracefully nodding in bud but becoming erect with maturity, of crowded starry white flowers. *Zones 4–10*.

Lysimachia nummularia
Creeping Jenny, moneywort
Various medicinal properties were attributed to this vigorous creeping European perennial by herbalists. The prostrate stems take root wherever they touch damp ground, forming a dense, rapidly spreading mat usually no more than 3 in (8 cm) deep. The paired leaves are almost circular, hence *nummularia* from the Latin for coin-like, also the English 'moneywort'. The deep yellow bowl-shaped flowers are borne singly on short stalks from the leaf axils over a long summer period. 'Aurea' has pale yellow-green leaves and stems; when grown in shade it turns an interesting lime green. *Zones 4–10*.

Lysimachia nummularia 'Aurea'

Lysimachia punctata
Golden loosestrife, garden loosestrife

A vigorous clump-forming perennial, this species grows erect to a height of 3 ft (1 m) with broad mid-green leaves in whorls of 4, grading into floral bracts on the upper stems which carry in summer a massed display of brilliant yellow starry flowers. It looks best planted in large groups. It is suitable for bedding, large rock gardens, or pool and streamside plantings. *Zones 5–10.*

LYTHRUM
Loosestrife

This genus of annuals, perennials and subshrubs shares the common name 'loosestrife' with *Lysimachia*, though the 2 genera are quite unrelated; however, the long, erect flower spikes of some species and their boggy habitats resemble some lysimachias. There are around 35 species, scattered through all continents except South America. They vary from small creeping plants with

Lysimachia punctata

stems rooting in the mud of ditches, to plants 6 ft (1.8 m) or more tall with showy spikes of pink to purple flowers.

Cultivation

They grow in most soil conditions as long as moisture is adequate, and in bogs and

Lythrum virgatum

other wetlands some can be invasive. Propagate from seed or by division.

Lythrum virgatum
This species extends in the wild from central Europe through central Asia as far as northern China. It is a handsome, vigorous perennial growing to as much as 6 ft (1.8 m) tall, with pretty pinkish red flowers arranged rather loosely in erect spikes. Like *Lythrum salicaria*, it has become a weed in some parts of North America. Cultivars include 'Morden Gleam' with rich crimson-red flowers, 'Morden Pink' with pretty pink flowers, and 'The Rocket', which has purple-tinged foliage and deep mauve-pink flowers. *Zones 4–10.*

Macleaya cordata

Malva moschata 'Alba'

MACLEAYA
Plume poppy

This genus honors Alexander Macleay (1767–1848), who was for many years Colonial Secretary of New South Wales, Australia. The plants are sometimes offered under the name *Bocconia*, an allied genus whose members are American. The genus consists of 2 or so species of rhizomatous perennials from China and Japan that do not really resemble poppies; the deception arises because the tubular flowers shed their petals as they open. The heart-shaped leaves are gray-green to olive green.

Cultivation

These fully frost-hardy plants prefer full sun and moderately fertile, moist but well-drained soil. Protect from cold winds. Propagate from seed or cuttings or by division.

Macleaya cordata
syn. *Bocconia cordata*
This tall perennial, growing to 5–8 ft (1.5–2.4 m) high, has large, rounded, deeply veined, heart-shaped, gray-green leaves. Large, feathery, terminal flower spikes of cream tinted with pink are borne in summer. It suits the herbaceous border. It spreads from rhizomes and may become invasive. *Zones 3–10*.

MALVA
Mallow

This genus is made up of 30 species of annuals, biennials and perennials from Europe, North Africa and Asia. The flowers are similar to but smaller than the popular *Lavatera* to which they are related; they are single, 5-petaled flowers in shades of white, pink, blue or purple. They suit borders or wild gardens.

Cultivation

They flourish in sunny, well-drained aspects and tend to be more robust in not too rich soil. They are fully frost hardy. Cut plants back after the first flowers have faded. Propagate from cuttings or seed; the perennials often self-seed. Watch for rust disease in spring.

Malva moschata
Musk mallow

Useful for naturalizing in a wild garden
or odd corner, this perennial has narrow,
lobed, divided leaves with a sticky, hairy
texture which emit a musky, cheesy odor
when crushed. It bears profuse spikes of
saucer-shaped pink flowers in summer.
'Alba', a white cultivar, is very popular.
It has a bushy, branching habit and can
grow to a height of about 3 ft (1 m).
Zones 3–10.

MATTHIOLA
Stock, gillyflower

This is a genus of some 55 species of
annuals, biennials and subshrubby
perennials from Europe, central Asia
and South Africa. The leaves are usually
gray-green and the perfumed flowers
can be produced from spring to autumn.
They make good cut flowers but stocks
are prone to a few pests and diseases,
including downy mildew, club-root, gray
mold and cabbage root fly.

Cultivation

They prefer a sunny aspect in moist but
well-drained, neutral or alkaline soil.
Shelter from strong winds and stake the
larger forms. Propagate from seed sown
in situ for night-scented stock—this
should be staggered to increase the
flowering season.

Matthiola incana

This very popular, upright biennial or
short-lived European perennial is best
grown as an annual. It has a bushy habit
and grows up to 24 in (60 cm) high.
Fully frost hardy, it has lance-shaped,
gray-green leaves and fragrant spikes of
mauve flowers borne in spring. 'Mam-
moth Column' grows taller, and produces a single spike of scented flowers in
spring in mixed or separate colors.
Zones 6–10.

Matthiola incana

MIMULUS
syn. *Diplacus*
Monkey flower, musk

The 180 or so species of annuals,
perennials and shrubs are characterized
by tubular flowers with flared mouths,
often curiously spotted and mottled
which have been likened to monkey
faces. The flowers come in a large range
of colors, including brown, orange,
yellow, red, pink and crimson. Mainly
native to the cool Pacific coastal areas of
Chile and the USA, most prefer bog
gardens or other moist situations; some
are excellent rock garden plants.

Cultivation

Grow them in full sun or part-shade in
wet or moist soil. Propagate perennials
by division in spring and annuals from
seed in autumn or early spring.

Mimulus guttatus
syn. *Mimulus langsdorfii*
Common monkey flower

A vigorous, very frost-hardy, semi-
herbaceous perennial native to the
Americas from Alaska to Mexico, this

species grows well in damp to wet sites and has naturalized in areas well away from its natural habitat. It grows to about 12 in (30 cm) or so tall and spreads to at least 4 ft (1.2 m) and produces its bright yellow flowers, spotted or blotched brown-red, throughout the summer months. *Zones 6–10*.

Mimulus × hybridus Hybrids

These popular hybrids between *Mimulus guttatus* and *M. luteus* blend parental characters in various ways. The funnel-shaped, open-mouthed flowers come in red, yellow, cream and white, or mixed variations of these colors, plus red mottling, spotting or freckling. Although reasonably hardy and perennial, they rapidly deteriorate in hot sunlight and become straggly after a few months, and so are treated as annuals. 'Ruiter's Hybrid' bears orange trumpet-shaped flowers with wavy petal margins. *Zones 6–10*.

Mimulus luteus
Yellow musk, golden monkey flower

A spreading perennial often grown as an annual, this plant bears a profusion of

Mimulus guttatus

yellow flowers above mid-green foliage throughout summer. It grows to a height and spread of 12 in (30 cm). It is very frost hardy. *Zones 7–10*.

MISCANTHUS

This is a genus of ornamental grasses occurring naturally from Africa to eastern Asia. They are highly desirable and well-behaved herbaceous plants, ideal in a perennial border or by the edge of water. Most are tall-growing

Mimulus luteus

Mimulus × hybridus Hybrid 'Ruiter's Hybrid'

Monarda didyma

Miscanthus sinensis 'Gracillimus'

grasses that can reach up to 12 ft (3.5 m) or more. There are 17 to 20 species, usually neatly clump forming with upright reed-like stems and narrow arching leaves. The flowerheads are produced in late summer and autumn and make attractive fluffy plumes at the tops of the stems. They make good cut flowers.

Cultivation

Moderately frost hardy, they prefer full sun and fertile, moist but well-drained soil. Cut them down to ground level in late winter when the dead stems start to collapse. Propagate by dividing larger clumps in late winter.

Miscanthus sinensis
Eulalia

Probably one of the most beautiful and least invasive of ornamental grasses, this Asian species has undergone more selection of cultivars than probably any other grass. The wild form makes neat, upright to slightly arching clumps up to 12 ft (3.5 m) tall, although usually less. Its leaves have a white midrib and die to a soft straw color in winter. The flowerheads are usually soft gray tinted purple-brown. 'Gracillimus' has very fine leaves that color well in autumn, have a white midrib and arch elegantly; it rarely exceeds 4 ft (1.2 m) in height. 'Yaku Jima' is a dwarf form to about 30

in (75 cm) or so with narrow arching leaves. 'Zebrinus' is a tall variety with bands of gold irregularly positioned across the leaf blade, giving it the common name of zebra grass. *Zones 4–10.*

MONARDA
Bergamot, horsemint

This is a genus of 15 species of perennials or annuals with green, sometimes purple-tinged, veined, aromatic leaves. They are used for flavoring teas and in potpourris. Plants can be single stemmed or sparsely branching, and bear 2-lipped, tubular flowers from mid-summer to early autumn.

Cultivation

They are frost-hardy plants preferring full sun although some shade is acceptable. They must be well drained; annual species prefer sandy soil. The perennials like moist soil and in some climates some manure or compost. Annuals are sown directly into their permanent spot, and perennials are usually grown by division of established clumps.

Monarda didyma
Bee balm, Oswego tea

This herb was used by Native Americans and early colonists as a tea. It has spidery white, pink or red flowers borne in late summer. The young leaves may be used in salads, as a tea, or as a stuffing for roast meat. The species grows 3 ft (1 m) or more tall. 'Croftway Pink' grows to 30 in (75 cm) tall and has rose-pink flowers. *Zones 4–10*.

Monarda fistulosa
Wild bergamot

This perennial species from eastern North America has hybridized naturally and in gardens with *Monarda didyma* to produce a range of hybrids. The wild species grows to about 4 ft (1.2 m) tall and less than half that in width. The flowers are usually light purple or pale pink with purple-stained bracts. *Zones 4–10*.

MYOSOTIS
Forget-me-not

This genus of annuals and perennials includes 34 New Zealand natives among its 50 or so species, but the most commonly cultivated are from temperate regions of Europe, Asia and the Americas. Their dainty blue (sometimes pink or white) flowers bloom in spring and most suit rock gardens and borders. The plants fade after flowering. *Myosotis*, from the Greek for 'mouse ear', refers to

the pointed leaves. They have long been associated with love and remembrance.

Cultivation

Mostly quite frost hardy, they like a semi-shaded or a sunny spot protected by larger plants, and fertile, well-drained soil. Fertilize before flowering begins. Propagate from seed.

Myosotis alpestris
Alpine forget-me-not

This short-lived perennial from Europe (usually grown as an annual or biennial) forms clumps to a height and spread of 4–6 in (10–15 cm). In late spring and early summer, it bears clusters of dainty, bright blue, pink or white flowers with creamy yellow eyes. *Zones 4–10*.

Myosotis sylvatica
Garden forget-me-not

This short-lived perennial is usually grown as an annual. It bears lavender-blue, yellow-eyed flowers in spring and early summer. It forms mounds of fuzzy foliage 18 in (45 cm) tall and 12 in (30 cm) wide, with taller stems uncurling as the flower buds open. 'Blue Ball' has tiny, deep blue flowers. *Zones 5–10*.

Myosotis sylvatica 'Blue Ball'

Myosotis alpestris

N, O

Narcissus, Trumpet daffodils (Division 1)

Narcissus, Double-flowered daffodils (Division 4)

NARCISSUS
Daffodil, narcissus

Members of this well-known genus of bulbs from Europe, Asia and North Africa are easy to grow, multiply freely and bloom year after year. The wild species number about 50 and are mostly native to the western Mediterranean region. The many thousands of named cultivars have been grouped into 12 divisions or classes, the most important being: the Trumpet narcissi (Division 1) which have trumpets as long as the outer petals or perianth; the Large-cupped narcissi (Division 2), with trumpets from one-third to two-thirds as long; the Small-cupped narcissi (Division 3), with trumpets less than one-third the length of the petals; and the Double-flowered narcissi (Division 4) with double flowers, either one or several per stem. Divisions 5 to 9 cover hybrids and cultivars of important species such as *Narcissus triandrus*, *N. cyclamineus*, *N. jonquilla*, *N. tazetta* and *N. poeticus* respectively; Division 10 covers the wild species; Division 11 the split-corona hybrids; and Division 12 consists of daffodils not included in any other division, such as *N. bulbocodium* hybrids. Colors range from white to yellow, although individual varieties may have white, yellow, red, orange or pink trumpets.

Cultivation

Frost hardiness varies, but all tolerate at least light frosts and they grow best in cool areas. Plant in autumn, 4–6 in (10–15 cm) deep in rich, well-drained soil. They enjoy full sun in cool areas, and some shade in warmer areas. Water well during growth and allow to dry out once the leaves die down. Clumps multiply freely; leave undisturbed for a few years; thereafter, lift and divide in fall.

Narcissus, Trumpet daffodils (Division 1)

These are the best known of all the daffodils with their solitary large flowers and long trumpets. They are derived mainly from the wild daffodil *Narcissus pseudonarcissus*. There are innumerable named cultivars, which may be all yellow, white with yellow trumpets, all white, or white with pale pink trumpets. They are the first of the big daffodils to flower. The all-gold 'King Alfred', raised in 1890, is the classic cultivar, but its name has been very loosely applied, and some authorities consider the original variety may be extinct. 'Irish Luck' has deep golden-yellow flowers; 'Chivalry' has white flowers. *Zones 4–10.*

Narcissus, Double-flowered daffodils (Division 4)

These daffodils can have either a solitary large flower or several smaller ones, with

Nemophila maculata

Nemesia strumosa

the perianth segments or the corona, or both, doubled. Some of the oldest narcissus cultivars are the double-flowered daffodils. The buds will not open properly if they have undergone dry conditions while developing. 'Tahiti' has a yellow perianth with an orange corona; and 'Unique' has a white perianth and wavy, yellow corona segments. *Zones 4–10.*

NEMESIA

This genus of 50-odd species of annuals, perennials and subshrubs comes from South Africa. Their flowering period is short, although if they are cut back hard when flowering slows down they will flower again. The flowers are trumpet-shaped and 2-lipped, and are borne singly in the upper leaf axils or in terminal racemes. The leaves are opposite and simple.

Cultivation

They need a protected, sunny spot and fertile, well-drained soil. They do not like hot, humid climates. Pinch out growing shoots on young plants to ensure bushiness. Propagate from seed in early autumn or early spring.

Nemesia strumosa

This colorful, fast-growing, bushy annual is a popular bedding plant. It has lance-shaped, pale green, prominently toothed leaves, and grows to a height of 8–12 in (20–30 cm) and a spread of 10 in (25 cm). Large flowers in yellow, white, red or orange are borne in spring on short terminal racemes. 'Blue Gem' is a compact cultivar with small, clear blue flowers. 'Red and White' has flowers strikingly bicolored, the upper lip bright red and the lower lip white. *Zones 9–11.*

NEMOPHILA

This is a group of 11 species of annuals with bright, open, 5-petaled flowers. Originating from western USA, they produce colorful spring–summer blooms in a range of mainly blues.

Cultivation

These quick-growing annuals grow best in full sun or part-shade in friable, moisture-retentive soil. Protect from wind and position plants away from high-traffic pathways. Regular watering helps prolong blooming. Check for aphids. Propagate from seed which can be sown *in situ* during the autumn.

Nemophila maculata
Five spot

Commonly referred to as five spot because each veined, white petal has a prominent deep purple blotch at its tip, this plant grows to 12 in (30 cm) tall. It is used extensively in massed displays as plants hold their profusion of blooms above the ferny foliage over a long period during summer. *Zones 7–11.*

Nemophila menziesii
syn. *Nemophila insignis*
Baby blue-eyes

A charming little Californian wildflower, this spreading annual is a useful ground cover under shrubs such as roses, as well as in rock gardens and around edges; it is particularly effective overplanted in a bed with spring bulbs. It bears small, bowl-shaped, sapphire-blue flowers with a well-defined concentric ring of white in the center. It has dainty, serrated foliage, and grows to a height and width of 6–10 in (15–25 cm). These plants dislike heat and transplanting. *Zones 7–11.*

NEPETA

This large genus of more than 200 species of perennial, rarely annual, plants is used extensively in herbaceous

Nemophila menziesii

Nepeta × faassenii

borders and for edgings or as ground cover plants. Some species are naturally compact, while others tend to be taller growing plants and may need staking

Cultivation

Provide a well-drained soil in a sunny position. Some of the vigorous herbaceous species make good single species ground covers. Trim lightly during the growing season and cut back each year to prevent the plants from becoming too straggly. Propagate by division, from cuttings, or from seed.

Nepeta cataria
Catnip, catmint

A native of Europe, catnip is a frost-hardy perennial with branching, upright stems growing up to 3 ft (1 m). It has aromatic, gray-green leaves and whorls of white flowers from late spring through to autumn. Cats are attracted to this plant and will lie in it or play in it and sometimes dig it up. A tea made from the leaves is said to be relaxing. *Zones 3–10.*

Nepeta × faassenii
Catmint

This is a bushy, clump-forming perennial, which forms spreading mounds of grayish green leaves that are aromatic when crushed. The numerous flower stems carry hundreds of small, violet-blue flowers throughout summer. It

Nepeta cataria

grows to a height and spread of 18 in (45 cm). 'Dropmore Blue' has upright, tall flower spikes of lavender blue; 'Six Hills Giant' will bloom continuously throughout summer if spent flowers are kept clipped. *Zones 3–10.*

Nepeta racemosa

syn. *Nepeta mussinii*

Native to the Caucasus region and northern Iran, this ornamental species has generally been known as *Nepeta mussinii* in gardens, though many of the plants sold under that name are in fact the hybrid *N. × faassenii.* It is a vigorous perennial up to about 12 in (30 cm) high with gray-green, densely hairy leaves and lavender-blue summer flowers in long racemes. 'Blue Wonder' is a very free-flowering form of spreading habit with violet-blue flowers. *Zones 3–10.*

NICOTIANA
Flowering tobacco

The 67 species of annuals, biennials, perennials and shrubs in this genus are from America and Australia and include the commercial tobacco plant. Earlier introduced species have fragrant warm-weather flowers, usually opening at night; flowers of newer strains remain open all day but have limited perfume. They are good for cutting, although the plants are sticky to handle.

Cultivation

Marginally frost hardy to frost tender, they need full sun or light shade and fertile, moist but well-drained soil. Propagate from seed in early spring.

Nicotiana alata

syn. *Nicotiana affinis*

A short-lived South American perennial often grown as an annual, this marginally frost-hardy plant bears clusters of fragrant, tubular flowers in white, red or various shades of pink. Rosette forming, it has oval leaves and grows to a height of about 3 ft (1 m) with a spread of 12 in (30 cm). It flowers through summer and early autumn. *Zones 7–11.*

Nicotiana sylvestris

One of the few summer-flowering annuals which thrive in shade, the

Nepeta racemosa 'Blue Wonder'

Nicotiana sylvestris

Nicotiana alata

Nigella damascena

Nymphaea, Hardy Hybrid 'Lucida'

flowers of this species remain open even in deep shade or on overcast days. It grows to 5 ft (1.5 m) or more with tall, stately flowering stems that arise from a mass of large, bright green lush foliage. Terminal groups of long, tubular white flowers are particularly fragrant on warm summer evenings, so plant it where the scent can be appreciated. *Zones 8–11.*

NIGELLA

The nigellas are a genus of about 15 species of annuals from the Mediterranean countries and western Asia. They have long been used in folk medicine. The flowers are attractive and are suitable for cutting. They have ornamen-

tal seed pods which hold their shape and are popular for flower arrangements.

Cultivation

The seedlings hate being transplanted, but if seeds are sown where the plants are to grow and some flowers are allowed to go to seed, new plants will come up for years. Plant in full sun in fertile, well-drained soil and deadhead to prolong flowering if the seed pods are not needed. Propagate from seed.

Nigella damascena
Love-in-a-mist, devil-in-a-bush

This fully frost-hardy annual bears spurred, many-petaled, pale to lilac-blue or white flowers in spring and early summer, almost hidden in the bright green, feathery foliage; these are followed by rounded, green seed pods that mature to brown. Upright and fast growing, it reaches 24 in (60 cm) in height with a spread of 8 in (20 cm). 'Miss Jekyll' is a double blue form. *Zones 6–10.*

NYMPHAEA
Waterlily

This worldwide genus of 50 species of deciduous and evergreen perennial aquatic plants with fleshy roots have rounded, floating leaves which are cleft at the base, and attractive large flowers which come in shades of white and cream, brilliant yellows and oranges, pinks and deep reds, blues and purple. They may be night blooming, depending on species, and sometimes fragrant.

Cultivation

Frost-hardy waterlilies grow in most climates and flower freely throughout summer. Divide the tuber-like rhizomes and replant every 3 or 4 years. Tropical waterlilies are frost tender, requiring a very warm, sunny situation. They flower from mid-summer. All need still water

Ocimum basilicum

Nymphaea, Tropical Day-blooming Hybrid 'Blue Beauty'

and annual fertilizing. Propagate from seed or by separating plantlets. Check for insects, particularly aphids; goldfish will eat most pests.

Nymphaea, Hardy Hybrids

These cold-hardy and colorful hybrids have day-blooming flowers, mostly in shades of white, yellow, pink or red, set on or just above the surface of the water. 'Atropurpurea' has reddish purple foliage and dark red, wide-open flowers with golden stamens. 'Lucida' has attractive deep red flowers with paler outer petals. The elegant Marliacea hybrids have dark green leaves and star-shaped, semi-double, soft pink flowers with golden centers, which appear in summer. The large flowers stand slightly above the water. *Zones 5–10.*

Nymphaea, Tropical Day-blooming Hybrids

Tropical hybrids can bear day- or night-time flowers. 'Blue Beauty' is a decidu-ous or evergreen, day-blooming waterlily with large, brown-speckled, dark green leaves with purplish under-sides; the flowers are rounded, semi-double, 12 in (30 cm) across, and deep purple-blue with yellow centers and it spreads to 8 ft (2.4 m). 'St. Louis Gold', with abundant daytime blooms of deep gold, is a good variety for smaller pools or tubs. *Zones 10–11.*

OCIMUM
Basil

This genus of approximately 35 species of rather frost-tender annuals, perenni-als and shrubs is native to tropical Asia and Africa. They are now widely cultivated in many other countries for their highly aromatic leaves, which are used for medicinal purposes or to flavor salads, soups, sauces, stews and curries. They have mostly oval leaves in opposite pairs and small tubular flowers borne in whorls towards the ends of the stems in late summer.

Cultivation

Grow in a protected, warm, sunny position in a moist but well-drained soil. Regularly pinch back plants to encour-age bushy growth and to prevent them going to seed quickly. Propagate from seed in mid-spring. Protect from late frosts and check for chewing insects and snails.

Ocimum basilicum
Basil, sweet basil

This native of tropical Asia, together with its cultivars, is the most commonly grown and most widely used basil. A favorite with cooks, it is one of the most widely used herbs in Mediterranean cooking. Fresh leaves are best; freeze them for the winter as they lose their flavor when dried. It is a tender annual plant growing to about 18 in (45 cm) with light green, oval leaves that have a delicious warm, spicy fragrance. Small white flowers are carried in whorls towards the ends of the stems in late summer. There are a number of varieties of basil including a compact small leaf type; a crinkled, lettuce leaf variety and the beautiful 'Dark Opal', which has rich purple stems and leaves. There are perennial varieties also, but their flavor is inferior. 'Minimum' is a dwarf form with tiny leaves, used in the Greek Orthodox Church for sprinkling holy water. *Zones 10–12.*

OENOTHERA
Evening primrose

This genus, native to the Americas, consists of more than 120 species of annuals, biennials and perennials. Their short-lived flowers, borne during summer, have 4 delicate petals, yellow or less commonly pink, red or white, and a long basal tube. Most are pollinated by nocturnal insects and only release their fragrance at night. Some do not open their petals during the day. Evening primrose oil is extracted from the plants' tiny seeds; it contains certain fatty acids believed to be beneficial to health if consumed regularly in modest quantities.

Cultivation

They are mostly frost hardy and prefer a well-drained, sandy soil in an open, sunny situation. Propagate from seed or by division, or from softwood cuttings.

Oenothera macrocarpa
syn. *Oenothera missouriensis*
Ozark sundrops, Missouri primrose, fluttermills

This perennial is usually almost stemless with large rosettes of narrow tapering leaves. The flowers are large, reaching 4 in (10 cm) in diameter, lemon yellow in color and open in the evening in summer. This plant reaches a height of no more than 6 in (15 cm), but spreads to 24 in (60 cm) or more across, the flowers appearing singly from between the leaves. *Zones 5–9.*

Oenothera speciosa
White evening primrose, showy evening primrose

This short-lived, rhizomatous perennial bears spikes of profuse, fragrant, saucer-shaped, pink-tinted white flowers. Fresh flowerheads open daily during summer. Clump forming, it grows to 18–24 in (45–60 cm) in height with a spread of 18 in (45 cm) or more. 'Rosea' (syns 'Childsii', *Oenothera berlandieri*) is lower growing, with flowers edged and heavily veined rose pink, yellow in the center. *Zones 5–10.*

Oenothera speciosa 'Rosea'

Oenothera macrocarpa

OMPHALODES
Navelwort

From Europe, Asia and Mexico, this genus consists of 28 species of forget-me-not–like annuals and perennials that are either evergreen or semi-evergreen. They make excellent ground covers, and they are suitable for rock gardens.

Cultivation

They prefer shade or part-shade with moist but well-drained soil (except for *Omphalodes linifolia*, which prefers a sunny position). They are mostly frost hardy. Propagate from seed in spring or by division in autumn.

Omphalodes cappadocica

This spreading perennial from Turkey has creeping underground stems. It produces numerous sprays of flat, bright purple-blue flowers in spring that arise from clumps of densely hairy, oval to heart-shaped leaves that are found at the base of the plant. It reaches a height of 6–8 in (15–20 cm) and a spread of 10 in (25 cm) and is frost hardy. *Zones 6–9.*

Omphalodes verna
Blue-eyed Mary, creeping forget-me-not

This semi-evergreen thrives in shady conditions. During spring, it produces long, loose sprays of flat, bright blue flowers with white eyes. This plant has heart-shaped, mid-green leaves that form clumps. It reaches a height and spread of 8 in (20 cm). *Zones 6–9.*

OPHIOPOGON
Mondo grass, snakebeard, lilyturf

This genus contains 50 or so species of evergreen perennials from eastern Asia. They have attractive, long-lived clumps of grass-like foliage springing from underground rhizomes. They are not grasses but lilies, allied to lily-of-the-valley *(Convallaria)*. The summer flowers are small and can be white or blue through to purple. The berry-like fruits each contain one seed. They are trouble-free and provide an attractive ground cover that effectively suppresses leaves.

Cultivation

They are mostly fairly frost hardy and tolerate sun or part-shade in moist, well-drained soil. Propagate by division of clumps, or from seed.

Ophiopogon japonicus
syn. *Liriope japonica*
Mondo grass

This fine-leafed species is native to Japan and Korea. The dark green

Omphalodes cappadocica

Omphalodes verna

Ophiopogon japonicus

Origanum vulgare 'Aureum'

Ophiopogon planiscapus 'Nigrescens'

recurving foliage arises from deep rhizomes, spreading to form dense, soft mats up to about 8 in (20 cm) deep. Pale purple flowers are hidden among the leaves in mid-summer, followed by bright blue, pea-sized fruit. The cultivar 'Kyoto Dwarf' is only 2–4 in (5–10 cm) high, with very short leaves. *Zones 8–11.*

Ophiopogon planiscapus 'Nigrescens'
syn. *Ophiopogon planiscapus* 'Ebony Night'
Black mondo grass
This striking cultivar is grown particularly for its distinctive purple-black, rather stiff leaves about ¼ in (6 mm) wide which form slow-growing, sparse clumps. Its lilac flowers appear in clusters along the flowering stem in summer. These are followed by black fruit. It reaches a height of 10 in (25 cm) and a spread of 12 in (30 cm). *Ophiopogon planiscapus* 'Nigrescens' is native to Japan. *Zones 6–10.*

ORIGANUM
syn. *Majorana*
Marjoram, oregano
Native to the Mediterranean region and temperate Asia, these perennials and subshrubs in the mint family have aromatic leaves and stalked spikes or heads of small tubular flowers with crowded, overlapping bracts. Some are grown as culinary herbs; others are grown for their decorative pink flowerheads. With arching or prostrate stems arising from vigorously spreading rhizomes, they are useful for trailing over rocks, banks and walls.

Cultivation
They like full sun and a moderately fertile, well-drained soil. Trim excess growth regularly and propagate from seed in spring or by root division in autumn or spring.

Origanum vulgare
Common oregano, wild marjoram
The common oregano has a sharper, more pungent flavor than marjoram. It has a sprawling habit and grows to 24 in (60 cm) high with dark green, oval leaves and small, white or pink flowers in summer. The leaves are used, fresh or dried, in many Mediterranean-inspired dishes. In Italy, oregano is used in pizza toppings and pasta dishes. 'Aureum' has a less sprawling habit and bright greenish gold leaves. *Zones 5–9.*

OSMUNDA

This is a genus of about 12 species of large, deciduous ferns that occur naturally near water in the Americas, Europe and Asia. The fronds are erect and rather narrow in outline, forming dense tufts or rosettes and turning yellow or golden brown in autumn. Spore-bearing fronds (or portions of fronds in some species) are very distinct, the green leaflets replaced by reddish brown spore cases. Osmunda fiber is used as a potting medium for orchids among other uses, and consists of the densely matted roots of *Osmunda regalis*.

Cultivation

These fully frost-hardy ferns require a position in shade, except for *Osmunda regalis*, which tolerates sun and very wet conditions. Propagate by division in fall or winter or from spores as soon as they ripen.

Osmunda regalis
Royal fern

Native to Asia, the Americas and Europe, this is the largest species of the genus. It grows to a height of 6 ft (1.8 m) with long bipinnate fronds. It is commonly found in large groups in swamps and other boggy areas, and so is suitable for wet gardens. The inner fronds in the crown are divided into a sterile, leafy lower portion and a crown spore-bearing upper portion. *Zones 3–9.*

OSTEOSPERMUM

This genus of 70 or so species of evergreen shrubs, semi-woody perennials and annuals is mostly indigenous to South Africa. Allied to *Dimorphotheca*, they have irregularly toothed leaves and produce a profusion of large, daisy-like flowerheads in the white, pink, violet and purple range. Most are cultivars of uncertain origin, suspected to be

Osmunda regalis

hybrids. Tough plants, they are useful for rock gardens, dry embankments or the front rows of shrub borders.

Cultivation

They are marginally to moderately frost hardy and prefer open, well-drained soil of medium fertility in an open, sunny spot. Propagate from cuttings or seed.

Osteospermum ecklonis
syn. *Dimorphotheca ecklonis*
Blue-and-white daisybush, sailor boy daisy

This shrub is variable in growth habit, with some erect forms of up to 5 ft (1.5 m) tall and other forms that are lower and more spreading, or even semi-prostrate. From late spring to autumn, it bears profuse 3 in (8 cm) wide daisies, sparkling white with deep reddish violet centers and streaked bluish mauve on the undersides of petals. 'Starshine' has white flowers with bluish centers. *Zones 8–10.*

OXALIS
Wood-sorrel

This is a genus of some 500 species of bulbous, rhizomatous and fibrous-rooted perennials and a few shrubs. Some have become garden weeds. The leaves are always compound, divided into 3 or more heart-shaped or more deeply 2-lobed leaflets in a palmate arrangement.

Osteospermum ecklonis 'Starshine'

Oxalis hirta

The funnel-shaped flowers are usually pink, white or yellow, and are carried in an umbel-like cluster on slender stalks.

Cultivation

Most grow from bulbs or corms, which multiply readily. A position in sun or part-shade suits most, along with a mulched, well-drained soil and moderate water. Propagate by division of the bulbs or from seed in autumn.

Oxalis hirta

Most oxalises have leaves like clovers, but this perennial from South Africa's western Cape Province is different. Growing from bulbs, it produces elongated, closely crowded stems, to about 8 in (20 cm) long, making a bushy, crinkly leafed plant that covers itself for weeks in autumn and winter with deep pink flowers with yellow throats about ³⁄₄ in (18 mm) wide. *Zones 9–11.*

Oxalis purpurea
syn. *Oxalis variabilis*

This showy South African native has large flowers in pink, rose, lilac or white; all have soft yellow centers. Clover-like leaves arise from bulbs to form a mound only 4 in (10 cm) high; the deep green leaflets have purple undersides and the flowers appear from late autumn until early spring. *Zones 8–10.*

Oxalis purpurea

P

Paeonia lactiflora Hybrid

Paeonia suffruticosa

Paeonia officinalis 'Rubra Plena'

PAEONIA
Peony

There are 33 species in this genus of deciduous perennials and shrubs from Europe, Asia, North America and China. The centers of the rose-like flowers have a mass of short stamens almost conceal-ing the large ovaries that develop into seed pods. Flowers are mostly in shades of pink or red, but there are also white and yellow-flowered species. The majority are herbaceous, but 'tree peonies' have aboveground woody stems, and are no more than about 8 ft (2.4 m) high.

Cultivation

Most will only succeed in climates with a cold winter. They like full or filtered sunlight, and cool, moist soil. Propagate from seed, or by division for cultivars.

Paeonia lactiflora **Hybrids**

The herbaceous Chinese peonies have handsome foliage—maroon tinted when it first appears in spring—and usually scented flowers in a huge range of colors and forms. 'Beacon Flame' has deep red semi-double flowers. 'Cora Stubbs' has broad outer petals and smaller central ones in contrasting tones. *Zones 6–9.*

Paeonia officinalis

Of European origin, this herbaceous perennial reaches a height of 24 in (60 cm) and from spring to mid-summer bears single, purple or red, rose-like flowers. Although poisonous, it has been used medicinally. 'Rubra Plena' bears flowers that consist of clusters of many small, mid-magenta petals. *Zones 8–10.*

Paeonia suffruticosa
Tree peony, moutan

Native to China, this handsome decidu-ous shrub has been so enthusiastically transplanted into gardens it is probably extinct in the wild. It reaches a height and width of 3–6 ft (1–1.8 m) and produces very large single or double cup-shaped flowers in spring. Depend-ing on the variety, these are white, pink, red or yellow, and are set among attractive, large, mid-green leaves. *P. suffruticosa* subsp. *rockii* has semi-double white flowers with a maroon blotch at the base of each petal. *Zones 4–9.*

Papaver nudicaule

Panicum virgatum

PANICUM
Panic grass, crab grass

This genus of around 470 species of annual and perennial grasses is found throughout the tropics and in warm-temperate parts of the northern hemisphere. Some are cropped, others are ornamental and more than a few are weeds. They range in size from 2–10 ft (0.6–3 m) tall and form clumps of fine stems with long, very narrow leaves often covered with fine hairs when young. Erect to nodding panicles of loose flower spikes open in summer. The flower panicles, which are up to 18 in (45 cm) long, are often bronze or red tinted.

Cultivation

They grow in any moist, well-drained soil in full sun. Most perennial species tolerate heavy frost. Propagate species from seed and cultivated forms by division.

Panicum virgatum
Switch grass

Found from Central America to southern Canada, this 6 ft (1.8 m) tall perennial forms clumps of blue-green to purple-green stems with sticky, bright green leaves up to 24 in (60 cm) long. Stiff, 18 in (45 cm) long flower panicles open from late summer. The leaves yellow in autumn; the flowers develop red to bronze tones. 'Heavy Metal' has erect blue-green leaves that yellow in fall. 'Rubrum' has red-green leaves that turn bright red in fall and fine sprays of deep brown flower spikelets. *Zones 5–10.*

PAPAVER
Poppy

The 50 or so annual, biennial or perennial species of this genus are mainly from temperate parts of Eurasia and Africa and eastern USA. They have characteristic cupped petals and nodding buds turning skywards upon opening. Several of their close relatives take their common name, such as the tree poppy (*Romneya*), the Californian poppy (*Eschscholzia*) or the blue poppy (*Meconopsis*).

Cultivation

Poppies are fully frost hardy and prefer little or no shade and deep, moist, well-drained soil. Sow seed in spring or autumn; many self-seed readily.

Papaver nudicaule
Iceland poppy

This tuft-forming perennial from North America and Asia Minor is almost always grown as an annual. Large scented flowers, borne in winter and spring, are white, yellow, orange or pink, and have a crinkled texture; the leaves are pale green, the stems long and hairy. It grows 12–24 in (30–60 cm) tall with a 6–8 in (15–20 cm) spread. *Zones 2–10.*

Papaver orientale
Oriental poppy

In summer this herbaceous perennial bears spectacular flowers as big as peonies in shades of pink through to red. The cultivated varieties, sometimes double, come in a wide range of colors and many feature a dark basal blotch on each petal. According to variety, it grows from 18 in (45 cm) to more than 3 ft (1 m) tall. 'Cedric Morris' has shell-pink flowers with frilly petals, each with an almost black blotch at the base. *Zones 3–9.*

Papaver rhoeas
Corn poppy, field poppy, Flanders poppy

The cupped flowers on this fast-growing annual are small, delicate, scarlet and single. The cultivated varieties (Shirley Series) come in reds, pinks, whites and

Papaver rhoeas (Shirley Series)

Papaver orientale

bicolors; they have a pale heart instead of the black cross that marks the center of the wild poppy. It grows to 24 in (60 cm) high with a 12 in (30 cm) spread. Double flowered strains are also available. *Zones 5–9.*

PELARGONIUM

The popular hybrid pelargoniums are known as 'geraniums', but should not be confused with members of the genus *Geranium* of the same family. The genus *Pelargonium* consists of perhaps 280 species from South Africa, Australasia and the Middle East. Common garden 'geraniums' are the Zonal pelargoniums. They have almost circular leaves with scalloped margins, often with horseshoe-shaped zones of brown, red or purple, and flower almost continuously.

Cultivation

These frost-tender plants are often treated like annuals for summer bedding in colder climates. In warmer climates they flower almost all the time, although they do not like extreme heat and humidity. They prefer light, well-drained, neutral soil. Avoid over-watering; Zonals rot at the base if soil remains wet. Propagate from softwood cuttings.

Pelargonium, Ivy-leafed Hybrids

These are derived mainly from the South African *P. peltatum*, which has a scram-

Pelargonium, Ivy-leafed Hybrid 'Blooming Gem'

bling or trailing habit with fleshy, pointed-lobed, hairless leaves and small pink flowers. The many cultivars retain the leaf characteristics, but have larger flowers in conspicuous long-stalked heads, often double and in a wide range of colors. Easily grown, they tolerate wetter conditions than the Zonals, and are especially suited to hanging baskets, window boxes and the tops of retaining walls. Recent developments include variegated leaves and compact or miniature plants. Hybridizing of Ivy-leafed and Zonal pelargoniums has resulted in plants with leaves like the former and flowers more like the latter. 'Blooming Gem' has bright pink flowers. The Cascade Series of miniature ivy-leafed pelargoniums have small leaves and masses of small flowers — 'Chic' has deep pink double flowers. *Zones 9–11.*

Pelargonium odoratissimum
Apple geranium

A strong, sweet smell of apples comes off the small, roughly heart-shaped, lobed, gray-green leaves of this bushy South African geranium. It reaches a height and spread of 12 in (30 cm). Flowers are small and white, sometimes with red veins in the upper petals. In warm-temperate climates, flowers may be borne

almost continuously, although it dislikes hot, humid conditions. *Zones 10–11.*

PENSTEMON

This large genus consists of 250 species of deciduous, evergreen or semi-evergreen subshrubs and perennials native to the cold temperate to subtropical northern hemisphere. The leaves appear in opposite pairs in whorls, while the flowers have 2 lobes on the upper lip and 3 on the lower. Hybrids have showy flower spikes in blues, reds, white and bicolors.

Cultivation

These marginally to very frost-hardy plants prefer fertile, well-drained soil and full sun. Propagate from seed, by division, or from cuttings of non-flowering shoots (the only method for cultivars).

Penstemon barbatus
syn. *Chelone barbata*
Coral penstemon, beard-lip penstemon

The scarlet flowers on this semi-ever-green, very frost-hardy perennial are tubular with 2 lips. They bloom on racemes from mid-summer to early autumn above narrow, lance-shaped, green leaves. The plant grows to 3 ft (1 m) high, with a spread of 12 in (30 cm). *Zones 3–10.*

Pelargonium odoratissimum

Penstemon barbatus

Penstemon heterophyllus

Penstemon digitalis 'Husker's Red'

Penstemon 'Evelyn'

Penstemon digitalis

Native to eastern North America, this very frost-hardy perennial species is usually seen with white or pale lavender flowers, neither particularly exciting. 'Husker's Red', however, is notable for its deep reddish purple foliage. A robust plant, it reaches a height of 30 in (75 cm) and spread of 24 in (60 cm), and is attractive to hummingbirds. *Zones 3–9.*

Penstemon 'Evelyn'

This is a 30 in (75 cm) tall perennial hybrid with very narrow leaves and masses of slightly curved pale pink flowers. It was raised by the famous Slieve Donard nursery of Northern Ireland and is very frost hardy. *Zones 7–10.*

Penstemon heterophyllus
Foothill penstemon, blue bedder penstemon

This very frost-hardy, summer-flowering subshrub grows to about 18 in (45 cm) tall. Its leaves are lance-shaped and slightly blue-green. The flowers vary from deep violet-pink to near blue. *Penstemon heterophyllus* subsp. *purdyi* (syn. *P. h.* 'Blue Bedder') is semi-evergreen with blue tube-shaped flowers. *Zones 8–10.*

PEROVSKIA

Found in western Asia and the Himalayan region, the 7 species of deciduous subshrubs in this genus have gray-white stems and aromatic leaves that are covered with gray felt when young. As they mature, the deeply lobed leaves lose the felting and become gray-green. The stems form large clumps, grow 3–5 ft (1–1.5 m) tall and are topped in late summer with 12–18 in (30–45 cm) panicles of tiny purple-blue flowers.

Cultivation

Grow in any well-drained, rather dry soil in a sunny position. These vigorous plants are very frost hardy. Propagate from seed or cuttings of non-flowering stems.

Petunia × *hybrida*

Perovskia atriplicifolia

Perovskia atriplicifolia
Russian sage

This tall, tough species produces soft, gray-green foliage that beautifully complements the haze of pale lavender-blue flowers that appear on panicles in late summer and autumn. The plants are upright to 5 ft (1.5 m), with a spread of 3 ft (1 m) or more. They are long lived. *Zones 6–9.*

PETUNIA

There are around 35 species in the genus, including annuals, biennials and shrubby perennials. They have dark green, rather hairy, smooth-edged leaves and trumpet-shaped flowers in white, purple, red, blue, pink or mixed hues.

Cultivation

They are fairly fast growing, frost-tender plants, and like well-drained, fertile soil and a sunny location. They thrive where summers are hot. Sow seed under glass in early spring, or plant purchased seedlings at beginning of summer. Fertilize every month until flowering is advanced.

Petunia × *hybrida*

The 2 most important hybrid groups are the Grandiflora and Multiflora petunias, both with plants around 12 in (30 cm) tall at maturity. Grandifloras are very wide and shallow, while Multifloras are more compact with densely massed and somewhat narrower blooms. Nana

Compacta petunias are generally less than 6 in (15 cm) high. Pendula petunias have prostrate, trailing stems. The Grandiflora petunias are very popular, with a dazzling range of newer F1 hybrids, although they are easily rain damaged and susceptible to disfiguring botrytis rot; they include the Cascade and Supercascade Series (or Magic Series), with single flowers and somewhat trailing stems. *Zones 9–11.*

PHLOMIS

This genus of around 100 species of often downy-leafed perennials, sub-shrubs and shrubs occurs from the Mediterranean to China. Leaves are mostly large, and densely covered with hair-like felting. The tubular flowers, borne on upright verticils, curl downwards and have 2 lips at the tip, the upper lip hooded over the lower. They occur in clusters of 2 to 40 blooms, depending on species, and are usually in shades of cream, yellow, pink, mauve or purple.

Cultivation

Hardiness varies, though most tolerate moderate frosts. Plant in well-drained soil in full sun or part-shade. Propagate from seed, cuttings or by division.

Phlomis fruticosa
Jerusalem sage

This evergreen shrub, a native of southern Europe, is grown for the strikingly beautiful yellow flowers it bears in whorls from early to mid-summer, among oval, wrinkled, felty green leaves. It tolerates coastal areas quite well and grows to a height and spread of 30 in (75 cm). To keep its habit neat, prune to about half its size in autumn. *Zones 7–10.*

Phlomis russeliana

This perennial thrives in any ordinary soil given a reasonable amount of sun. The large, heart-shaped, fresh green leaves make excellent ground cover, forming clumps around 12 in (30 cm) high and up to 24 in (60 cm) across. In summer, it bears stout stems 3 ft (1 m) high topped with several whorls of hooded, butter-yellow flowers. *Zones 7–10.*

PHLOX

This North American genus contains more than 60 species of evergreen and semi-evergreen annuals and perennials. They have profuse, fragrant flowers and symmetrical flower clusters. *Phlox* means 'flame', an appropriate epithet for these brightly colored, showy flowers.

Cultivation

The tall perennial phloxes like any temperate climate, though they need a lot of water while growing. The annuals grow in almost any climate. Grow in moist, well-drained, fertile soil in a sunny or part-shaded spot. Propagate from seed, cuttings or by division.

Phlox divaricata
Wild sweet William, blue phlox

A perennial found from Quebec to south-central USA, this species has leafy stems to 12 in (30 cm) tall that develop from spreading underground stems. Its leaves are oval and around 2 in (5 cm) long. The flowers are blue, lavender or white, up to 1½ in (35 mm) wide, slightly fragrant and carried in open clusters. It blooms in spring. *Zones 4–9.*

Phlox drummondii
Annual phlox

This annual grows quickly to a bushy shrub 15 in (38 cm) high, half that in spread. In summer and fall, it bears clustered, small, flattish flowers with 5 petals in reds, pinks, purples and creams. It has lanceolate, light green leaves and is frost resistant. 'Sternenzauber' (syn. 'Twinkle') has star-like flowers with pointed petals. Dwarf strains grow to 4 in (10 cm). *Zones 6–10.*

Phlox maculata
Meadow phlox

Phlox maculata is an herbaceous perennial that grows to 3 ft (1 m) tall and bears

Phlomis russeliana

Phlomis fruticosa

scented, white, pink or purple flowers in mid-summer. 'Alpha' is around 30 in (75 cm) tall with deep pink flowers. 'Miss Lingard' is up to 3 ft (1 m) tall with fragrant white flowers that some-times have a central pink ring. 'Omega' is around 30 in (75 cm) tall with fragrant white, lilac-centered flowers. *Zones 5–10.*

Phlox paniculata
Summer phlox, perennial phlox
This tall perennial can grow to more than 3 ft (1 m) high. In summer, it bears long-lasting, terminal flowerheads comprising many small, 5-lobed flowers. Colors range through violet, red, salmon and white according to variety. 'Mother of Pearl' has white to pale pink flowers suffused pink on stems up to 30 in (75 cm) tall 'Amethyst' has violet flowers. *Zones 4–10.*

Phlox drummondii

Phlox subulata

Phlox subulata
Moss phlox
Throughout spring, this prostrate alpine perennial produces terminal masses of star-shaped flowers in blue, mauve, carmine, pink and white, the petals being notched and open. Fully frost hardy and evergreen, it is suitable for sunny rock gardens. 'McDaniel's Cushion' (syn. 'Daniel's Cushion') is best in small groups among shrubs or taller perennials. 'Marjorie' has glowing deep pink flowers. *Zones 3–10.*

PHYGELIUS
Cape fuchsia
Related to *Penstemon* and *Antirrhinum* (the snapdragons) rather than *Fuchsia*, these 2 species of erect, evergreen shrubs or subshrubs—perennials in some winter conditions—are good rock

Phlox maculata 'Omega'

Phlox paniculata

Phygelius aequalis 'Yellow Trumpet'

Physalis alkekengi var. franchetii

garden plants. They grow to 3 ft (1 m) high and 18 in (45 cm) wide, and bear handsome, red flowers in summer.

Cultivation
They do best in sun or part-shade and like a fertile, well-drained soil that is not too dry. Propagate from cuttings in summer.

Phygelius aequalis
This species is a suckering shrub to 3 ft (1 m) tall with dark green leaves and pale pink flowers. 'Yellow Trumpet' has leaves that are a paler green and creamy yellow flowers. *Zones 8–11.*

PHYSALIS
Ground cherry
This is a genus of around 80 species of annuals and perennials with a wide-spread distribution, especially in the Americas. Most form a clump of upright leafy stems 2–4 ft (0.6–1.2 m) tall. The flowers are small, usually white or yellow blotched purple, and are backed by calyces that enlarge to enclose the fruits—yellow, orange or red berries—as they develop. The fruits are often edible.

Cultivation
Hardiness varies, but most tolerate moderate frosts. They like moist, well-drained soil and a spot in sun or part-shade. Propagate from seed or by division.

Physalis alkekengi
Chinese lantern, winter cherry
This 24 in (60 cm) tall perennial found from southern Europe to Japan is notable for the vivid orange calyx that surrounds the ripening fruit. The flowers are small and white with yellow centers. The fruiting stems are often used fresh in floral arrangements or dried for winter decoration. *Physalis alkekengi* var. *franchetii* has minute, creamy white flowers. *Zones 6–10.*

PHYSOSTEGIA
Obedient plant, false dragon head
This is a genus of some 12 species of vigorous, rhizomatous perennials. They form clumps of unbranched, upright stems clothed in narrow, lance-shaped, long leaves with toothed edges. Plant size varies from 2–6 ft (0.6–1.8 m) tall. From midsummer, spikes of flowers develop at the stem tips. The flowers are tubular to bell-shaped with 2 upper lobes and 3 lower lobes. They come in shades of lavender, pink or purple and white.

Cultivation
They prefer moist, well-drained soil in sun or very light shade. Hardiness varies, though all tolerate moderate

Physostegia virginiana 'Summer Spire'

Platycodon grandiflorus

buds that open into broad, bell-shaped, white, pink, blue or purple flowers.

Cultivation
Very frost hardy, it likes any well-drained soil in full sun, but may take a few years to become established. Propagate from seed or by division. Because it resents disturbance, do not divide regularly.

Platycodon grandiflorus
On this species, balloon-like buds open out into 5-petaled flowers like bells, colored blue, purple, pink or white, in summer. The serrated elliptical leaves with a silvery blue cast form in a neat clump up to 24 in (60 cm) high and half that in spread. *Platycodon grandiflorus* var. *mariesii* was introduced in the late 1800s. More compact than the species, it grows to 18 in (45 cm) tall and has glossy, lance-shaped leaves. *Zones 4–10.*

PLECTRANTHUS
This genus contains more than 350 species of annuals, perennials and shrubs native to Africa, Asia and Australia. Most are rather frost tender and several species are grown as

frosts. Propagate from seed or small basal cuttings or by division.

Physostegia virginiana
The showy flowers of this herbaceous perennial, which bloom in erect terminal spikes late in summer, are available in pale pink, magenta ('Vivid') or white. This native of eastern and central North America grows to 3 ft (1 m). 'Summer Spire' is around 24 in (60 cm) tall with deep pink flowers. *Zones 3–10.*

PLATYCODON
Balloon flower, Chinese bellflower
The sole species in this genus is a semi-tuberous perennial with flower stems up to 30 in (75 cm) tall. Native to China, Japan, Korea and eastern Siberia, in spring it forms a clump of toothed-edged, elliptical to lance-shaped light blue-green foliage. The leafy flower stems develop quickly from mid-summer and are topped with heads of inflated

houseplants, others are garden ornamentals or herbs. They generally have succulent or semi-succulent stems. The leaves are often fleshy and frequently oval to heart-shaped. The flowers are small and tubular, but are borne in sometimes showy spikes that extend above the foliage.

Cultivation

Grow these plants in moist, well-drained soil in a part shaded position. They need protection from frost and prolonged dry conditions. Propagation is from seed or cuttings or by layering. Many will self-layer.

Plectranthus australis
Swedish ivy

Commonly grown as an indoor plant, Swedish ivy has quilted leaves and sprays of tubular lilac and white flowers which look very pretty cascading from a hanging basket. It grows to 8 in (20 cm) in height and spreads widely. Its glossy green leaves have attractive scalloped edges. It will thrive if given some direct sunlight and plenty of moisture. Tips should be cut back when the plant becomes untidy. *Zones 9–11.*

Plectranthus ciliatus

Plectranthus ciliatus

This evergreen perennial with creeping, branched stems with upturned ends reaches a height of about 18 in (45 cm). *Plectranthus ciliatus* is a South African species that will make a rapidly spreading ground cover in the shade of trees. The leaves are bronze-green above, deep purple beneath, with a row of fine, soft bristle-tipped teeth along the margin. In summer and autumn, it bears short sprays of tubular pale mauve flowers. *Zones 9–11.*

POLEMONIUM
Jacob's ladder

This genus of around 25 species of annuals and perennials is distributed over the Arctic and temperate regions of the northern hemisphere. They form clumps of soft, bright green, ferny, pinnate leaves from which emerge upright stems topped with heads of short, tubular, bell- or funnel-shaped flowers usually in white or shades of blue or pink. Dormant in winter, they develop quickly in spring and are in flower by early summer.

Cultivation

Most are very frost hardy and easily cultivated in moist, well-drained soil in sun or part-shade. Propagate annuals from seed; perennials from seed or cuttings of young shoots or by division. Some self-sow freely.

Polemonium caeruleum

Yellowy orange stamens provide a colorful contrast against the blue of this perennial's bell-shaped flowers when they open in summer. The flowers cluster among lance-shaped leaflets arranged in many pairs like the rungs of a ladder. The plant grows in a clump to a height and spread of up to 24 in (60 cm) or more. The stem is hollow and upstanding. It suits cooler climates. *Zones 2–9.*

POLIANTHES

This is a sun-loving Mexican genus of about 13 clump-forming perennials, most of which are tender to both frost and dry conditions. The garden-grown species present their leaves from a basal rosette and their flowers on straight, upright stems. The genus includes the well-known tuberose, *Polianthes tuberosa*, which has been grown as a cut flower for centuries and is used extensively in the manufacture of perfumes.

Cultivation

They prefer open positions in good, well-drained garden loams and adequate moisture during the summer growing phase. The clumps should be lifted annually and the large bulbs, which once they flower will not flower again, removed. Propagate from seed.

Polianthes tuberosa
Tuberose

This species produces a mass of sweetly scented blooms in summer or early fall A tall stem up to 3 ft (1 m) high is topped with a spike bearing clusters of tubular, star-shaped, creamy white flowers. A double variety, 'The Pearl', is more widely available than the single. *Zones 9–11.*

Polemonium caeruleum

POLYGONUM

syns *Aconogonon, Bistorta, Tovara, Persicaria affinis*
Knotweed

This is a genus of 50 to 80 species of evergreen, semi-evergreen or deciduous annuals, perennials or subshrubs. They have rounded, lance- or heart-shaped leaves 1½–10 in (3.5–25 cm) long depending on the species. The foliage often has purple-gray markings and may develop red and gold tints in autumn. The flowers, usually pink or cream, are borne in sometimes showy panicles or spikes in the leaf axils and at stem tips.

Cultivation

These frost hardy plants like any well-drained soil in sun or part-shade; some may become invasive. Plant stronger growers where they can be contained. Propagate from seed or by division.

Polygonum affine
syn. *Persicaria affinis*
This evergreen Himalayan perennial has small, lance-shaped leaves that become

Polianthes tuberosa

Polygonum affine

Pontederia cordata

bronze in winter. It forms a mat 12 in (30 cm) or more high with a similar spread. In late summer and fall, it bears dense spikes of small, red, funnel-shaped flowers. 'Darjeeling Red' has elongated leaves that turn bright red in fall. 'Donald Lowndes' is a compact cultivar with salmon-pink flowers that age to deep pink. *Zones 3–9*.

POLYSTICHUM
Shield fern

This genus of 200 species of ground- or rock-dwelling ferns is found worldwide in anything from tropical to subantarctic regions. Their fronds are either pinnate or simple and ribbon-shaped. They are known as shield ferns because groups of the spores are covered with a fragile, shield-shaped growth. Some of the ornamental species have become very popular.

Cultivation

They prefer part- to full shade and fertile, humus-rich, well-drained soil. The frond tips usually bear an abundance of small buds that become plantlets in their own right when conditions are favorable. Otherwise, shield ferns can be propagated by sowing spores in summer or by division of the rhizomes in spring.

Polystichum acrostichoides
Christmas fern

From the North American woodlands, this terrestrial fern grows from tufted crowns arising from slowly spreading rhizomes. The leathery, evergreen fronds emerge as silvery white 'fiddleheads' in early spring and mature to lustrous, dark green, pinnate leaves 12–36 in (30–90 cm) tall. It is excellent for naturalizing among low to medium shrubs. *Zones 3–9*.

PONTEDERIA
Pickerel weed

The 5 or so aquatic perennials in this genus are native to river shallows in North and South America. They have distinctive, lance-shaped leaves and bell-shaped, usually blue flowers in terminal spikes. The name honors Guilio Pontedera (1688–1757), who was a professor of botany at the University of Padua.

Cultivation

Pickerel weed flourishes in almost any climate, from cold to subtropical. Plant in full sun in up to 10 in (25 cm) of water. Prune only spent flower stems, to encourage successive batches of flowers. Propagate from seed or by division in spring.

Pontederia cordata
Pickerel rush

This species grows from Nova Scotia to Florida. A very frost-hardy, marginal water plant, it grows to 30 in (75 cm) with an 18 in (45 cm) spread. Its tapered, heart-shaped leaves are dark green and shiny. In summer it produces intense blue flowers in dense, terminal spikes. *Zones 3–10.*

PORTULACA

There are about 100 species of semi-succulent annuals or perennials in this genus, indigenous to the warm, dry regions of the world. The fleshy leaves vary in color from white to green or red. The flowers are cup-shaped, white, yellow, apricot, pink, purple or scarlet in color, and resemble roses in form.

Cultivation

They are easily grown in all climates. In cooler areas they should not be planted out until the danger of frost has passed. They need sun, well-drained soil and occasional watering. Propagate from seed or cuttings. Check for aphids.

Portulaca grandiflora
Rose moss, sun plant

This annual South American succulent is a low-growing plant which reaches 8 in (20 cm) high and spreads to 6 in (15 cm). It has small, lance-shaped, fleshy leaves and reddish stems. Its large, open flowers, usually double and borne in summer, come in bright colors including yellow, pink, red or orange. They close at night and on cloudy days. *Zones 10–11.*

POTENTILLA
Cinquefoil

This genus consists of 500 or so perennials, some annuals and biennials, and deciduous shrubs. Many have 5-parted leaves (hence the common name,

Portulaca grandiflora

Potentilla nepalensis 'Miss Willmott'

cinquefoil), and range from about 1 in (25 mm) tall to about 18 in (45 cm). They bear profuse clusters of rounded, bright flowers through spring and summer. Some are used medicinally— the root bark of one species is said to stop nose bleeds and internal bleeding.

Cultivation

Plant in well-drained, fertile soil. They thrive in full sun in temperate climates. Perennials are generally frost hardy. Propagate by division or from seed; propagate shrubs from seed or from cuttings.

Potentilla nepalensis

A profusion of flowers in shades of pink or apricot with cherry red centers appears throughout summer on the slim branching stems of this Himalayan perennial. With bright green, strawberry-like leaves, this species grows to 12 in (30 cm) or more high and twice that in width. 'Miss Willmott' is an 18 in (45 cm) high cultivar with deep cerise-red flowers. *Zones 5–9.*

PRIMULA
Primrose

This popular genus of perennials consists of around 400 species. They are mainly rhizomatous, though some have poorly developed rhizomes and are short lived. The leaves are usually crowded into a basal tuft or rosette: mostly broadest toward their tips, they generally have toothed or scalloped margins. Flower shape, size and color vary so much that it is hard to generalize, though basically all have a tubular flower that opens abruptly into a funnel or flat disc, with five or more petals that are often notched at their tips.

Cultivation

Primulas like fertile, well-drained soil, part-shade and ample water. Propagate from seed or by division, or from root cuttings.

Primula japonica

Primula auricula

This small central European perennial has yellow flowers in spring and furry leaves. Garden varieties come in a wide range of colors. In the mid-18th century a mutation resulted in flowers in shades of gray, pale green and almost black with centers covered with a white powder called 'paste'. Such flowers, called show auriculas, were once great favorites, but now have few devotees. *Zones 3–9.*

Primula denticulata
Drumstick primrose

The botanical name of this very frost-hardy Himalayan perennial refers to the toothed profile of the mid-green, broadly lanceolate leaves. A vigorous grower, it reaches a height and spread of 12 in

Primula auricula

Primula denticulata

(30 cm). In early to mid-spring its open, yellow-centered flowers of pink, purple or lilac crowd in rounded terminal clusters atop thick hairy stems. *Primula denticulata* subsp. *alba* has white flowers usually on slightly shorter stems. *Zones 6–9.*

Primula japonica
Japanese primrose

Forming a clump up to 24 in (60 cm) high and 18 in (45 cm) across, this fully frost-hardy perennial flowers in tiers on tall, sturdy stems like a candelabra in spring and early summer. Its shiny flowers range through pink, crimson and purple to nearly pure white, usually with a distinct eye of another color. It prefers a moist situation. *Zones 5–10.*

Primula juliae

This low-growing, rosette-forming miniature primrose from the Caucasus has 4 in (10 cm) long, dark green leaves. It bears bright purple, yellow-centered flowers and has given rise to a series of garden varieties. *Zones 5–9.*

Primula malacoides
Fairy primrose

This is a native of China. Small, open flowers bloom in spiral masses on this frost-tender perennial, sometimes grown as an annual. The single or double flowers range from white to pink to magenta. Its oval, light green leaves and erect stem have a hairy texture. It reaches a height and spread of 12 in (30 cm) or more. *Zones 8–11.*

Primula, Polyanthus Group

syn. *Primula × polyantha*

These frost-hardy perennials, sometimes grown as annuals, reach 12 in (30 cm) in spread and height. Large, flat, scented flowers in every color but green bloom on dense umbels from winter to spring. Polyanthus are cultivars derived from *P. vulgaris* crossed with *P. veris*, and have been grown since the 17th century. *Zones 6–10.*

Primula sieboldii

This species from Japan and northeast Asia has large, scalloped-edged leaves

Primula, Polyanthus Group

Primula sieboldii

Primula malacoides

Primula veris

Primula vulgaris

4–15 in (10–38 cm) long. Its flowers, which may be white, pink or purple, are carried in 6- to 20-flowered heads on 6–15 in (10–38 cm) stems. There are several cultivated forms, grown mainly in Japan. *Zones 5–9.*

Primula veris
Cowslip
A European wildflower of open woods and meadows, this species blooms a little later than the common primrose does. It is easily distinguished by the clusters of flowers carried on 6 in (15 cm) tall stalks and its sweeter scent. *Zones 5–9.*

Primula vulgaris
English primrose, common primrose
This common European wildflower likes its cultivated conditions to resemble the cool woodland conditions of its native environment. Low growing to 8 in (20 cm) and usually frost hardy, it produces a carpet of bright flowers in spring. The flattish flowers are pale yellow with dark eyes (but garden forms come in every color), and bloom singly on hairy stems above rosettes of crinkled, lance-shaped, serrated leaves. Both the leaves and flowers are edible. The cultivar 'Gigha White' has white flowers with yellow centers. *Zones 6–9.*

PRUNELLA
Self-heal
This is a genus of 7 species of semi-evergreen perennials from Europe, Asia, North Africa and North America. They form low, spreading clumps and bear opposite pairs of ovate to oblong, sometimes deeply lobed leaves. Erect flowering stems bear whorled spikes of 2-lipped tubular flowers in shades of white, pink or purple.

Cultivation
Most spread from creeping stems that readily take root at the nodes, making them excellent ground covers. They are fully frost hardy and grow in sun or part-shade in moist, well-drained soil. Propagate from seed or by division.

Prunella grandiflora
Large self-heal
Purple, 2-lipped flowers grow in erect spikes above leafy stubs in spring and summer on this European native. It has a spread and height of 18 in (45 cm). *Zones 5–9.*

PSYLLIOSTACHYS
Statice

This genus of 6 to 8 species of annuals is found in the Middle East and central Asia. Once included with *Statice* (*Limonium*), they are now classified separately. Rarely over 15 in (38 cm) tall in flower, they form a clump of basal leaves, sometimes hairy, that are often deeply cut so they are almost pinnate. The papery flowers are white, pink or mauve, tiny and borne on upright spikes that only rarely branch.

Cultivation

Plant in moist, well-drained soil in full sun and allow to dry off after flowering. Propagate from seed.

Psylliostachys suworowii

syn. *Limonium suworowii*

Russian statice, rat's tail statice

Native to Iran, Afghanistan and Asia, this species has sticky 2–6 in (5–15 cm) leaves and large pink flowers on wavy 6 in (15 cm) spikes. *Zones 6–10*.

Psylliostachys suworowii

PULMONARIA
Lungwort

Lungwort is an unappealing name for this European genus of 14 species of perennial, rhizomatous, forget-me-not like plants—it refers to their former medicinal use. The most common species are low, spreading plants 6–10 in (15–25 cm) high with a spread of 24 in (60 cm) or more. The simple oval to lance-shaped leaves are sometimes slightly downy and often spotted silver-white. From early spring small deep blue, pink or white flowers open from pink or white buds.

Cultivation

They like cool, moist, humus-rich soil in light shade. All are very frost hardy. Propagate from seed or cuttings or by division.

Pulmonaria angustifolia
Blue cowslip, blue lungwort

Dark blue flowers, sometimes tinged pink, bloom throughout spring on this

Prunella grandiflora

frost-resistant European deciduous perennial. The flowerheads have a 5-lobed tubular shape and are held above basal rosettes of mid-green foliage. The plant grows to a height and spread of 10–12 in (25–30 cm). 'Blaues Meer' produces an extra generous display of big, very bright blue flowers. *Zones 3–9.*

Pulmonaria saccharata
Jerusalem sage, Bethlehem sage

This evergreen perennial has heavily spotted, hairy, 10 in (25 cm) leaves and has given rise to numerous cultivars with flowers in white and all shades of pink and blue. 'Highdown' is a 12 in (30 cm) cultivar with silver-frosted leaves and pendulous clusters of deep blue flowers. The Argentea Group consists of cultivars with silver leaves and red flowers that turn dark purple with age. *Zones 3–9.*

PULSATILLA
Pasque flower

These 30 species of spring-flowering, deciduous perennials are closely related to the anemones and were once included in that genus. They form mounding clumps of finely divided, almost ferny foliaged rosettes. The leaves and flower stems are covered with downy silver-gray hairs. The flower color range includes white, pink, purple and red.

Cultivation

Most often grown in rock gardens, these very frost-hardy plants also suit borders and troughs and prefer a moist, gritty, scree soil in sun or part-shade. They prefer cool to cold winters and cool summers and tend to be short lived in mild areas. Propagate from seed or by division.

Pulsatilla vulgaris

syns *Anemone pulsatilla, A. vulgaris*
Nodding, 6-petaled flowers bloom in spring on this European species. The yellow centers of the flowers are a stark color contrast to the petals, which can range through white, pink and red to purple. The finely divided leaves are pale green and very hairy. It reaches 10 in (25 cm) in height and spread. Avoid disturbing the roots. 'Alba' has pure white flowers and needs protection from sun and frost. 'Rode Klokke' (syn. 'Rote Glocke') is a free-flowering form with dark red blooms. 'Rubra' has purplish red or rusty flowers. *Zones 5–9.*

Pulmonaria saccharata

Pulsatilla vulgaris

Q, R

Ranunculus repens

Ranunculus acris 'Flore Pleno'

RANUNCULUS
Buttercup

This is a genus of some 400 species, mostly annuals and perennials from temperate regions worldwide. The flowers are bowl- or cup-shaped, 5-petaled and yellow, white, red, orange or pink. The name derives from the Latin for 'frog', due to the tendency of some to grow in bogs or shallow water. Two species are popular folk cures for arthritis, sciatica, rheumatism and the removal of warts.

Cultivation
Most thrive in well-drained soil, cool, moist conditions and sunny or shady locations. They are mostly fully frost hardy. Propagate from fresh seed or by division.

Ranunculus acris
Meadow buttercup
This clump-forming perennial from Europe and western Asia has wiry stems with lobed and cut leaves. Panicles of saucer-shaped, bright yellow flowers appear in mid-summer. It grows from 8–36 in (20–90 cm) in height. 'Flore Pleno' has double, rosetted, golden-yellow flowers. *Zones 5–9.*

Ranunculus repens
Creeping buttercup
From Europe, Asia and Africa, this perennial has open, glossy yellow flowers

Reseda odorata

Rheum palmatum 'Atrosanguineum'

Reseda odorata
Common mignonette
From northern Africa, this moderately fast-growing annual is renowned for the strong fragrance of its flowers. The conical heads of tiny greenish flowers, with touches of red, and dark orange stamens are otherwise unspectacular. The plants will grow to 24 in (60 cm) high and about half that in spread. *Zones 6–10.*

RHEUM
This genus contains 50 species of rhizomatous perennials, including the edible rhubarb and several ornamental plants. From eastern Europe and central Asia to the Himalayas and China, they have a striking appearance; their large basal leaves are coarsely toothed and have prominent midribs and veins. The minute, star-shaped flowers appear in summer and are followed by winged fruits.

Cultivation
These very frost-hardy plants prefer full sun or part-shade and deep, moist, humus-rich soil. Propagate from seed or by division. Watch for slugs and crown rot.

Rheum palmatum
Chinese rhubarb
This Chinese species bears panicles of small, dark red to creamy green flowers

that appear in spring and summer. It has 3-lobed leaves and narrow, entire upper leaves, both appearing on prostrate, creeping stems. It grows to 12 in (30 cm) in height. 'Pleniflorus' is an erect cultivar to 24 in (60 cm) with yellow, double flowers. *Zones 3–10.*

RESEDA
Mignonette
This genus from Asia, Africa and Europe contains about 60 species of erect or spreading, branching annuals and perennials. They bear star-shaped, greenish white or greenish yellow flowers in spike-like racemes from spring to autumn. These are attractive to bees. Mignonette used to be a favorite with perfumers and it is still cultivated in France for its essential oils.

Cultivation
Plant in full sun or part-shade in well-drained, fertile, preferably alkaline soil. Deadheading will prolong flowering. Propagate from seed in late winter.

that open early in summer. It has deep green leaves with decoratively cut edges, and reaches up to 8 ft (2.4 m) in height and 6 ft (1.8 m) in spread. 'Atrosanguineum' has dark pink flowers and crimson leaves that fade to dark green. *Zones 6–10*.

RHODANTHE
Strawflower

The 40 species of erect annuals, perennials and subshrubs in this genus all come from arid areas of Australia and recently have mostly been classified in the genus *Helipterum*. Their daisy-like, everlasting, pink, yellow or white summer flowers are used for cut flowers and in

Rhodanthe chlorocephala subsp. *rosea*

Rhodanthe 'Paper Star'

dried arrangements. They have alternate, mid-green to gray-green leaves.

Cultivation

These marginally frost-hardy plants prefer full sun and well-drained soil of poor quality. Propagate from seed.

Rhodanthe chlorocephala subsp. *rosea*

syns *Helipterum roseum, Acroclinium roseum* This annual from southwestern Australia grows to a height of 24 in (60 cm) and a spread of 6 in (15 cm). The flowerheads are composed of white to pale pink bracts surrounding a yellow center, and close in cloudy weather. It is widely grown for cut flowers. *Zones 9–11*.

Rhodanthe 'Paper Star'

This cultivar, possibly a form of *Rhodanthe anthemoides*, has profuse white flowerheads. While not very long lasting as a cut flower, it is an impressive, long-flowering garden specimen of semi-prostrate habit. *Zones 7–11*.

RICINUS

This genus from northeastern Africa and southwestern Asia contains a single species, a fast-growing, tree-like shrub grown for its foliage. The spikes of small, cup-shaped flowers appear in summer. All parts of the plant, especially the seeds, are extremely poisonous and can cause death in children; however, the seed oil is used medicinally after heat treatment and purification.

Cultivation

This marginally frost-hardy plant prefers full sun and fertile, humus-rich, well-drained soil. It may need staking. Propagate from seed.

Ricinus communis
Castor oil plant

The purgative of universal renown comes from the seeds of this species,

Ricinus communis 'Carmencita'

which is mostly grown as an annual. Rounded, prickly seed pods follow the summer display of felty clusters of red and greenish flowers. The plant's leaves are large, glossy and divided deeply into elliptical lobes. *Ricinus communis* grows rapidly, reaching 12 ft (3.5 m) in height and in warm climates it often becomes a weed. 'Carmencita' is a tall form that grows to 10 ft (3 m) with bronze-red foliage and red female flowers. *Zones 9–11.*

Rodgersia aesculifolia

Romneya coulteri

RODGERSIA

Native to Burma, China, Korea and Japan, this genus consists of 6 species of moisture-loving perennials. They tend to be grown more for their bold leaves than for their plumes of fluffy flowers, borne in mid- to late summer. The stems unfurl in mid-spring and spread out to form a fan of leaves on top of stout stems.

Cultivation

They are excellent plants for marshy ground at the edge of a pond or in a bog garden in sun or part-shade. They do best in a site sheltered from strong winds, which can damage the foliage. Propagate by division or from seed.

Rodgersia aesculifolia

This Chinese species has lobed, 10 in (25 cm) wide leaves that are borne on hairy stalks, forming a clump 24 in (60 cm) high and wide. The large, cone-shaped clusters of small, starry flowers are cream or pale pink, and are borne on stout stems up to 4 ft (1.2 m) tall. *Zones 5–9.*

ROMNEYA

Tree poppy

The 2 species in this genus from North America and Mexico are summer-flowering, woody based perennials and deciduous subshrubs. They have blue-green foliage composed of alternate leaves and poppy-like, 6-petaled flowers with glossy yellow stamens.

Cultivation

They prefer a warm, sunny position and fertile, well-drained soil. They are difficult to establish (although once established they may become invasive), and they resent transplanting. Protect the roots in very cold areas in winter. Propagate from seed or cuttings.

Romneya coulteri
California tree poppy, Matilija poppy

This shrubby Californian perennial produces large, sweetly scented, poppy-like white flowers highlighted with fluffy gold stamens. The silvery green leaves are deeply divided, their edges sparsely fringed with hairs. Fully frost hardy, it forms a bush up to 8 ft (2.4 m) high with a spread of 3 ft (1 m). *Romneya coulteri* var. *trichocalyx* has pointed, rather bristly sepals. *Zones 7–10.*

ROSCOEA

These 18 species of tuberous perennials are related to ginger (*Zingiber*), but in appearance are more reminiscent of irises. They have orchid-like flowers, which have hooded upper petals, wide-lobed lower lips and 2 narrower petals. The leaves are lance-shaped and erect.

Roscoea cautleoides

Rudbeckia fulgida var. *sullivantii* 'Goldsturm'

Cultivation

They prefer part-shade and cool, fertile, humus-rich soil that should be kept moist but well drained in summer. Provide a top-dressing of leafmold or well-rotted compost in winter. Propagate from seed or by division.

Roscoea cautleoides

Bearing its yellow or orange flowers in summer, this frost-hardy species from China grows to 10 in (25 cm) tall with a 6 in (15 cm) spread. The glossy leaves are lance-shaped and erect and wrap into a hollow stem-like structure at their base. *Zones 6–9.*

RUDBECKIA
Coneflower

This popular genus from North America has about 15 species of annuals, biennials and perennials. The plants have bright, daisy-like, composite flowers with prominent central cones (hence the common name). The single, double or semi-double flowers are usually in tones of yellow; cones, however, vary from green through rust, purple and black. Species range in height from 24 in (60 cm) to 10 ft (3 m).

Cultivation

Coneflowers prefer loamy, moisture-retentive soil in full sun or part-shade.

Propagate from seed or by division in spring or autumn. They are moderately to fully frost hardy. Watch for aphids.

Rudbeckia fulgida
Black-eyed Susan, orange coneflower

This rhizomatous perennial, which reaches 3 ft (1 m) high, has branched stems, mid-green, slightly hairy leaves with prominent veins, and daisy-like, orange yellow flowers with dark brown centers. *Rudbeckia fulgida* var. *sullivantii* 'Goldsturm' (syn. *R.* 'Goldsturm') grows 24 in (60 cm) tall with crowded stems and narrow, lanceolate, green leaves. *Zones 3–10.*

Rudbeckia hirta
Black-eyed Susan

The flowerheads on this biennial or short-lived perennial are bright yellow, with central cones of purplish brown, and its lanceolate leaves are mid-green and hairy. It reaches between 12–36 in (30–90 cm) tall, with a spread of 12 in (30 cm). 'Irish Eyes' is noteworthy for its olive-green center. 'Marmalade' has large flowerheads with golden-orange ray florets. Many dwarf strains of cultivars such as 'Becky Mixed' are available in a range of colors from pale lemon to orange and red; they are usually treated as annuals. *Zones 3–10.*

Rudbeckia laciniata
Cutleaf coneflower

This is a summer-flowering perennial that can reach 10 ft (3 m) tall, though 6 ft (1.8 m) is more usual. The drooping ray florets give the flowerhead an informal elegance. 'Golden Glow' is a striking, if somewhat floppy, double cultivar. 'Goldquelle' grows to around 30 in (75 cm) tall and has large, bright yellow, double flowers. *Zones 3–10.*

RUTA
Rue

This genus consists of 8 species of subshrubs and shrubs and woody

Rudbeckia laciniata

Rudbeckia hirta 'Irish Eyes'

perennials with deeply divided aromatic leaves and small yellow flowers produced in terminal sprays. They are sometimes used as a medicinal and strewing herb or as an insect repellent. Take care when picking or weeding around rue as the foliage can cause an irritating rash in hot weather.

Cultivation

Marginally to fully frost hardy, they prefer slightly alkaline, well-drained soil in full sun. Protect from strong winds and severe frost in cold climates. Trim after flowering to encourage compact growth. Propagate by division in spring or from stem cuttings in late summer.

Ruta graveolens
Common rue

One of the bitter herbs of classical times believed to ward off disease, this species is also very decorative with very pretty, gray-green, lacy leaves. It is a frost-hardy, evergreen shrub that grows 24 in (60 cm) high, with clusters of small yellow-green flowers in summer. The leaves and flowers make attractive posies. Common rue has been used in the past for medicinal purposes, but can be dangerous if taken in large doses and during pregnancy. *Zones 5–10.*

Ruta graveolens

S

Salvia elegans 'Scarlet Pineapple'

Salpiglossis sinuata

SALPIGLOSSIS

These natives from the southern Andes can be tricky to grow, but patient gardeners who live in mild climates with fairly cool summers will be rewarded by a short but beautiful display of flowers. They come in rich shades of crimson, scarlet, orange, blue, purple and white, all veined and laced with gold. There are 2 species of annuals and perennials providing color in borders or as green-house plants in cold climates.

Cultivation

Plant in full sun in rich, well-drained soil. Deadhead regularly. They are best sown directly from seed in early spring in the place they are to grow. Watch for aphids.

Salpiglossis sinuata
Painted tongue
Offering a variety of flower colors including red, orange, yellow, blue and purple, this annual blooms in summer and early autumn. The 2 in (5 cm) wide, heavily veined flowers are like small flaring trumpets, while the lanceolate leaves are light green. A fast grower, it reaches a height of 18–24 in (45–60 cm) and a spread of at least 15 in

(38 cm). It is frost tender and dislikes dry conditions. *Zones 8–11.*

SALVIA
Sage
Salvia consists of some 900 species of annuals, perennials and soft-wooded shrubs with a cosmopolitan distribution. Their distinguishing feature is the tubular, 2-lipped flower with the lower lip flat but the upper lip helmet- or boat-shaped; the calyx is also 2-lipped and may be colored. Some with aromatic leaves are grown as culinary herbs. The genus name is from the Latin *salvus*, 'safe' or 'well', referring to the supposed healing properties of *Salvia officinalis*.

Cultivation

Most shrubby species tolerate only light frosts, but some perennials are more frost-hardy. Sages prefer full sun in well drained, light-textured soil with adequate summer water. Propagate from seed or cuttings, or division of rhizomatous species.

Salvia elegans
Pineapple-scented sage
This open-branched perennial or subshrub which can reach 6 ft (1.8 m) in milder areas, has a distinctive pineapple scent and flavor. Its whorls of small bright red flowers are borne in late summer and autumn. The leaves are used fresh but sparingly in fruit salads,

Salvia farinacea

Salvia involucrata 'Bethellii'

summer drinks and teas. The flowers are delicious, and may be added to desserts and salads for color and flavor. 'Scarlet Pineapple' (syn. *Salvia rutilans*) is more floriferous with larger scarlet flowers which, in milder areas, will persist to mid-winter. *Zones 8–11.*

Salvia farinacea
Mealy-cup sage
This species is grown as an annual in regions that have cold winters. It is a short-lived perennial in warmer climates. Although it planted in a little shade to protect it from hot afternoon sun and pruned hard in mid-autumn it can live up to 5 years. Growing to some 24–36 in (60–90 cm), it bears lavender-like, deep violet-blue flowers on slender stems. It is a good cut flower. 'Victoria' has deep blue flowers. *Zones 8–11.*

Salvia involucrata
Roseleaf sage
This tall Mexican perennial remains evergreen in mild climates but is best cut back to the ground every year to promote flowering. It has erect cane-like stems to about 5 ft (1.5 m) high and broad, long-stalked leaves that often develop red veining. The loose flower spikes terminate in groups of large mauve to magenta bracts, which are shed one by one to reveal a trio of developing flowers of the same or deeper

Salvia officinalis

color. It blooms over a long summer– autumn season. 'Bethellii' is a popular cultivar. *Zones 9–10.*

Salvia officinalis
Common sage, garden sage
From Spain, the Balkans and North Africa, common sage is a decorative, frost-hardy, short-lived perennial that grows to 30 in (75 cm) high and wide, with downy gray-green oval leaves and short racemes of bluish mauve flowers in summer. Its culinary merits are well known, and it has entered folklore over the centuries for its real and supposed medicinal qualities. 'Purpurascens' has

gray-green leaves invested with a purplish hue and pale mauve flowers; 'Tricolor' is a garish combination of green, cream and beetroot red leaves; 'Icterina' has gold and green leaves; and 'Berggarten' is a lower-growing form with larger leaves and blue flowers. *Zones 5–10.*

Salvia sclarea
Biennial clary, clary sage

This native of southern Europe and Syria is a biennial and grows 3 ft (1 m) tall. Moderately fast growing and erect, it has long, loose, terminal spikes of tubular, greenish white tinged with purple flowers in summer and velvety, heart-shaped leaves. *Salvia sclarea* var.

Salvia sclarea

Salvia splendens 'Van Houttei'

turkestanica has pink stems and white, pink-flecked flowers. *Zones 5–10.*

Salvia splendens
Scarlet sage

This native of Brazil, which is grown as an annual, produces dense terminal spikes of scarlet flowers in summer through early fall. It grows 3–4 ft (1–1.2 m) tall with a similar spread. In hotter climates, give some shade; it is moderately frost hardy. 'Salsa Burgundy' has deep burgundy flowers, while 'Van Houttei' has a deep dull red calyx with large lighter red flowers. *Zones 9–12.*

Salvia × superba

This hybrid between *Salvia × sylvestris* and *S. villicaulis* is a clump-forming, erect, branched perennial that bears slender, terminal racemes of purple flowers from mid-summer to early autumn. Reaching a height of 3 ft (1 m), it has lance-shaped, scalloped, mid green leaves that are 4 in (10 cm) long and slightly hairy underneath. *Zones 5–10.*

SANGUINARIA
Bloodroot, red puccoon

The single species of the genus is a widespread woodland plant occurring from Nova Scotia through to Florida. It is a low-growing perennial herb grown for its spring display of cup-shaped flowers.

Cultivation

Bloodroot prefers sandy soil but will tolerate clay soil if not too wet. It does well in sun or part-shade, and especially under deciduous trees. Propagation is by division in late summer when the leaves have died back.

Sanguinaria canadensis

This perennial has a long stout horizontal rootstock. Each bud on the stock sends up a heart-shaped leaf with scalloped edges on stalks 6 in (15 cm) long. Each leaf is up to 12 in (30 cm) across. The solitary white or pink-tinged flowers are up to 3 in (8 cm) across, single, with 8 to 12 petals and many yellow central anthers. They appear in the folds of the leaves in spring before the gray leaves fully expand, and last for about 3 weeks. *Zones 3–9.*

SANTOLINA

Small, aromatic, frost-hardy evergreens from the Mediterranean region, the 18 shrub species in this genus are grown for their scented, usually silvery gray foliage and dainty, button-like yellow flowerheads. They are useful for covering banks and as a ground cover.

Cultivation

They require well-drained soil and a sunny situation. Cut back old wood to encourage new growth from the base immediately after flowering, and remove dead flowerheads and stems in autumn. Propagate from cuttings in summer.

Santolina chamaecyparissus
Cotton lavender, lavender cotton

This low-spreading, aromatic shrub, native to mild, coastal areas of the Mediterranean, grows to a height of 18 in (45 cm) and spread of 3 ft (1 m). It bears bright yellow, rounded

flowerheads on long stalks in summer, set among oblong, grayish green leaves divided into tiny segments. 'Lemon Queen' is a compact form—to 24 in (60 cm)—with lemon-yellow flowerheads. *Zones 7–10.*

SANVITALIA
Creeping zinnia

From the southwestern USA and Mexico come these 7 species of annuals or short-lived perennials of the daisy family. The ovate leaves come in pairs and the small white or yellow flowers have a dark purplish black or white center. They make good ground covers, rock garden plants and hanging basket specimens.

Cultivation

Plants do best in full sun in humus-rich, well-drained soil. They are grown as annuals, sown *in situ* or in small pots for transplanting with minimal root disturbance. Propagate from seed.

Sanvitalia procumbens

A native of Mexico, this summer-flowering, frost-hardy annual produces masses of bright yellow flowerheads like daisies with blackish centers. It is a prostrate species with mid-green, ovate

Santolina chamaecyparissus 'Lemon Queen'

Sanguinaria canadensis

Saponaria ocymoides

Saxifraga exarata subsp. moschata

Sanvitalia procumbens

leaves, growing to 8 in (20 cm) high
and spreading at least 15 in (38 cm).
Zones 7–11.

SAPONARIA
Soapwort
The common name of this genus consisting of 20 species of annuals and perennials comes from the old custom of using
the roots for washing clothes. They
contain a glucoside called saponin,
which dissolves grease and dirt and
which, being edible, has been used as an
additive to beer to ensure that it develops a good head when poured.

Cultivation
Fully frost-hardy, they need sun and
well-drained soil. Propagate from seed in
spring or autumn or from cuttings.

Saponaria ocymoides
Rock soapwort
This alpine perennial from Europe forms
a thick carpet from which profuse
terminal clusters of small, flattish
flowers, colored pink to deep red, bloom
in late spring and early summer. It has
sprawling mats of hairy oval leaves.
Zones 4–10.

SAXIFRAGA
Saxifrage
Both the foliage and blooms on these
perennials, biennials and annuals are
equally appealing. The genus comprises
some 440 species of evergreens and
semi-evergreens from Eurasia and the
Americas. The flowers are mostly white,
sometimes spotted with pink, but other
colors are also available. The genus
name combines two Latin terms, 'rock'
and 'to break', suggestive of either the
hardiness of their rooting system or their
reputed medicinal effect on bladder
stones.

Cultivation
Soil, light requirements and frost
hardiness vary greatly depending on the
species. Propagate from seed in autumn,
by division or from rooted offsets in
winter.

Saxifraga exarata subsp. moschata
syn. *Saxifraga moschata*
This is a delightful downy-leafed cushion-forming plant from central and southern Europe with many round-petaled flowers on 4 in (10 cm) stems. The colors range from white or creamy yellow to pink through to strong carmine pink or red. The tricky combination of full sun and moist soil with perfect drainage in winter will keep it robust and healthy. *Zones 6–9.*

Saxifraga paniculata
syn. *Saxifraga aizoon*
Livelong saxifrage
This summer-flowering evergreen perennial from Europe grows to a height and spread of 8–10 in (20–25 cm) and bears terminal clusters of 5-petaled white flowers, often with spots of reddish purple, on erect stalks. Other colors include pale pinks and yellows. The bluish green leaves form a rosette below the flower stems. Grow in full sun in well-drained, alkaline soil. 'Rosea' has bright pink flowers. 'Minima' has very small foliage and flowers. *Zones 3–9.*

Saxifraga 'Ruth Draper'
Ruth Draper was a British comedienne of the 1930s, famous for her monologue, 'You should have seen my garden last week'. Her namesake is a pretty example of a mossy saxifrage, a group that likes a moist and lightly shaded position. It bears large, cup-shaped, purple-pink flowers in early spring and grows to 2 in (5 cm) in height. *Zones 6–9.*

SCABIOSA
Scabious, pincushion flower
This genus of 80 species of annuals, biennials and perennials, from Eurasia and north Africa, bears tall-stemmed, honey-scented flowers ideal for cutting. The blooms, bearing multiple florets with protruding filaments giving a pincushion effect, range from white, yellow, red, blue and mauve to deep purple.

Cultivation
Most *Scabiosa* species will thrive in full sun in well-drained, alkaline soil. Propagate annuals from seed in spring, and perennials from cuttings in summer, seed in autumn or by division in early spring.

Scabiosa atropurpurea
This bushy biennial or short-lived perennial from southern Europe produces flowers from summer through to early autumn, provided blooms are cut or deadheaded. The dome-shaped flowerheads are about 2 in (5 cm) wide and are fragrant; they are mainly crimson but also come in white, pink,

Saxifraga paniculata

Saxifraga 'Ruth Draper'

purple and blue. Size varies from 18 in (45 cm) for dwarf forms up to 3 ft (1 m) for taller plants. This fully frost-hardy species has lobed, lance-shaped foliage. *Zones 7–11.*

Scabiosa caucasica

Flat, many-petaled flowerheads in pink, red, purple or blue hues with pincush-ion-like centers often in a contrasting color make this summer-flowering perennial popular for borders and as cut flowers. A bushy plant with lobed mid-green leaves, it reaches a height and spread of 18–24 in (45–60 cm). 'Clive Greaves' has lilac-blue flowers; 'Staefa' is a strong grower with blue flowers; and 'Mrs. Isaac House' has creamy white flowers. *Zones 4–10.*

Scabiosa caucasica

Schizanthus × wisetonensis

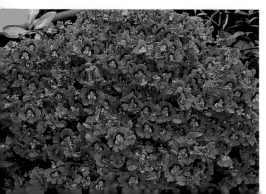

SCHIZANTHUS
Poor man's orchid, butterfly flower

These 12 to 15 species of annuals are from the Chilean mountains. They come in shades of pink, mauve, red, purple and white, all with gold-speckled throats. They grow to about 3 ft (1 m) high and 12 in (30 cm) wide. Most of the flowers seen in gardens are hybrids, giving a colorful display over a short spring to summer season.

Cultivation

These plants do not like extremes of heat or cold, and grow best outdoors in a mild, frost-free climate; in colder climates they should be grown in a greenhouse. They prefer full sun and fertile, well-drained soil. Propagate from seed.

Schizanthus × wisetonensis

This erect species bears tubular to flared, 2-lipped, white, blue, pink or reddish brown flowers often flushed with yellow from spring to summer. It has lance-shaped, light green leaves and grows to 18 in (45 cm) high with a spread of 12 in (30 cm). Most garden strains are derived from this species. *Zones 7–11.*

SCHIZOSTYLIS

A single species of grassy leafed rhizo-matous perennial in the iris family makes up this genus. *Schizostylis* is widely distributed in South Africa where it grows along banks of streams. The long-flowering stems terminate in clusters of bowl-shaped 6-petaled flowers in deep scarlet and pink.

Cultivation

Frost hardy, it prefers full sun and fertile, moist soil with shelter from the cold in cool-temperate climates. Divide every couple of years when it becomes crowded or propagate from seed in spring.

Schizostylis coccinea
Crimson flag

This variable species can fail in prolonged dry conditions. The sword-shaped leaves are untidy unless pruned regularly and protected from thrips and slugs. It has a late summer and autumn display which in some climates, conditions and seasons can extend into winter and beyond. *Coccinea* means scarlet, and that is the usual color of this species. It is a dainty plant reaching a height of 24 in (60 cm) and spread of 12 in (30 cm). 'Mrs. Hegarty' is rose pink. *Zones 6–10.*

SCUTELLARIA
Skullcap, helmet flower

The name of this cosmopolitan genus comes from the Latin *scutella*, meaning a small shield or cup, which is a rough description of the pouch of the upper calyx. There are some 300 known species consisting mainly of summer-flowering perennials, most on a rhizomatous root system; a few are annuals and rarely subshrubs.

Cultivation

They like full sun in most reasonable garden soil. They do not like parched soil in summer, but are content with ordinary watering throughout dry weather. Propagate by division in winter

Scutellaria incana

or from seed sown fresh in autumn. Cuttings may be taken in summer.

Scutellaria incana

This is a rounded perennial to 4 ft (1.2 m) in height with lightly serrated oval leaves and large panicles of grayish blue flowers in summer. It is widespread throughout northeastern USA. *Zones 5–9.*

SEDUM
Stonecrop

This genus, from the temperate northern hemisphere and tropical mountains, contains about 400 species of succulent annuals, biennials, perennials, subshrubs and shrubs. Quick-growing plants, they vary in habit from carpet forming to upright up to 3 ft (1 m) tall.

Cultivation

They range from frost tender to fully frost hardy, and prefer fertile, porous soil and full sun. Propagate perennials from seed, by division or from cuttings. Propagate annuals and biennials from seed sown under glass in spring.

Sedum spectabile
syn. *Hylotelephium spectabile*
Showy sedum, ice plant

Spoon-shaped, fleshy, gray-green leaves grow in clusters on the erect stems of

Schizostylis coccinea 'Mrs. Hegarty'

Sidalcea 'Rose Queen'

Sidalcea malviflora

Sedum spectabile

this perennial. Flattish heads of small, pink, star-like flowers appear in late summer. It grows to a height and spread of 18 in (45 cm) and is resistant to both frost and dry conditions. *Zones 5–10.*

SIDALCEA
Prairie mallow, checker mallow

The 20 to 25 species of upright annuals or perennials with lobed, rounded leaves in this genus are found in western USA, from open grasslands to mountain forests. Pink, purple or white flowers have a silky appearance and feel, and last well as cut flowers.

Cultivation

They prefer cool summers and mild winters in good, deep, moisture-retentive soil. They tolerate some shade in hot climates. Cutting back after flowering will produce a second flush of blooms. Propagate from seed or by division.

Sidalcea malviflora
Checkerbloom

This erect perennial grows to 4 ft (1.2 m) tall with spreading fibrous roots. It has lobed leaves and loose heads of pink or white flowers resembling hollyhocks during spring and summer. Most cultivars included under this name are now believed to be hybrids with other species. *Zones 6–10.*

Sidalcea 'Rose Queen'

syn. *Sidalcea malviflora* 'Rose Queen' Large, deep pink, cupped flowers are borne in spikes in summer on this fully frost-hardy perennial. The divided leaves form a basal clump with a spread of 24 in (60 cm). The overall height is 4 ft (1.2 m) and tall plants may need staking. 'William Smith' is similar but grows only 3 ft (1 m) tall and produces flowers in 2 tones of deep pink. *Zones 6–10.*

SILENE
Campion, catchfly

This genus contains over 500 species of annuals, biennials and deciduous or evergreen perennials featuring 5-petaled summer flowers, baggy calyces and a multitude of small, elliptical, often silky leaves. They are widespread in the northern hemisphere with a few in

Silene coeli-rosa

Silene armeria

Silene vulgaris

South America and Africa. Some exude gum from their stems; passing flies get stuck to this, hence the common name catchfly.

Cultivation

These marginally to fully frost-hardy plants like fertile, well-drained soil and full or part-sun. Propagate from seed or from cuttings.

Silene armeria

This European annual or biennial has pink, bell-shaped flowers with 5 notched petals. Growing to a height of 12 in (30 cm) with a spread of 6 in (15 cm), it has slender, erect, branching stems and linear leaves. *Zones 6–10.*

Silene coeli-rosa

syns *Agrostemma coeli-rosa, Lychnis coeli-rosa, Viscaria elegans*

Rose of heaven

This upright annual from the Mediterranean bears pinkish purple flowers in summer. Its lance-shaped, green leaves have a grayish cast. It grows rapidly to 18 in (45 cm). *Zones 6–11.*

Silene vulgaris

syn. *Silene uniflora*

Bladder campion, maiden's tears

This perennial has stems up to 24 in (60 cm) tall, oval leaves and white flowers with 2-lobed petals; the flowers are either solitary or in heads. It is found throughout northern Africa, temperate Asia and Europe. However, most plants sold as *Silene vulgaris* are, in fact, *S. uniflora. Zones 5–10.*

SISYRINCHIUM

These natives of South and North America can self-destruct in seasons of prolific blooming, because the flower stem kills off the leaf stem from which it sprouts. The genus includes 90 species of annuals and rhizomatous perennials. It is easy to mistake the narrow leaves of the seedlings for grass.

Cultivation

Establish them in poor to moderately fertile, moist but well-drained soil.

Although tolerant of part-shade, they prefer sun. They readily self-seed, otherwise propagate by division in late summer.

Sisyrinchium bellum
California blue-eyed grass

Branched stems rise up to 18 in (45 cm) on this perennial species to form a tuft with linear leaves and amethyst-purple (rarely white) flowers. It comes from California. *Zones 8–11.*

Sisyrinchium striatum
syn. *Phaiophleps nigricans*
Satin flower

Long, narrow and sword-shaped, the leaves on this fully frost-hardy, evergreen perennial are gray-green. In summer it bears slender spikes of small cream flowers, striped purple. The species, which originates in Chile and Argentina, grows 18–24 in (45–60 cm) high with a 12 in (30 cm) spread. There is also an attractive variegated form. *Zones 8–10.*

SOLENOSTEMON
Coleus, flame nettle, painted nettle

This genus comprises 60 species of low shrubby perennials, often hairy and with variegated leaves, from tropical Africa and Asia. The stems are 4-angled and the opposite leaves are often toothed. The flowers are small with an elongated lower lip.

Cultivation

These frost-tender plants are easily grown in milder climates with adequate summer moisture and protection from hot sun. They prefer humus-rich, moist but well-drained soil and need to be

Solenostemon scutellarioides

Sisyrinchium striatum

Sisyrinchium bellum

Solidago 'Golden Wings'

pinched back to promote bushiness. Propagate from seed or cuttings.

Solenostemon scutellarioides
syns *Coleus blumei* var. *verschaffeltii, C. scutellarioides*
Native to Southeast Asia, this bushy, fast-growing perennial is grown as an annual in more temperate climates. The leaves are a bright mixture of pink, green, red or yellow and are a pointed, oval shape with serrated edges. It grows 24 in (60 cm) high and 12 in (30 cm) wide. *Zones 10–12.*

SOLIDAGO
Goldenrod
The goldenrods are a genus of about 100 species of woody based perennials, related to the asters. They flower in autumn. The small, individual flowers are bright yellow. Most are too weedy to be allowed into even the wildest garden, but some are worth cultivating for their big flower clusters and there are some very attractive hybrids.

Cultivation
These fully frost-hardy plants grow well in sun or shade in any fertile, well-drained soil. Most self-seed, or they can be propagated by dividing the clumps in fall or spring.

Solidago 'Golden Wings'
This perennial grows to 5 ft (1.5 m) high with a spread of 3 ft (1 m). It has downy, lance-shaped leaves with serrated margins, and produces small, bright yellow flowers in feathery panicles early in autumn. *Zones 5–10.*

Stachys byzantina

Stachys byzantina 'Primrose Heron'

STACHYS
Betony, woundwort, hedge nettle
This genus, in the mint family, contains about 300 species of annuals, perennials and evergreen shrubs. They are widespread in temperate zones and have long been used in herb gardens, many of them having supposed medicinal value, and come from a range of habitats mostly in northern temperate regions. Many are aromatic, and attract bees and butterflies. They bear tubular, 2-lipped, purple, red, pink, yellow or white flowers.

Cultivation
They like well-drained, moderately fertile soil in full sun. Propagate from seed or cuttings or by division.

Stachys byzantina
syns *Stachys lanata*, *S. olympica*
Lambs' ears, lambs' tails, lambs' tongues
The leaves give this perennial its common names: they are lance-shaped and have the same white, downy feel of a lamb. Unfortunately, the leaves turn to mush in very cold, humid or wet weather. It makes a good ground cover or border plant, growing to about 12–18 in (30–45 cm) high, with a 24 in (60 cm) spread. Mauve-pink flowers appear in summer. 'Primrose Heron' has yellowish green leaves. 'Big Ears' (syn. 'Countess Helen von Stein') is a large growing cultivar which bears tall spikes of purple flowers. *Zones 5–10.*

Stachys officinalis

Stokesia laevis

Stachys officinalis
Bishop's wort, wood betony

This stately erect perennial from Europe grows to 3 ft (1 m) in height. The basal rosette leaves are oblong or heart-shaped. The red-purple flowers are held in dense spikes, although white and pink forms also occur. *Zones 5–10.*

STOKESIA
Stokes' aster

This genus of a single perennial species native to the southeastern United States was named after Englishman Dr. Jonathan Stokes (1755–1831). An attractive late-flowering perennial, it grows about 18 in (45 cm) high and flowers from late summer to autumn if the spent flower stems are promptly removed. It is very good for cutting.

Cultivation

Plant in full sun or part-shade and fertile, well-drained soil. Water well in summer. Propagate from seed in fall or by division in spring.

Stokesia laevis

syn. *Stokesia cyanea*
This fully frost-hardy perennial has evergreen rosettes, its narrow leaves green, basal and divided. The blue-mauve or white blooms have a shaggy appearance reminiscent of cornflowers and are borne freely on erect stems. *Zones 7–10.*

STREPTOCARPUS

This genus consists of 130 species of annuals, perennials and rarely subshrubs from tropical Africa, Madagascar, Thailand, China and Indonesia. There are 3 main groups: shrubby bushy species with vigorous growth; rosetted plants; and single-leafed species producing one very large leaf up to 3 ft (1 m) long. They all bear tubular flowers with 5 lobes and hairy, veined, crinkly leaves.

Cultivation

Frost tender, they prefer part-shade and leafy, humus-rich, moist but well-drained soil. Seeding will be prevented if flowers are deadheaded and stalks are removed. Propagate from seed or cuttings or by division.

Streptocarpus Hybrids

Most *Streptocarpus* hybrids have *S. rexii* as a major parent. They generally have a rosette growth habit and large, showy, trumpet-shaped flowers in bright colors with a white throat. 'Blue Heaven' has flowers that are a strong mid-blue to pale purple. *Zones 10–11.*

SYMPHYTUM
Comfrey

This genus comprises 25 to 35 species of hairy perennials from damp and shaded places in Europe, North Africa and western Asia. They grow rapidly and may become invasive. The leaves are alternate and rather crowded at the base of the plant. The flowers are held in shortly branched heads of pink, blue, white or cream. Each flower consists of a tube terminating in 5 triangular lobes.

Cultivation

They are easily grown in sun or part-shade in moist, well-dug soil with added manure. Propagate from seed or cuttings, or by division.

Symphytum 'Goldsmith'

syn. *Symphytum* 'Jubilee'

'Goldsmith' grows to 12 in (30 cm) and has leaves edged and blotched with cream and gold; the flowers are blue, pink or white. *Zones 5–10.*

Streptocarpus Hybrid 'Blue Heaven'

Symphytum 'Goldsmith'

T

Tagetes patula

TAGETES
Marigold

These familiar summer plants have single or double flowers in shades of orange, yellow, mahogany, brown and red, which contrast brightly with the deep green leaves. Some of the 50 or so species have aromatic foliage, hence *Tagetes minuta*'s common name of stinking Roger. It is said that the roots exude substances fatal to soil-borne pests, leading to their extensive use as companion plants.

Cultivation

These fast-growing plants thrive in warm, frost-free climates. Grow in full sun in fertile, well-drained soil. Deadhead regularly. Propagate from seed in spring after frost has passed. Watch for slugs, snails and botrytis.

Tagetes erecta
African marigold, American marigold, Aztec marigold

The aromatic, glossy, dark green leaves of this bushy annual from Mexico have deeply incised margins. With its upstanding, branching stems, it grows to 18 in (45 cm) in height and spread. Orange or yellow daisy-like flowers bloom in summer and early autumn. The flowers can be as large as 4 in (10 cm) across. 'Crackerjack' has double flowers and grows to a height of 24 in (60 cm). This species is used as a culinary and medicinal herb. *Zones 9–11*.

Tagetes patula
French marigold

This fast-growing, bushy annual reaches 12 in (30 cm) in height and spread. It was introduced to Europe from its native Mexico via France, hence its common name. The double flowerheads, produced in summer and early fall, resemble carnations. They bloom in red, yellow and orange. The leaves are deep green and aromatic. 'Dainty Marietta' is an all-yellow cultivar with single flowerheads. *Zones 9–11*.

TANACETUM
syn. *Pyrethrum*

In Greek mythology, immortality came to Ganymede as a result of drinking tansy, a species of this genus of rhizomatous perennial daisies. Even in recent times, it has been used (despite being potentially quite poisonous) for promoting menstruation and treating hysteria, skin conditions, sprains, bruises and rheumatism. The 70 or so species of this genus from northern temperate zones have daisy-like flowers.

Cultivation

Moderately to very frost hardy, they prefer full sun in well-drained, dryish soil. Do not overwater. They spread readily and need to be kept under control. Propagate by division in spring or from seed in late winter or early spring.

Tanacetum coccineum
syns *Chrysanthemum coccineum*, *Pyrethrum roseum*
Painted daisy, pyrethrum

This frost-hardy, erect perennial has dark green, feathery, scented leaves that

Tanacetum parthenium 'Golden Moss'

Tanacetum coccineum

are finely dissected. Its single, or sometimes double, long-stalked flowerheads may be pink, red, purple or white, appearing from late spring to early summer. The species grows 2–3 ft (60–90 cm) tall with a spread of 18 in (45 cm) or more. 'Brenda' has striking magenta single flowers. 'Eileen May Robinson' is one of the best single pinks. 'James Kelway' has deep crimson-pink flowers. *Zones 5–9.*

Tanacetum parthenium
syn. *Chrysanthemum parthenium*
Feverfew
Feverfew is an aromatic plant which was once used to dispel fevers and agues, and as an antidote for over-indulgence in opium. It bears clusters of single or double white-petaled, daisy-like flowers over a long summer period. This short-lived perennial is frost hardy, and reaches 24 in (60 cm) high. 'Golden Moss' is a dwarf cultivar with a height and spread of 6 in (15 cm); it has golden, moss-like foliage and is often grown as an edging or bedding plant. *Zones 6–10.*

TEUCRIUM
Germander
Mainly native to the Mediterranean region, this genus of around 100 species in the mint family was named for King Teucer of Troy, who reputedly used the plants medicinally. Evergreen or deciduous shrubs, subshrubs and perennials, they have 2-lipped flowers and slightly aromatic foliage. They are able to withstand hot, dry conditions and poor soils. They can be used as hedges and will grow in sheltered maritime conditions.

Cultivation
Mostly fairly frost hardy, they prefer light, well-drained soil and sun. Low-growing species do best in poor soils. Propagate shrubs and subshrubs from cuttings in summer; perennials are propagated by division in autumn or from seed in spring.

Teucrium chamaedrys
Wall germander
This hardy, evergreen alpine species of subshrub is native to Europe and southwestern Asia. It grows 1–2 ft (30–60 cm) tall with a spread of 2–3 ft (60–90 cm). The toothed, ovate leaves are glossy deep green above and gray beneath. It is suitable for walls, steep banks and edging, and has long been used as a medicinal herb. Spikes of pale

to deep rosy purple flowers are produced in summer and autumn.
'Prostratum' is, as its name suggests, a
prostrate form. *Zones 5–10.*

THALICTRUM
Meadow rue

Over 300 species make up this genus of
perennials known for their fluffy, showy
flowers. The branches of their slender,
upstanding stems often intertwine. The
leaves are finely divided. Blooming in
spring and summer, the flowers have no
petals, but instead have 4 or 5 sepals and
conspicuous stamen tufts. They serve
well in borders.

Cultivation
Grow these frost-hardy plants in sun or
part-shade in any well-drained soil; some
species need cool conditions. Propagate
from fresh seed or by division.

Thalictrum aquilegiifolium
Greater meadow rue

This clump-forming Eurasian perennial
grows to 3 ft (1 m) tall and has a spread

Teucrium chamaedrys

Thalictrum aquilegiifolium

Thalictrum delavayi

of 18 in (45 cm). Pink, lilac or greenish white flowers in fluffy clusters on strong stems are produced in summer. Each gray-green leaf comprises 3 to 7 small, elliptical, toothed leaflets in a feather-like arrangement, resembling the leaves of some *Aquilegia* species. *Zones 6–10.*

Thalictrum delavayi
syn. *Thalictrum dipterocarpum* of gardens
Lavender shower
Rather than fluffy heads, this graceful, clump-forming perennial from western China bears a multitude of nodding, lilac flowers in loose panicles, with prominent yellow stamens. The flowers are borne from the middle to the end of summer. The finely divided leaves give the mid-green foliage a dainty appearance. Reaching 4 ft (1.2 m) high, this species has a spread of 24 in (60 cm). *Zones 7–10.*

THUNBERGIA
This genus of 90 to 100 species of mainly twining climbers and evergreen, clump-forming shrubs, was named after the 18th-century Swedish botanist Dr. Carl Peter Thunberg. Native to Africa, Asia and Madagascar, their leaves are entire or lobed, and the mostly trumpet-shaped blooms are borne individually from the leaf axils or in trusses.

Cultivation
They range from marginally frost hardy to frost tender, and prefer temperatures above 50°F (10°C). They like any reasonably rich soil and adequate drainage. Full sun is preferred, except during summer, when part-shade and liberal water should be provided. Propagate from seed or cuttings.

Thunbergia alata
Black-eyed Susan
Native to tropical Africa, this vigorous annual or perennial (in frost-free areas)

climber grows quickly to 10 ft (3 m). It is marginally frost hardy. Its deep green, cordate leaves are up to 3 in (8 cm) long. The plant bears masses of 2 in (5 cm) wide orange flowers with black throats from early summer to autumn. *Zones 9–12.*

THYMUS
Thyme
This Eurasian genus consists of over 300 evergreen species of herbaceous perennials and subshrubs, ranging from prostrate to 8 in (20 cm) high. Chosen for their aromatic leaves, they are frequently featured in rock gardens, between stepping stones or for a display on banks. Some are used in cooking. The flowers are often tubular and vary from white through pink to mauve. Thyme has been associated with courage, strength, happiness and wellbeing.

Cultivation
They are mostly frost hardy. Plant out from early autumn through to early

Thunbergia alata

Tiarella cordifolia

Thymus × citriodorus 'Anderson's Gold'

spring in a sunny site with moist, well-drained soil. Propagate from cuttings in summer or by division.

Thymus × citriodorus

syn. *Thymus serpyllum* var. *citriodorus*
Lemon-scented thyme
This delightful rounded, frost-hardy shrub grows 12 in (30 cm) high and has tiny oval lemon-scented leaves and pale lilac flowers. The leaves are used fresh or dry in poultry stuffings or to add lemon flavor to fish, meat and vegetables. 'Anderson's Gold' is a yellow-foliaged spreader that is inclined to revert to green. *Zones 7–10.*

Thymus serpyllum

Wild thyme, creeping thyme, mother of thyme
This European native grows to a height of 10 in (25 cm) and spread of 18 in (45 cm), forming a useful ground cover. Its creeping stem is woody and branching, and the scented, bright green leaves are elliptical to lanceolate. The bluish purple flowers are small and tubular with 2 lips, and are borne in spring and summer. It is frost hardy and will take moderate foot traffic, but needs replanting every few years to maintain a dense cover. 'Pink Ripple' has bronze-pink flowers. *Zones 3–9.*

Thymus serpyllum 'Pink Ripple'

TIARELLA
Foamflower
The foamflowers are a genus of 5 species of forest-floor perennials native to North America. They resemble their relatives, the heucheras, and can be hybridized with them. They grow from thick rootstocks, with their decorative leaves growing close to the ground. The airy sprays of small white flowers are borne on bare stems about 12 in (30 cm) tall.

Cultivation
Very frost hardy, they like cool-temperate climates, and make good ground

covers for a woodland-style garden. Plant in part- to deep shade in moist, well-drained soil. Propagate from seed or by division in early spring.

Tiarella cordifolia
Foamflower, coolwort

This vigorous spreading evergreen blooms profusely in early to late spring, producing terminal spikes of tiny, creamy white flowers with 5 petals. Its leaves are mostly pale green, lobed and toothed, with dark red marbling and spots; the basal leaves take on an orange-red hue in winter. When in flower, it has a height and spread of 12 in (30 cm) or more. *Zones 3–9.*

TITHONIA
Mexican sunflower

This genus of 10 species consists mainly of annuals, biennials and perennials. Originating in Central America and the West Indies, they are related to sunflowers and bear large, vivid yellow, orange or scarlet daisy-like flowerheads in summer and autumn. The leaves are often hairy on the undersides and sharply lobed.

Cultivation

Marginally frost hardy, they thrive in hot, dry conditions, but need plenty of water. They prefer well-drained soil and full sun. Deadhead regularly and prune hard after flowering to encourage new growth. Propagate from seed sown under glass in late winter or early spring.

Tithonia rotundifolia

This bulky annual needs plenty of room in the garden as it can easily grow to 5 ft (1.5 m) tall with a spread of 3 ft (1 m). Its leaves are heart-shaped. It is a great plant for hot color schemes, both in the garden and as a cut flower, with its 4 in (10 cm) wide, zinnia-like flowers of orange or scarlet. 'Torch' bears bright orange or red flowerheads and grows to 3 ft (1 m). *Zones 8–11.*

TORENIA
Wishbone flower

This genus of 40 to 50 species of erect to spreading, bushy annuals and perennials comes from tropical African and Asian woodlands. They have oval to lance-shaped, entire or toothed, opposite leaves. In summer, they bear racemes of trumpet-shaped, 2-lipped flowers with 2-lobed upper lips and 3-lobed lower lips.

Cultivation

Torenias prefer a warm, frost-free climate. In cooler climates, they should not be planted out until after the last frost. Grow in fertile, well-drained soil in part-shade in a sheltered position. Pinch out the growing shoots of young plants to encourage a bushy habit. Propagate from seed in spring.

Tithonia rotundifolia

Torenia fournieri
Bluewings

This branching annual has ovate or elliptical leaves with toothed edges. Frost tender, it grows fairly rapidly to a height of 12 in (30 cm). Its flowers, borne in summer and early fall, are pansy-like and a deep purplish blue, turning abruptly paler nearer the center, and with a touch of yellow. *Zones 9–12.*

TRADESCANTIA
syns *Rhoeo, Setcreasea, Zebrina*
Spiderwort

This genus consists of 50 or more species of perennials, some evergreen, from the

Torenia fournieri

Tradescantia, Andersoniana Group hybrid

Americas. Some are rather weedy, but the creeping species (wandering Jew) make useful ground covers. Some upright species have pure blue flowers, a hard color to find for the late-summer garden. Most trailing types are frost tender and are usually grown as greenhouse potted plants, except in mild-winter climates where they make good ground cover.

Cultivation
Grow in full sun or part-shade in fertile, moist to dry soil. Cut back ruthlessly when they become straggly. Propagate by division or from tip cuttings.

Tradescantia, Andersoniana Group
This group of hybrids covers a range of plants formerly listed under *Tradescantia × andersoniana* or *T. virginiana*. They are mainly low-growing perennials with fleshy, strap-like leaves and heads of 3-petaled flowers. Although the foliage clump seldom exceeds 18 in (45 cm) high, the flower stems can reach 24 in (60 cm). There are many hybrids in a range of white, mauve, pink and purple flower shades. 'Alba' has white flowers. *Zones 7–10.*

Tradescantia virginia
This is the most widely grown species and grows to about 3 ft (1 m) tall. It

Tradescantia, Andersoniana Group 'Alba'

bears its flowers in long succession from summer until well into autumn. Garden varieties have been selected with larger flowers and a wide color range, from white through to deep blue and purple. They like a shaded spot and a rich moist soil. Cut them down ruthlessly at the end of autumn. *Zones 4–9.*

TRICYRTIS
Toad lilies

The common name of this genus of about 20 species seems to have biased gardeners against the toad lilies, but these clumping rhizomatous summer-flowering perennials from the woodlands of Asia are quite attractive in their quiet colorings and markings. The flowers, which are star-, bell- or funnel-shaped, with opened-out tips, are held in the axils of the leaves. The leaves are pointed and appear on erect or arching, hairy stems.

Cultivation

Grow these very frost-hardy plants in part-shade in humus-rich, moist soil; in areas with cool summers, they need a warm spot. Propagate from seed in autumn or by division in spring.

Trillium grandiflorum

Tricyrtis hirta

This upright Japanese species bears 2 in (5 cm) wide, star-shaped white flowers spotted with purple from late summer to autumn. The branching stems are 3 ft (1 m) long. *Zones 5–9.*

TRILLIUM
Wake robin, wood lily

Among North America's most beautiful wildflowers, this genus in the lily family contains 30 species of rhizomatous, deciduous perennials; they also occur naturally in northeastern Asia. Upright or nodding, solitary, funnel-shaped flowers with 3 simple petals are held just above a whorl of 3 leaves. They flower in spring and make good ornamentals.

Cultivation

Very frost hardy, they prefer a cool, moist soil with ample water and shade from the hot afternoon sun. Slow to propagate from seed in fall or by division in summer, they are long lived once established.

Trillium grandiflorum
Snow trillium, wake robin

This showy, clump-forming trillium is the easiest to grow, reaching 12–18 in

Tricyrtis hirta

Trollius chinensis

Tropaeolum majus

Trollius chinensis
syn. *Trollius ledebourii*
Chinese globe flower
This species grows 2–3 ft (60–90 cm) tall and bears its shining flowers in spring above handsomely slashed foliage. The flower color varies from light to deep yellow. It is a fast grower, but is not invasive. *Zones 5–9.*

TROPAEOLUM
Nasturtium
The 87 species of annuals, perennials and twining climbers in this genus are from Chile to Mexico. In warm areas, nasturtiums can survive for several years, self-sowing freely and flowering all year. The flowers can be single or double, about 2 in (5 cm) across, and come in red, orange, russet, yellow, cream and even blue.

Cultivation
Frost hardy to frost tender, most prefer moist, well-drained soil in full sun or part-shade. Propagate from seed, basal stem cuttings or tubers in spring. Watch out for aphids and cabbage moth caterpillars.

Tropaeolum majus
Garden nasturtium, Indian cress
The stem is trailing and climbing on this fast-growing, bushy South American

(30–45 cm) in height. The pure white flowers, borne in spring, fade to pink as they age. The double-flowered white form, 'Flore Pleno', is beautiful but rare, and has arching stems and oval, dark green leaves. *Zones 3–9.*

TROLLIUS
Globe flower
The perennial globe flowers resemble their cousins the buttercups in their bright yellow flowers and their liking for wet ground, but they have a more sedate habit. The flowers are also often bigger, and their larger number of petals gives them the appearance of being double. Spring is the main flowering season, but they often flower in autumn too. They are native to northern temperate regions.

Cultivation
Very frost hardy, they grow in moist soil provided they are watered generously, but the boggy edge of a pond or stream suits them better. They like some shade. Propagate from seed in spring or fall or by division.

annual. Its leaves are rounded and marked with radial veins. It blooms in summer and fall; its 5-petaled flowers spurred, open and trumpet-shaped, come in many shades from deep red to pale yellow. It grows to a spread of 3 ft (1 m) and a height of up to 18 in (45 cm). The spicy-tasting leaves and flowers of this species are sometimes added to salads. The Alaska Hybrids have single flowers in a range of colors and prettily variegated leaves. *Zones 8–11.*

TULIPA
Tulip

Tulips are one of the world's major commercial flower crops. Wild species come from central and western Asia. They were introduced into Europe around 1554 and have been popular ever since. There are more than 100 species, but most of those are cultivars of only a few species, chiefly *Tulipa gesneriana*. Cultivars run into thousands, and new ones are developed every year. Cultivars are classified into 15 groups or divisions. The Royal General Bulbgrowers' Association (KAVB) trial garden in Holland classifies tulips according to characteristics such as stem length, flower features and time of flowering. They range in height from 4 in (10 cm) up to 27 in (70 cm). The blooms come in a wide range of colors.

Cultivation

Tulips require dry, warm summers but cold winters, and are not recommended for warm climates. Plant in late autumn, in a sunny position, about 6 in (15 cm) deep in rich, alkaline, well-drained soil. Water well during the growth period. Remove spent flowers, but allow leaves to die off naturally in order to replenish the bulb. In areas with wet summers, lift bulbs and store under cool, dry, well-ventilated conditions. Tulips are prone to aphid attack and the fungal disease tulip fire. Propagate from offsets or seed in fall.

Tulipa, Darwin Hybrid Group

This group consists of the single-flowered, long-stemmed cultivars that flower mid-season. These are the most frequently grown varieties for the cut-flower market. They are hybrids either between cultivars of the former Darwin Group with *Tulipa fosteriana*, or between other cultivars and botanical tulips which have the same habit and in which the wild plant is not evident. 'Charles' is orange-red; 'Apeldoorn' is very tall and is best used as a background to a mixed border or alone as a feature. With black anthers, an outside of cherry red edged in signal red, with a yellow base and its inside signal red with a black base edged with yellow, it is very striking. 'Oxford', a fragrant tulip, has a scarlet exterior flushed purple-red and is pepper red inside with a base of sulfur yellow. It grows to 22 in (55 cm) tall and has produced several sports. *Zones 5–9.*

Tulipa, Darwin Hybrid Group 'Charles'

Tulipa, Single Early Group 'Beauty Queen'

Tulipa, **Single Early Group**

These single-flowered cultivars, mainly short stemmed and early flowering, are mostly derived from *Tulipa gesneriana*. 'Apricot Beauty' is a fragrant cultivar dating from 1953; salmon rose tinged red, it reaches 18 in (45 cm) high and is suitable as a bedding plant. A mutation of 'Imperator', it has itself produced several sports, including 'Beauty Queen' which has an exterior of feathered rose on a salmon ground with a red midrib. Its outer base is whitish; the star-shaped inner base is yellowish green edged with yellow, sitting within a cup of scarlet, edged in red and supporting gray anthers. *Zones 5–9.*

Tulipa, **Single Late Group**

This late-flowering group, which includes the former Darwin and Cottage Groups, comprises single-flowered, mainly long-stemmed cultivars. They are generally excellent garden plants and cut flowers. 'Grand Style' has a strong red exterior and pale yellow anthers inside a purple interior on a yellow base edged with blue; it grows about 26 in (65 cm) tall. 'Halcro' has large, carmine flowers with yellow bases edged in green. It grows to more than 27 in (70 cm) tall and is excellent for naturalizing. 'Queen of Night' is one of the best of the 'black' tulips. Its beautiful, stately cups are actually a deep velvety maroon and it grows 24 in (60 cm) tall. *Zones 5–9.*

Tulipa, Single Late Group 'Grand Style'

U, V

Valeriana officinalis

VALERIANA
Valerian

This genus consists of more than 150 species of herbaceous perennials, herbs and subshrubs, few of which have any ornamental value. Those that do, are suitable for borders and rock gardens. The name is from the Latin *valere* (keep well) in recognition of the medicinal properties of some species. Before modern tranquilizers were introduced, the root from *Valeriana officinalis* was used to treat nervous conditions.

Cultivation

Very frost hardy, they thrive in almost any soil, in sun or part-shade. Propagate from seed or by division of established plants in autumn.

Valeriana officinalis
Cat's valerian, common valerian, garden heliotrophe

This clump-forming, fleshy perennial, which is attractive to cats, grows to 4 ft (1.2 m) tall with a spread of 3 ft (1 m). It occurs naturally throughout Europe and eastwards to Russia and western Asia. It bears rounded flowerheads of white to dark pink flowers in summer on erect hairy stems. The leaves are opposite with serrated margins. *Zones 3–9.*

VERBASCUM
Mullein

This genus consists of semi-evergreen to evergreen perennials, biennials and shrubs from Europe and the more temperate zones of Asia. Foliage ranges from glossy to velvety. Many of the 250 or so species are considered weeds. However, several are desirable in the garden for their stately habit and long summer-flowering season—the flowers do not open from the bottom up, but a few at a time along the spike.

Cultivation

They are fully to moderately frost hardy but will not tolerate winter-wet conditions. Plant in well-drained soil in an open, sunny location. Propagate from seed in spring or late summer or by division in winter. Some self-seed readily.

Verbascum bombyciferum

This biennial from Asia Minor has silvery gray, furry, large leaves and grows 6 ft (1.8 m) tall. It bears golden-yellow, cup-shaped flowers in summer, sometimes in terminal spikes. *Zones 6–10.*

Verbascum bombyciferum

Verbascum thapsus

Verbascum chaixii

This species from southern Europe can
be relied on to live long enough to form
clumps. The flowers, borne on 3 ft (1 m)
tall stems in summer, are normally
yellow. The white form 'Album' is
usually finer. *Zones 5–10.*

Verbascum thapsus

This species has soft, velvety, pale green
leaves and yellow, stalkless flowers in
dense, terminal spikes in summer. It
grows on freely draining hillsides, often
in very poor soil. The flowers, once
dried, form an ingredient in herbal teas
and cough mixtures. *Zones 3–9.*

Verbascum chaixii 'Album'

VERBENA

Originating in Europe, South America and North America, this genus of 250 or more species of biennials and perennials is characterized by small, dark, irregularly shaped and toothed leaves. They bloom in late spring, summer and autumn. An agreeably spicy aroma is associated with most verbenas.

Cultivation

Marginally frost hardy to frost tender, they do best where winters are not severe. Establish in medium, well-drained soil in full sun or part-shade. Propagate from seed in fall or spring, stem cuttings in summer or fall, or by division in late winter.

Verbena bonariensis

This tall South American perennial is often grown as an annual, primarily for its deep purple flowers which top the sparsely foliaged 4–5 ft (1.2–1.5 m) stems from summer to autumn. The deeply toothed leaves cluster in a mounded rosette, which easily fits in the front or middle of a border; the floral stems give a vertical line without much

Verbena bonariensis

mass. Frost hardy, it self-seeds readily and survives with minimal water, even in dry areas. *Zones 7–10.*

Verbena × hybrida
Garden verbena

This trailing perennial blooms in summer to autumn. Its fragrant flowers appear in dense clusters, many showing off white centers among the hues of red, mauve, violet, white and pink. It suits summer beds and containers. 'Homestead Purple' is a sturdy cultivar with rich red-purple flowers. 'La France' has bright pink flowerheads. 'Silver Ann' has heads of light pink flowers with darker blooms at the center. 'Sissinghurst' has mid-green leaves and bears stems of brilliant pink flowerheads in summer. *Zones 9–10.*

Verbena × hybrida

Verbena rigida

Verbena rigida

syn. *Verbena venosa*

A South American native, this tuberous-rooted perennial is an excellent species for seaside cultivation. It reaches a height of 18–24 in (45–60 cm) with a spread of 12 in (30 cm). The dense spikes of pale violet to magenta flowers are borne from mid-summer. 'Silver Jubilee' bears a mass of red flowers right through the growing season. *Zones 8–10.*

VERONICA
Speedwell

The genus was named after Saint Veronica who, pious legend relates, wiped the face of Christ with her veil and was rewarded with having his image imprinted on it. The 200 or so species are herbaceous perennials, ranging from prostrate, creeping plants to 6 ft (1.8 m) high giants. The small flowers are gathered in clusters of various sizes and are borne in abundance in summer, mainly in blue, although white and pink are also common.

Veronica austriaca

Cultivation

Fully to moderately frost hardy, they like any temperate climate, and are not fussy about soil or position. Propagate from seed in autumn or spring, from cuttings in summer or by division in early spring or early autumn.

Veronica austriaca

syn. *Veronica teucrium*

This clump-forming European perennial grows to 10–18 in (25–45 cm) tall with long, slender stems bearing bright blue, saucer-shaped flowers in late spring. The leaves vary in shape from broadly oval to narrow and are either entire or deeply cut. Propagate by division in autumn or from softwood cuttings in summer. *Zones 6–10.*

Veronica gentianoides
Gentian speedwell

This mat-forming perennial found from the Caucasus to southwest Asia has wide, dark green leaves from which rise spikes of pale blue or white flowers in spring. It reaches 18 in (45 cm) in height. *Zones 4–9.*

Veronica gentianoides

Veronica spicata

Veronica spicata
Digger's speedwell, spike speedwell

This very frost-hardy European perennial reaches a height of 24 in (60 cm)
and a spread of up to 3 ft (1 m). Its
stems are erect, hairy and branching.
Spikes of small, star-shaped, blue
flowers with purple stamens bloom in
summer. *Veronica spicata* subsp. *incana* has
spreading clumps of silvery, felty leaves
and deep violet-blue flowers. 'Rosea' is a
pink-flowered form. *Zones 3–9.*

Viola cornuta

VIOLA
Violet, heartsease, pansy

This genus of annuals, perennials and subshrubs has up to 500 species occurring in temperate zones. Most are creeping plants, either deciduous or evergreen, with slender to thick rhizomes. Flowers of wild species have 3 spreading lower petals and 2 erect upper petals, with a short nectar spur projecting to the rear of the flower. Many species produce *cleistogamous* flowers, with smaller petals that do not open properly, and able to set seed without cross-pollination. Hybridization has produced garden pansies, violas and violettas, with showy flowers in very bright or deep colors.

Cultivation

Most cultivated species tolerate light frosts; many are fully frost hardy. Pansies and violas are grown as annuals or potted plants in full sun, but appreciate shelter from wind; sow seed in late winter or early spring, planting in late spring in well-drained soil. Propagate perennials by division or from cuttings.

Viola cornuta
Horned violet

Native to the Pyrenees, this is a broad-faced violet with a short spur at the back, in shades of pale blue to deeper violet and borne in spring and summer. The plants spread by rhizomes, sending up flowering stems to 6 in (15 cm) long. The horned violet is one of the major parent species of pansies and violas. 'Minor' has smaller leaves and flowers. *Zones 6–9.*

Viola odorata
Sweet violet

A sweet perfume wafts from the flowers of these well-known florists' violets, sold in small bunches for their scent. It is a spreading, rhizomatous perennial from Europe, which grows 3 in (8 cm) tall and may spread indefinitely on cool, moist ground. Its dark green

Viola odorata

leaves are a pointed kidney shape with shallowly toothed edges. Spurred, flat-faced flowers in violet, white or rose appear from late winter through early spring. It boasts many cultivars. *Zones 6–10.*

Viola pedata
Bird's-foot viola

A beautiful and variable species found in eastern North America, it has a tufted habit with the basal leaves divided into segments like a bird's foot. The flowers have 2 upper petals of dark violet and the 3 lower ones are pale lilac with darker veins. Unlike most violets, it thrives in a sunny, dry position in acidic sandy soil, although it needs some shade in hot conditions. It flowers in early spring and again in late summer, and can be propagated from seed. *Zones 4–9.*

Viola, Perennial Cultivars

Primarily of *Viola lutea*, *V. amoena* and *V. cornuta* parentage, these hardy perennial plants are long flowering, year round in mild climates. 'Jackanapes' has brown upper petals and yellow lower petals; 'Maggie Mott' has bright purple-blue flowers; and 'Magic' is rich purple with a small eye of dark purple and yellow. *Zones 6–10.*

Viola, Perennial Cultivar 'Jackanapes'

Left: *Viola tricolor*

Viola × wittrockiana

Viola tricolor
Wild pansy, Johnny jump up, love-in-idleness

Of wide occurrence in Europe and temperate Asia, this annual, biennial or short-lived perennial produces neat flowers with appealing faces, in shades of yellow, blue, violet and white, in autumn and winter in mild climates if cut back in late summer. It has soft, angular, branching stems and lobed oval to lance-shaped leaves. It grows to a height and spread of 6 in (15 cm) and self-seeds readily. *Viola tricolor* 'Bowles' Black' is a striking cultivar with black velvety petals and a yellow center. *Zones 4–10.*

Viola × wittrockiana
Viola

This hybrid group of compactly branched perennials are almost always grown as biennials or annuals. Offering flowers of a great many hues, the numerous cultivars bloom in late winter through spring and possibly into summer in cooler climates. The flowers are up to 4 in (10 cm) across and have 5 petals in a somewhat flat-faced arrangement. They grow slowly, reaching about 8 in (20 cm) in height and spread. This is a complex hybrid group, including both pansies and violas, the latter traditionally distinguished by the flowers lacking

Viola × wittrockiana 'Universal True Blue'

dark blotches, but there are now intermediate types with pale-colored markings. Hybrids in the Imperial Series are large-flowered pansies. The Joker Series are of an intermediate type, with a range of very bright contrasting colors such as orange and purple. The Accord Series of pansies covers most colors and has a very dark central blotch. Other seedling strains include the Universal and Sky Series. 'Universal Orange' has bronze-orange flowers; 'Universal True Blue' has rich purple-blue flowers with a yellow center. *Zones 5–10.*

Viola × wittrockiana 'Universal Orange'

W, X, Y, Z

Xeranthemum annuum

XERANTHEMUM
Immortelle

The 5 or 6 annuals in this genus are natives of the Mediterranean region, extending to Iran. They are called immortelles or everlasting flowers because the dried flowerheads retain their color and form for many years. The erect, branching stems have narrow, hoary leaves. The pretty flowerheads are solitary on long stems and the small fertile flowers are surrounded by papery bracts which may be white, purple or pink.

Cultivation

Moderately frost hardy, they grow best in a sunny position in fertile, well-drained soil. Propagate from seed which should be sown in spring where the plants are to grow.

Xeranthemum annuum
Immortelle

A good source of dried flowers, this annual blooms in summer, producing heads of purple daisy-like flowers; whites, pinks and mauves, some with a 'double' appearance are also available. The leaves are silvery and lance-shaped and the plants grow to around 24 in (60 cm) high and 18 in (45 cm) wide. Mixed Hybrids include singles and doubles in shades of pink, purple, mauve, red or white. *Zones 7–10.*

Yucca filamentosa

YUCCA

The 40 or so species of unusual ever-green perennials, shrubs and trees in this genus are found in drier regions of North America. Often slow growing, they form rosettes of stiff, swordlike leaves usually tipped with a sharp spine; as the plants mature, some species develop an upright woody trunk, often branched. Yuccas bear showy, tall panicles of drooping, white or cream, bell- to cup-shaped flowers. The fruits are either fleshy or dry capsules, but in most species are rarely seen away from the plants' native lands, as the flowers must be pollinated by the yucca moth.

Cultivation

Yuccas prefer low humidity, full sun and sandy soil with good drainage. Depend-ing on the species, they are frost hardy to frost tender. Propagate from seed (if available), cuttings or suckers in spring.

Yucca filamentosa
Adam's needle-and-thread

The leaves on this plant form basal rosettes and are edged with white threads. Up to 3 ft (1 m) long, they are

Yucca glauca

Zantedeschia aethiopica

thin-textured and a slightly bluish gray-green. The nodding, white flowers are 2 in (5 cm) long, borne on erect panicles to 6 ft (1.8 m) tall in summer. It is native to eastern USA and is the most frost hardy of the yuccas. *Zones 4–10.*

Yucca glauca
syn. *Yucca angustifolia*
Dwarf yucca, soapweed
Native to central USA, this small, stemless clump-forming species has glaucous, blue-green, narrow spearlike leaves with white margins and a few gray threads. In summer, the flower spike, up to 3 ft (1 m) tall, bears fragrant greenish white flowers that are often tinged reddish brown. *Zones 4–9.*

ZANTEDESCHIA
Arum lily, calla lily, pig lily
Indigenous to southern and eastern Africa and Lesotho, this well-known genus of the arum family consists of 6 species of tuberous perennials. The inflorescence consists of a showy white, yellow or pink spathe shaped like a funnel, with a central finger-like, yellow spadix. The leaves are glossy green and usually arrowhead-shaped.

Cultivation
Consisting of both evergreen and deciduous species, this genus includes frost-tender to moderately frost-hardy plants; most are intolerant of dry conditions. Most prefer well-drained soil in full sun or part-shade, although *Zantedeschia aethiopica* will grow as a semi-aquatic plant in boggy ground that is often inundated. Propagate from offsets in winter.

Zantedeschia aethiopica
White arum lily, lily of the Nile
Although normally deciduous, in summer and early autumn this species can stay evergreen if given enough moisture. It can also be grown in water up to 6–12 in (15–30 cm) deep. This species reaches 24–36 in (60–90 cm) in height and spread, with large clumps of broad, dark green leaves. The large flowers, produced in spring, summer and autumn, are pure white with a yellow spadix. 'Green Goddess' has interesting green markings on the spathes. *Zones 8–11.*

Zantedeschia elliottiana
Golden arum lily
This summer-flowering hybrid species has a yellow spathe surrounding a yellow spadix, sometimes followed by a spike of bright yellow berries. It grows 24–36 in (60–90 cm) tall with a spread of 24 in (60 cm). The heart-shaped,

semi-erect leaves have numerous white spots or streaks. *Zones 8–11*.

Zantedeschia rehmannii
Pink arum lily, pink calla

The spathe on this summer-flowering plant is mauve to rose-purple with paler margins, enclosing a yellow spadix. Its green, unmarked leaves are semierect and not arrowhead-shaped as in other species. It grows 15 in (38 cm) tall and 12 in (30 cm) wide. Marginally frost hardy, it likes well-composted soil, a protected location and part-shade. *Zones 8–11*.

ZEPHYRANTHES
Windflower, zephyr lily, rain lily

There are about 70 species in this bulb genus, all indigenous to the Americas. Most species have open flowers like small Asiatic lilies and are deciduous. They vary in height from about 6–15 in (15–38 cm) and can be white, yellow or various shades of warm pink. All bear one flower to a stem; most close up their petals at night.

Cultivation
Moderately to marginally frost hardy, they do well in sun or part-shade. They

Zantedeschia elliottiana

like fertile, well-drained but moist soil, but usually flower best when they have had a chance to thicken into clumps. In colder climates, they do well in pots in a mildly warmed greenhouse. Propagate from seed in autumn or spring.

Zephyranthes candida
syn. *Argyropsis candida*
Flower of the west wind, storm lily

Indigenous to Uruguay and Argentina, this vigorous species grows to a height of 6 in (15 cm). The starry, cup-shaped, white flowers, 2 in (5 cm) wide, are borne singly on the slender stems in summer and early autumn. It is said to flower mainly in cloudy weather. The grasslike foliage is evergreen. *Zones 9–10*.

Zantedeschia rehmannii

Zephyranthes candida

Zephyranthes grandiflora

Zinnia elegans

Zephyranthes grandiflora
syns *Zephyranthes carinata, Z. rosea*
Pink storm lily
A native of Mexico, this popular species grows to 10 in (25 cm) tall. The 4 in (10 cm) flowers, produced in summer, are funnel shaped, white throated and dusky pink, while the slender leaves are strap shaped. There are many forms, some with smaller flowers. *Zones 9–10.*

ZINNIA
Zinnia
This genus of 20 species of erect to spreading annuals, perennials and sub-shrubs has daisy-like, terminal flower-heads in many colors including white, yellow, orange, red, purple and lilac. Found throughout Mexico and Central and South America, some are grown for cut flowers and in mixed borders.

Cultivation
These plants are marginally frost hardy and should be grown in a sunny position in fertile soil that drains well. They need frequent deadheading. Propagate from seed sown under glass early in spring.

Zinnia elegans
Youth-and-old-age
This sturdy Mexican annual is the best known of the zinnias. The wild form has purple flowerheads, and blooms from summer to fall. It grows fairly rapidly to 21–30 in (60–76 cm), with a smaller spread. Garden varieties offer hues of white, red, pink, yellow, violet, orange or crimson in flowers up to 6 in (15 cm) across. The Dreamland series is compact and heavy flowering—typical of F1 Hybrid bedding zinnias. 'F1 Dreamland Ivy' has pale greenish yellow flowers. The Thumbelina series has 2 in (5 cm) wide flowerheads on plants only 6 in (15 cm) high. *Zones 8–11.*

Zinnia haageana
syn. *Zinnia mexicana, Z. angustifolia*
This Mexican annual reaches 24 in (60 cm) in height with a spread of 8 in (20 cm). The small but profuse yellow, orange and bronze flowerheads, more than 1½ in (35 mm) wide, appear in summer and early autumn. 'Old Mexico' is an old but valuable cultivar that is drought resistant. *Zones 8–11.*

REFERENCE TABLE

Name	Type*	Zone	Color	Planting time	Flowering season
Acaena 'Blue Haze'	P	7–10	blue-gray	spring	late spring–early summer
Acanthus mollis	P	5–10	white, purple, gray	autumn	summer
Acanthus spinosus	P	7–10	white, purple-red	autumn	summer
Achillea 'Coronation Gold'	P	4–10	golden yellow	winter	summer
Achillea 'Moonshine'	P	3–10	yellow	winter	summer
Achillea tomentosa	P	4–10	yellow	winter	summer
Aconitum napellus	P	5–9	blue, purple	autumn	summer–autumn
Actaea alba	P	3–9	white	autumn	summer
Actaea rubra	P	3–9	white with mauve tints	autumn	summer
Adiantum pedatum	P	4–9	–	autumn, winter, spring	–
Aegopodium podagraria	P	3–9	white	any time	summer
Agapanthus praecox	P	9–11	lavender-blue	spring, autumn	summer
Agastache foeniculum	P	8–10	purple	spring	summer
Ageratum houstonianum	A	9–11	blue	spring	summer–autumn
Ajuga roptans	P	3–10	deep blue	spring, autumn	spring
Alcea rosea	A	4–10	pink, purple, cream, yellow	late summer–spring	spring–summer
Alchemilla mollis	P	4–9	greenish yellow	late winter–early spring	summer
Allium giganteum	P	6–10	violet to deep purple	autumn	mid-summer
Allium moly	P	3–8	yellow	autumn	summer
Allium schoenoprasum	P	3–10	mauve	autumn	late spring–summer
Aloysia triphylla	P	8–11	pale lavender	spring, summer	summer–autumn
Alstroemeria aurea	P	7–9	orange	spring	summer
Alstroemeria Ligtu Hybrids	P	7–9	cream, orange, red, yellow	spring	summer
Alstroemeria psittacina	P	8–10	crimson, green	spring	summer
Amaranthus caudatus	A	8–11	dark red	spring	summer
Amaranthus tricolor	A	8–11	red	spring	summer
Ammi majus	P	6–10	white	spring	summer–autumn
Ampelopsis brevipedunculata	P	4–9	greenish	summer, autumn	summer
Amsonia tabernaemontana	P	3–9	pale blue	spring	summer
Anaphalis margaritacea	P	4–9	yellow	spring	summer
Anchusa azurea	P	3–9	blue	autumn, spring	spring–summer
Anchusa capensis	P	8–10	blue	autumn, spring	early summer
Androsace carnea	P	5–9	pink	autumn	spring
Androsace sarmentosa	P	3–8	pink with yellow centers	autumn	spring
Anemone blanda	P	5–9	white, pink, blue	summer	spring
Anemone coronaria	P	8–10	pink, scarlet, purple, blue	summer	spring

Name	Type*	Zone	Color	Planting time	Flowering season
Anemone hupehensis	P	6–10	white-mauve	summer	autumn
Anemone × hybrida	P	5–10	white to deep rose	summer	spring
Anethum graveolens	A	4–10	yellow	spring	summer
Angelica archangelica	P	4–9	green	spring	summer
Anigozanthos Bush Gems Series	P	9–11	yellow, gold, green, orange, red, burgundy	spring	spring
Anigozanthos 'Regal Claw'	P	9–11	orange	spring	spring
Antennaria dioica	P	5–9	white, pink, yellow	autumn	summer
Anthemis tinctoria	P	4–10	bright golden	spring, autumn	spring–summer
Antigonon leptopus	P	9–11	deep pink	autumn	summer–autumn
Aquilegia canadensis	P	3–9	red, yellow	spring, autumn	spring–summer
Aquilegia 'Crimson Star'	P	3–10	crimson	spring, autumn	spring–summer
Aquilegia, McKana Hybrids	P	3–10	pink, blue, yellow, white, red, purple	spring, autumn	spring–summer
Aquilegia vulgaris	P	3–10	pink, crimson, white, purple	spring, autumn	spring–summer
Arabis blepharophylla	P	7–10	pink-purple	summer	spring
Arabis caucasica	P	4–10	white	summer	spring
Arctotis fastuosa	P	9–11	orange	spring, autumn	summer
Arctotis hybrids	P	9–11	yellow, orange	spring, autumn	summer–autumn
Arenaria montana	P	4–9	white	late winter, spring	summer
Arisaema triphyllum	P	4–9	white	autumn	spring
Armeria maritima	P	4–9	white-pink	spring, autumn	spring–summer
Artemisia ludoviciana	P	4–10	brownish-green	spring	summer
Artemisia 'Powis Castle'	P	5–10	–	spring	–
Arum italicum	P	6–10	yellow	autumn	spring
Aruncus dioicus	P	3–9	greenish, creamy white	late winter, spring	summer
Asarum caudatum	P	6–9	brownish purple	spring	spring–summer
Asarum europaeum	P	4–9	dull purple	spring	spring–summer
Asclepias speciosa	P	2–9	pinkish red, white	autumn	summer
Asclepias tuberosa	P	3–9	orange	autumn	summer
Asperula arcadiensis	P	5–9	pink-pale purple	spring	summer
Aster ericoides	P	4–10	white	spring, autumn	summer–autumn
Aster novae-angliae	P	4–9	pink, cerise	spring, autumn	summer–autumn
Aster novi-belgii	P	3–9	pale mauve, violet, deep pink	spring, autumn	summer–autumn
Astilbe, Arendsii Hybrids	P	4–10	range from red to pink to white	winter	late spring–early summer
Astrantia major	P	6–9	pink, white	spring	summer
Athyrium nipponicum 'Pictum'	P	4–9	–	autumn	–
Aubrieta deltoidea	P	4–9	mauve-pink	late winter–spring	spring
Aurinia saxatilis	P	4–9	yellow	late winter–spring	spring–summer

Name	Type*	Zone	Color	Planting time	Flowering season
Baptisia australis	P	3–10	purple-blue	autumn	summer
Begonia grandis subsp. *evansiana*	P	6–11	pink	spring	summer
B.Semperflorens-cultorum Group	P	9–11	pink, white, red	spring	summer–autumn
Begonia, Tuberhybrida Group	P	9–11	most colors, except blues	spring	summer
Belamcanda chinensis	P	8–11	cream, yellow, apricot, orange-red	late winter–spring	summer
Bellis perennis	P	3–10	white	autumn–spring	winter–summer
Bergenia cordifolia	P	3–9	purple-pink	spring	winter–spring
Bergenia crassifolia	P	3–9	deep pink	spring	early spring
Boltonia asteroides	P	4–9	white, pale pink, mauve	late winter–spring	spring–summer
Borago officinalis	A/B	5–10	sky-blue	late winter–spring	spring–summer
Bougainvillea 'Scarlett O'Hara'	P	10–11	red bracts	summer	summer–autumn
Brachycome iberidifolia	A/P	9–11	mauve-blue, white, pink, purple	spring, autumn	summer–autumn
Brachycome multifida	P	9–11	mauve-pink	spring, autumn	spring–summer
Bracteantha bracteata	A/P	8–11	golden-yellow	spring	summer–autumn
Brassica oleracea, Acephala Group	A	6–11	yellow to white	spring	summer–autumn
Browallia speciosa	P	9–11	purple-blue	spring	summer–autumn
Brunnera macrophylla	P	3–9	violet	spring	spring–summer
Caladium bicolor	A	10–11	green with pink center; combinations of green,white, pink, red	spring	summer
Calendula officinalis	A	6–11	orange, yellow, cream	spring–autumn	spring–autumn
Callistephus chinensis	A	6–10	purple, blue, pink, white	spring	summer–autumn
Caltha palustris	P	3–8	golden-yellow	autumn–early spring	spring
Campanula carpatica	A	3–9	blue, lavender, white	late winter–spring	spring–summer
Campanula glomerata	P	3–9	purple-blue	late winter–spring	summer
Campanula lactiflora	P	5–9	lilac-blue	late winter–spring	summer
Campanula medium	B	6–10	violet-blue, pink, white	winter–spring	spring–early summer
Campanula persicifolia	P	3–9	white, purplish blue	winter–spring	spring–summer
Campanula portenschlagiana	P	5–10	violet-blue	late winter–spring	late spring–summer
Campanula rotundifolia	P	3–9	lilac-blue, white	late winter–spring	summer
Canna × *generalis*	P	9–11	orange-red, yellow, apricot, cream	spring–early summer	summer–autumn
Catananche caerula	P	6–10	lavender-blue	late winter–spring	summer
Celosia argentea	A	10–11	silvery-white	spring	summer
Centaurea cyanus	A	5–10	blue, pink, white	late winter–spring	spring–summer
Centaurea macrocephala	P	4–9	yellow	spring–early summer	summer
Centranthus ruber	P	4–10	red, pink, white	late winter–spring	spring–autumn
Cerastium tomentosum	P	3–10	white	late winter–spring	late spring–summer
Chelone obliqua	P	6–9	rosy-purple	late winter–spring	summer–autumn

Name	Type*	Zone	Color	Planting time	Flowering season
Chrysanthemum carinatum	A	8–10	multicolored	late winter–spring	spring–summer
Cimicifuga racemosa	P	3–9	cream	spring–early summer	summer–autumn
Cimicifuga simplex	P	3–9	white	spring–early summer	late autumn
Clarkia amoena	A	7–11	pink shades	autumn	summer
Clematis integrifolia	P	3–9	purple-blue	summer	spring
Cleome hassleriana	A	9–11	rose-pink to white	spring	summer–autumn
Clintonia umbellata	P	4–9	white	late winter–spring	late spring–summer
Colchicum autumnale	A	4–9	lilac-pink	summer	late summer–mid-autumn
Consolida ambigua	A	7–11	pink, white, purple	spring, autumn	summer
Convallaria majalis	P	3–9	white	autumn	spring
Convolvulus tricolor	A	8–11	purple-blue, white	all year	late spring–early autumn
Coreopsis grandiflora	P	6–10	golden-yellow	spring, autumn	spring–summer
Coreopsis lanceolata	P	3–11	golden-yellow	spring, autumn	summer
Coreopsis verticillata	P	6–10	yellow	spring, autumn	spring–autumn
Corydalis lutea	P	6–10	yellow	late winter–spring	spring–autumn
Cosmos atrosanguineus	P	8–10	dark maroon	spring	summer–autumn
Cosmos bipinnatus	A	8–11	pink, red, purple, white	spring–early summer	summer–autumn
Crocosmia × crocosmiiflora	P	6–11	orange-red	spring	spring
Crocus chrysanthus	P	4–9	orange	autumn	late winter–early spring
Crocus sativus	P	6–9	lilac, purple	autumn	autumn
Crocus vernus	P	4–9	white, pink, purple	autumn	spring–early summer
Cynoglossum amabile	A	5–9	blue, white, pink	late winter–spring	spring–summer
Dahlia × hortensis	A	8–10	scarlet	late winter–spring	autumn
Dahlia, Waterlily	A	8–10	white, pink	late winter–spring	summer–autumn
Dahlia, Semi-cactus	A	8–10	bronze, orange, yellow, purple-pink	late winter–spring	summer–autumn
Delosperma nubigenum	P	8–11	yellow to orange-red	autumn	summer
Delphinium, Belladonna	P	3–9	blue, white	spring	summer
Delphinium grandiflorum	P	3–9	blue	spring	summer
Delphinium, Pacific Hybrids	P	7–9	blue, purple, white	late winter–early summer	summer
Dendranthema × grandiflorum	P	4–10	white, yellow, bronze, pink, purple, red	spring–autumn	autumn
Deschampia caespitosa	P	4–10	greenish yellow, gold, silver, bronze	autumn	summer
Dianthus barbatus	P	4–10	white, pink, carmine, crimson-purple	summer	spring–summer
Dianthus chinensis	A	7–10	pink, red, lavender, white	autumn, spring	spring–summer
Dianthus, Modern Pinks	P	5–10	white, pink, crimson	summer	spring–autumn
Dianthus, Old-fashioned Pinks	P	5–9	white, pale pink, magenta, red	summer	spring–summer
Dianthus superbus	P	4–10	purple-pink	summer	summer
Dicentra eximia	P	4–9	pink	autumn	spring

Name	Type*	Zone	Color	Planting time	Flowering season
Dicentra formosa	P	4–9	pink, red	autumn	spring–summer
Dicentra spectabilis	P	2–9	pink, white	autumn	spring–summer
Dictamnus albus	P	3–9	white, pink, lilac	summer	summer
Digitalis × mertonensis	P	4–9	pink, salmon	autumn	summer
Digitalis purpurea	P	5–10	purple, pink, magenta, white, yellow	autumn	summer
Dimorphotheca pluvialis	A	8–10	white & purple	spring	winter–spring
Disporum flavens	P	5–9	yellow	autumn	spring
Dodecatheon meadia	P	3–9	white, pink	autumn	spring
Doronicum columnae	P	5–9	yellow	autumn–early summer	spring
Doronicum pardalianches	P	5–9	yellow	autumn–early summer	spring–summer
Dorotheanthus bellidiformis	A	9–11	yellow, white, red, pink	spring–early summer	summer
Dryas octopetala	P	2–9	white	spring	late spring–summer
Dryopteris erythrosora	P	5–9	–	summer, autumn, winter	–
Dryopteris filix-mas	P	4–9	–	summer, autumn, winter	–
Dryopteris marginalis	P	4–8	–	summer, autumn, winter	–
Echinacea purpurea	P	3–10	rosy purple	winter–spring	summer
Echinops ritro	P	3–10	purple-blue	late winter–spring	summer
Echium vulgare	B	7–10	violet	spring, summer	spring–summer
Epilobium angustifolium	P	2–9	rose-pink	spring, autumn	summer
Epilobium canum subsp. canum	P	8–10	bright red	spring, autumn	summer–autumn
Epimedium × rubrum	P	4–9	crimson and white	autumn	spring
Epimedium × versicolor	P	5–9	pink, yellow	autumn	spring
Eranthis hyemalis	P	5–9	yellow	spring	winter–spring
Eremurus × isabellinus	P	5–9	white, pink, salmon, yellow, apricot, copper	autumn	summer
Erigeron 'Foersters Liebling'	P	5–9	dark pink	spring	summer
Erigeron foliosus	P	5–9	blue, yellow center	spring	spring–summer
Erigeron karvinskianthus	P	7–11	white, pink, red	spring	spring–summer
Eryngium bourgatii	P	5–9	blue, gray-green	late winter–spring	summer–autumn
Eryngium giganteum	P	6–9	blue, pale green	late winter–spring	summer
Erysimum × allionii	P	3–10	yellow, orange	spring	spring
Erysimum 'Golden Bedder'	P	8–10	cream, yellow, orange, red	spring	winter–spring
Erysimum linifolium	P	6–10	deep mauve	spring	all year in mild areas
Erythronium californicum	P	5–9	white	summer, autumn	spring
Erythronium revolutum	P	5–9	pink, purple, white	summer, autumn	spring
Eschscholzia caespitosa	A	7–10	yellow	spring	summer–autumn
Eschscholzia californica	P	6–11	orange, bronze, yellow, scarlet, cream, mauve, rose	spring	summer–autumn
Eucomis comosa	P	8–10	white, green	autumn	late summer–autumn

Name	Type*	Zone	Color	Planting time	Flowering season
Eupatorium coelestinum	P	5–9	blue	spring, autumn	late summer
Eupatorium fistulosum	P	4–10	rosy-mauve	spring, autumn	summer–autumn
Euphorbia characias	P	8–10	bracts yellow-green	spring–summer	summer
Euphorbia griffithii	P	4–9	yellow, bracts orange	spring–summer	summer
Euphorbia marginata	A	4–10	bracts white	spring–summer	summer
Euphorbia myrsinites	P	5–10	chartreuse	spring–summer	spring
Euphorbia polychroma	P	6–9	chrome-yellow	spring–summer	spring–summer
Eustoma grandiflorum	B	9–11	purple, pink, blue, white	spring	spring & autumn
Exacum affine	B	10–11	purple-blue	spring	summer
Felicia amelloides	P	9–11	blue	spring	spring–autumn
Festuca glauca	P	3–10	–	spring, autumn	summer
Festuca ovina	P	5–10	purple-tinged	spring, autumn	summer
Filipendula ulmaria	P	2–9	creamy white	spring, autumn	summer
Fragaria 'Pink Panda'	P	4–10	pink	late winter–spring	spring–autumn
Fritillaria imperialis	P	4–9	yellow, orange, red	summer	late spring–early summer
Fritillaria meleagris	P	4–9	maroon, green, white	summer	late spring–early summer
Fuchsia magellanica	P	7–10	red, purple petals	autumn	summer
Fuchsia Hybrids	P	9–11	pink, red shades	autumn	summer
Gaillardia aristata	P	6–10	yellow, red-center	spring	summer–autumn
Gaillardia × grandiflora	P	5–10	red, orange, yellow, burgundy	spring	summer
Galanthus elwesii	A	6–9	white	autumn	late winter–spring
Galanthus nivalis	A	4–9	white, green markings	autumn	late winter
Galanthus endressii	P	5–9	pink	autumn	summer–autumn
Gaura lindheimeri	P	5–10	white, pink	autumn	spring–autumn
Gazania rigens	P	9–11	orange	winter–spring	spring–summer
Gazania, Sunshine Hybrids	P	9–11	yellow, orange, cream, chocolate striped	winter–spring	spring–summer
Geranium himalyense	P	4–9	violet-blue	spring	summer
Geranium 'Johnson's Blue'	P	5–9	lavender-blue	spring	summer
Geranium macrorrhizum	P	4–9	pink, purple, white	spring	spring–summer
Geranium maculatum	P	6–9	lilac-pink	spring	late spring–mid-summer
Geranium sanguineum	P	4–9	magenta	spring	summer
Geranium sylvaticum	P	4–9	purple-blue	spring	spring–summer
Gerbera jamesonii	P	8–11	white, pink, yellow, orange, red	autumn & spring	spring–summer
Geum chiloense	P	5–9	scarlet	autumn	summer
Gladiolus × colvillei	P	8–10	dark pink, yellow, white	spring	late spring
Gladiolus communis	P	6–10	pink, blotched white or red	spring	late spring–early summer
Gladiolus, Grandiflorus Group	P	9–11	various	spring	summer

Name	Type*	Zone	Color	Planting time	Flowering season
Glaucium flavum	P	7–10	golden-yellow, orange	spring, autumn	summer
Goodenia macmillanii	P	9–11	pink, purple streaks	spring–autumn	spring–summer
Gypsophila paniculata	P	4–10	white	spring, autumn	summer
Gypsophila repens	P	4–9	white, lilac, purple	spring, autumn	summer
Hakonechloa macra 'Aureola'	P	5–11	–	autumn	–
Helenium 'Moerheim Beauty'	P	5–9	orange-red	late winter–spring	summer–autumn
Helianthemum nummularium	P	5–10	yellow, cream, pink, orange	late winter–spring	spring–summer
Helianthus annuus	A	4–11	yellow	autumn, spring	summer
Helianthus × multiflorus	P	5–9	yellow, gold, lemon, bronze	autumn, spring	summer–autumn
Helictotrichon sempervirens	P	4–9	white	spring	summer
Heliopsis helianthoides	P	4–9	golden-yellow	spring	summer
Helleborus foetidus	P	6–10	pale green	autumn, spring	winter–spring
Helleborus orientalis	P	6–10	white, green, pink, rose, purple	autumn, spring	winter–spring
Hemerocallis 'Apricot Queen'	P	4–9	apricot	autumn, spring	summer–autumn
Hemerocallis lilioasphodelus	P	4–9	lemon-yellow	autumn, spring	summer–autumn
Hemerocallis Hybrids	P	5–11	orange, brick red, yellow, pink, cream	autumn, spring	summer–autumn
Hepatica nobilis	P	5–9	blue, pink, white	spring	summer
Hesperis matronalis	P	3–9	white to lilac	spring, autumn	summer
Heuchera micrantha var. diversifolia	P	5–10	white	autumn, spring	summer
Heuchera sanguinea	P	4–10	scarlet, coral red	autumn, spring	summer
× Heucherella tiarelloides	P	5–9	pink	autumn	summer
Hibiscus coccineus	P	7–11	red	autumn	summer
Hibiscus moscheutos	P	5–9	white to pink	autumn	summer
Hosta fortunei	P	6–10	lavender	spring	summer
Hosta 'Krossa Regal'	P	6–10	white to pale mauve or violet	spring	summer–autumn
Hosta plantaginea	P	3–10	white	spring	summer–autumn
Hosta sieboldiana	P	3–10	mauve-white	spring	summer
Hosta undulata	P	3–10	mauve	spring	summer
Houttuynia cordata	P	5–11	yellow	winter–spring	summer
Hypericum 'Hidcote'	P	7–10	golden yellow	autumn, summer	mid-summer–early autumn
Hypericum olympicum	P	6–10	yellow	autumn, summer	summer
Iberis sempervirens	P	4–11	white	spring, autumn	spring–summer
Iberis umbellata	A	7–11	mauve, lilac, pink, red, purple, white	spring, autumn	spring–summer
Impatiens, New Guinea Hybrids	P	10–11	pink, orange, red, cerise	spring	most of year
Impatiens usambarensis	P	10–11	red, pink, white	spring	most of year
Impatiens walleriana	P	9–11	crimson, red, pink, orange, lavender, white	spring	most of year
Imperata cylindrica	P	6–11	–	autumn	–

Name	Type*	Zone	Color	Planting time	Flowering season
Ipomoea tricolor	P	8–11	blue, mauve	spring, summer	summer–autumn
Iresine herbstii	P	10–11	deep red & pink foliage	spring	summer
Iris, Bearded Hybrids	P	3–10	all colors except true red	autumn	spring–summer
Iris cristata	P	3–9	pale blue, lavender, purple	autumn	spring–summer
Iris ensata	P	4–10	white, lavender, blue, purple	autumn	spring–summer
Iris japonica	P	8–11	pale blue, white	autumn	winter–spring
Iris, Louisiana Hybrids	P	7–10	blue, mauve, white, purple, chocolate	autumn	summer
Iris pallida	P	5–10	pale blue	autumn	spring
Iris pseudacorus	P	5–9	yellow	autumn	spring
Iris sibirica	P	3–9	purple, blue, white	autumn	summer
Iris, Spuriac Hybrids	P	4–9	white to blue, yellow	autumn	early summer
Kalanchoe blossfeldiana	P	10–11	red	spring	spring
Kniphofia ensifolia	P	8–10	lemon-yellow	spring	autumn–winter
Kniphofia 'Little Maid'	P	7–10	yellow	spring	winter–summer
Kniphofia 'Winter Cheer'	P	7–10	orange-yellow	spring	winter–summer
Lamium album	P	4–10	white	spring	spring–autumn
Lamium galeobdolon	P	6–10	bright yellow	autumn	summer
Lamium maculatum	P	4–10	pale pink to deep rose	spring	spring–summer
Lathyrus latifolius	P	5–10	pink, rose, white	autumn–early spring	spring–summer
Lathyrus odoratus	P	4–10	white, cream, pink, blue, mauve, lavender, maroon, scarlet	autumn–early spring	winter–summer
Lavandula angustifolia	P	5–10	purple	summer	summer
Lavandula × intermedia	P	6–10	mauve	summer	summer
Lavandula latifolia	P	6/7–10	light purple	summer	summer
Lavandula stoechas	P	7–10	deep purple	summer	summer
Lavatera 'Barnsley'	P	6–10	pale pink	spring, autumn	summer
Lavatera trimestris	A	8–11	white, pink	spring	summer–autumn
Leucanthemum × superbum	P	5–10	white	winter–spring	summer–autumn
Leucojum aestivum	P	4–10	white with green spot	spring, autumn	spring
Leucojum autumnale	P	5–10	white, flushed pink	spring, autumn	late summer–early autumn
Leucojum vernum	P	5–10	white	spring, autumn	late winter–early spring
Lewisia cotyledon	P	6–11	white, yellow, apricot, pink, purple	late winter–spring	summer
Liatris spicata	P	3–10	lilac-purple, pink, white	winter	summer
Ligularia dentata	P	4–9	orange-yellow	spring, autumn	summer
Lilium, American Hybrids	P	5–10	various	autumn	summer
Lilium, Asiatic Hybrids	P	5–10	various	autumn	spring, summer
Lilium candidum	P	4–10	white	autumn	summer

Name	Type*	Zone	Color	Planting time	Flowering season
Lilium lancifolium	P	4–10	orange	autumn	summer
Lilium regale	P	4–10	white and carmine	autumn	summer
Limonium latifolium	P	5–10	lavender-blue, white	spring, autumn	summer
Limonium sinuatum	P	9–10	yellow, white, cream, salmon-pink, purple, blue	spring, autumn	summer–autumn
Linaria purpurea	P	6–10	purple	autumn, spring	summer
Linum narbonense	P	5–10	violet	autumn	summer
Linum perenne	P	5–10	light blue	autumn	summer
Liriope muscari	P	6–10	violet	autumn	summer
Lobelia cardinalis	P	3–10	scarlet-red	winter–spring	summer–autumn
Lobelia erinus	A	7–11	pinkish purple	late winter–early spring	spring–autumn
Lobularia maritima	A	7–10	white	spring	spring–autumn
Lobelia siphilitica	P	5–9	violet-blue	winter–spring	summer–autumn
Lunaria annua	B	8–10	magenta, white, violet-purple	autumn, spring	spring–summer
Lunaria rediviva	P	8–10	pale violet	autumn, spring	spring–summer
Lupinus, Russell Hybrids	P	3–9	cream, pink, orange, blue, violet	late winter–spring, autumn	spring–summer
Lupinus texensis	A	8–10	dark blue & white	autumn, spring	late spring
Lychnis chalcedonica	P	4–10	orange-red	autumn, spring	summer
Lychnis coronaria	P	4–10	rose-pink, scarlet	autumn, spring	summer
Lychnis flos-jovis	P	5–9	pink	autumn, spring	summer
Lychnis viscaria	P	4–9	mauve to magenta	autumn, spring	early summer
Lysimachia clethroides	P	4–10	white	winter–spring	summer
Lysimachia nummularia	P	4–10	yellow	winter–spring	summer
Lysimachia punctata	P	5–10	yellow	winter–spring	summer
Lythrum virgatum	P	4–10	pinkish red	autumn	summer
Macleaya cordata	P	3–10	cream	spring	summer–autumn
Malva moschata	P	3–10	pink	spring	spring
Matthiola incana	B	6–10	mauve	spring	spring
Mimulus guttatus	P	6–10	yellow	spring	summer
Mimulus × *hybridus* Hybrids	P	6–10	red, yellow, cream, white	spring	summer
Mimulus luteus	P	7–10	yellow	spring	summer
Miscanthus sinensis	P	4–10	gray, tinted purple-brown	winter	summer–autumn
Monarda didyma	P	4–10	white, pink, red	spring	summer–autumn
Monarda fistulosa	P	4–10	light purple, pale pink	spring	summer–autumn
Myosotis alpestris	P	4–10	blue, pink, white	autumn	spring–summer
Myosotis sylvatica	P	5–10	lavender-blue	autumn	spring–summer
Narcissus, Trumpet daffodils	A	3–10	yellow, white	autumn	spring
Narcissus, Double-flowered daffodils	A	3–10	white, yellow	autumn	spring

Name	Type*	Zone	Color	Planting time	Flowering season
Nemesia strumosa	A	9–11	yellow, white, red, orange	autumn or spring	spring
Nemophila maculata	A	7–11	white & purple	autumn	summer
Nemophila menziesii	A	7–11	blue	autumn	spring–summer
Nepeta cataria	P	3–10	white	spring–summer	spring–autumn
Nepeta × faassenii	P	3–10	violet-blue	spring–summer	summer
Nepeta racemosa	P	3–10	lavender-blue	spring–summer	summer
Nicotiana alata	P	7–11	white, red, pink	early spring	summer–autumn
Nicotiana sylvestris	A	8–11	white	early spring	summer
Nigella damascena	A	6–10	lilac-blue, white	autumn or spring	spring–summer
Nymphaea, Hardy Hybrids	P	5–10	white, yellow, pink, red	spring	summer–autumn
Nymphaea, Tropical Day-blooming Hybrids	P	10–11	blue, purple, red, pink, yellow, white	spring	summer–autumn
Ocimum basilicum	P	10–11	white	mid-spring	late summer
Oenothera macrocarpa	P	5–9	lemon yellow	spring or autumn	summer
Oenothera speciosa	P	5–10	white, pink tips	spring or autumn	summer
Omphalodes cappodocica	P	6–9	purple-blue	spring	spring
Omphalodes verna	P	6–9	blue	spring	spring
Ophiopogon japonicus	P	8–11	pale purple	autumn	summer
Ophiopogon planiscapus 'Nigrescens'	P	6–10	lilac	autumn	summer
Origanum vulgare	P	5–9	pink	spring	summer
Osmunda regalis	P	3–9	–	autumn, winter	–
Osteospermum ecklonis	P	8–10	white, reddish centers	summer	spring–autumn
Oxalis hirta	P	9–11	deep pink	autumn	autumn–winter
Oxalis purpurea	P	8–10	pink, rose, lilac, white	autumn	autumn–spring
Paeonia lactiflora Hybrids	P	4–9	red, white, yellow, pink, apricot	winter–early spring	spring
Paeonia officinalis	P	4–10	purple, red	winter–early spring	spring–summer
Paeonia suffruticosa	P	4–9	white, pink red, yellow	winter–early spring	spring
Panicum virgatum	P	5–10	red-bronze	autumn	late summer
Papaver nudicaule	P	2–10	white, yellow, orange, pink	spring or autumn	winter–spring
Papaver orientale	P	3–9	scarlet, orange, dusky pink, blackish centers	spring or autumn	spring–summer
Papaver rhoeas	A	5–9	scarlet	spring or autumn	spring–summer
Pelargonium, Ivy-leafed Hybrids	P	9–11	pink	spring–autumn	summer
Pelargonium odoratissimum	P	10–11	white	spring–autumn	summer
Penstemon barbatus	P	3–10	scarlet	spring or autumn	summer–autumn
Penstemon digitalis	P	3–9	white, pale lavender	spring or autumn	summer–autumn
Penstemon 'Evelyn'	P	7–10	pale pink	spring or autumn	summer–autumn

Name	Type*	Zone	Color	Planting time	Flowering season
Penstemon heterophyllus	P	8–10	violet-pink, blue	spring or autumn	summer
Perovskia atriplicifolia	P	4–9	lavender-blue	autumn	summer–autumn
Petunia × hybrida	A	9–11	pink, purple, red, blue, white	spring	spring–autumn
Phlomis fruticosa	P	7–10	yellow	late winter–spring	summer
Phlomis russeliana	P	7–10	butter yellow	late winter–spring	summer
Phlox divaricata	P	4–9	blue, lavender, white	autumn	spring
Phlox drummondii	A	6–10	red, pink, purple, cream	spring	summer–autumn
Phlox maculata	P	5–10	white, pink, purple	late winter–spring	mid-summer
Phlox paniculata	P	4–10	violet, red, salmon, white	winter–spring	summer
Phlox subulata	P	3–10	blue, mauve, carmine, pink, white	late winter–spring	spring
Phygelius aequalis	P	8–11	pale pink	summer	summer
Physalis alkekengi	P	4–10	white, yellow centers	late winter–spring	summer
Physostegia virginiana	P	3–10	pale pink, magenta	winter–spring	summer
Platycodon grandiflorus	P	4–10	blue, purple, pink, white	winter–spring	summer
Plectranthus australis	P	9–11	lilac, white	autumn	spring–summer
Plectranthus ciliatus	P	9–11	mauve	autumn	spring–summer
Polemonium caeruleum	P	2–9	blue	spring	early summer
Polianthes tuberosa	P	9–11	creamy white	spring	summer–autumn
Polygonum affine	P	3–9	red	spring	summer–autumn
Polystichum acrostichoides	P	3–9	–	spring	–
Pontederia cordata	P	3–10	blue	spring	summer
Portulaca grandiflora	A	10–11	yellow, pink, red, orange	summer	summer
Potentilla nepalensis	P	5–9	pink, apricot, red centers	autumn	summer
Primula auricula	P	3–9	gray, pale green, almost black	late winter–spring	spring
Primula denticulata	P	6–9	pink, purple, lilac	late winter–spring	mid-spring
Primula japonica	P	5–10	pink, crimson, purple, white	late winter–spring	spring–summer
Primula juliae	P	5–9	purple, yellow centers	late winter–spring	spring
Primula malacoides	P	8–11	white, pink, magenta	late summer–spring	spring–summer
Primula, Polyanthus Group	P	6–10	all colors	late summer–spring	winter–spring
Primula sieboldii	P	5–9	white, pink, purple	late summer–spring	summer
Primula veris	P	5–9	orange-yellow	late summer–spring	spring–summer
Primula vulgaris	P	6–9	pale yellow, white, pink	autumn–early spring	late winter–summer
Prunella grandiflora	P	5–9	white, pink, purple	spring or autumn	spring–summer
Psylliostachys suworowii	A	6–10	pink	spring	summer
Pulmonaria angustifolia	P	3–9	dark blue	winter–early spring	spring
Pulmonaria saccharata	P	3–9	white, pink, blue	winter–early spring	early spring
Pulsatilla vulgaris	P	5–9	white, pink red, purple	late winter–early spring	spring

Name	Type*	Zone	Color	Planting time	Flowering season
Ranunculus acris	P	5–9	bright yellow	spring or autumn	mid-summer
Ranunculus repens	P	3–10	yellow	spring, autumn	spring–summer
Reseda odorata	A	6–10	greenish	late winter	summer–autumn
Rheum palmatum	P	6–10	dark red to creamy green	winter–early spring	summer
Rhodanthe chlorocephala subsp. *rosea*	A	9–11	pink, yellow, white	spring	summer
Rhodanthe 'Paper Star'	P	7–11	white	spring–early summer, autumn	most of year
Ricinus communis	A	9–11	red and greenish	autumn	summer
Rodgersia aesculifolia	P	5–9	cream, pale pink	autumn	mid-spring
Romneya coulteri	P	7–10	white, orange center	late winter–spring	late summer
Roscoea cautleoides	P	6–9	yellow, orange	late winter–spring	summer
Rudbeckia fulgida	P	3–10	orange-yellow	spring or autumn	summer–autumn
Rudbeckia hirta	P	3–10	orange-yellow, orange-red	spring or autumn	summer–autumn
Rudbeckia laciniata	P	3–10	golden yellow	spring or autumn	summer
Ruta graveolens	P	5–10	yellow-green	late summer	summer
Salpiglossis sinuata	A	8–11	red, orange, yellow, blue, purple	spring	summer–autumn
Salvia elegans	P	8–11	bright red	spring	summer–autumn
Salvia farinacea	A	8–11	violet-blue	spring	summer
Salvia involucrata	P	9–10	mauve, magenta	spring	summer–autumn
Salvia officinalis	P	4–10	blue-mauve	spring	summer
Salvia sclarea	B	5–10	greenish white, tinged purple	spring	summer
Salvia splendens	A	9–11	scarlet	spring	summer
Salvia × *superba*	P	5–10	purple	spring	mid-summer–early autumn
Sanguinaria canadensis	P	3–9	white	late summer	spring
Santolina chamaecyparissus	P	6–10	yellow	summer	summer
Sanvitalia procumbens	A	7–11	yellow	autumn	summer
Saponaria ocymoides	P	4–10	pink, deep red	spring or autumn	spring–summer
Saxifraga exarata subsp. *moschata*	P	6–9	white, creamy yellow, pink, red	autumn	spring
Saxifraga paniculata	P	3–9	white	autumn	spring
Saxifraga 'Ruth Draper'	P	6–9	purple-pink	autumn	early spring
Scabiosa atropurpurea	B/P	7–11	crimson, white, pink, purple, blue	autumn	summer–autumn
Scabiosa caucasica	P	4–10	pink, red, purple, blue	autumn	summer–autumn
Schizanthus × *wisetonensis*	A	7–11	white, blue, pink, reddish brown	summer, autumn	spring–summer
Schizostylis coccinea	P	6–10	scarlet	spring	summer–autumn
Scutellaria incana	P	5–9	grayish blue	autumn	summer
Sedum spectabile	P	4–10	pink	spring	late summer
Sidalcea malviflora	P	5–10	pink, white	late winter–spring	spring–summer

Name	Type*	Zone	Color	Planting time	Flowering season
Sidalcea 'Rose Queen'	P	5–10	deep pink	late winter–spring	summer
Silene armeria	P	5–10	pink	spring or autumn	summer–autumn
Silene coeli-rosa	A	6–11	pinkish purple	spring or autumn	summer
Sisryinchium bellum	P	8–11	amethyst-purple	summer	late spring
Sisryinchium striatum	P	8–10	cream, striped purple	summer	summer
Solenostemon scutellarioides	P	10–11	leaves pink, green, red, yellow	spring–summer	summer (winter houseplant)
Solidago 'Golden Wings'	P	3–10	yellow	spring or autumn	autumn
Stachys byzantina	P	5–10	mauve-pink	spring, early autumn	summer
Stachys officinalis	P	4–10	red-purple	spring, early autumn	summer
Stokesia laevis	P	7–10	blue-mauve, white	autumn	summer–autumn
Streptocarpus Hybrids	P	10–11	lilac, purple, blue, pink, crimson	spring, autumn	winter–early summer
Symphytum 'Goldsmith'	P	5–10	blue, pink, white	spring, autumn	spring
Tagetes erecta	A	9–11	orange, yellow	spring	summer–early autumn
Tagetes patula	A	9–11	red, yellow, orange	spring	summer–autumn
Tanacetum coccineum	P	5–9	pink, red, purple, white	late winter–early spring	spring–summer
Tanacetum parthenium	P	6–10	white	late winter–early spring	summer
Teucrium chamaedrys	P	5–10	rosy purple	autumn, spring	summer, autumn
Thalictrum aquilegiifolium	P	5–10	pink, lilac, greenish white	autumn	summer
Thalictrum delavayi	P	5–10	lilac	autumn	summer
Thunbergia alata	A	9–11	orange	spring	summer–autumn
Thymus × citriodorus	P	4–10	pale lilac	summer	spring–summer
Thymus serpyllum	P	3–9	bluish-purple	summer	spring–summer
Tiarella cordifolia	P	3–9	creamy white	spring	summer
Tithonia rotundifolia	A	8–11	orange, scarlet	late winter–early spring	summer–autumn
Torenia fournieri	A	9–11	purplish-blue	spring	summer–autumn
Tradescantia, Andersoniana Group	P	7–10	white, mauve, pink, purple	spring, summer or autumn	late summer
Tradescantia virginia	P	4–9	white to deep blue, purple	spring, summer or autumn	late summer
Tricyrtis hirta	P	5–9	white	autumn	summer
Trillium grandiflorum	P	3–9	white	autumn	spring
Trollius chinensis	P	5–9	light to deep yellow	spring	spring
Tropaeolum majus	A	8–11	red, orange, yellow, cream	spring	summer–autumn
Tulipa, Darwin Hybrid Group	A	3–9	orange, yellow, red shades	autumn	summer
Tulipa, Single Early Group	A	3–9	orange, yellow, red shades	autumn	summer
Tulipa, Single Late Group	A	3–9	orange, yellow, red shades	autumn	summer
Valeriana officinalis	P	3–9	white to dark pink	autumn	summer
Verbascum bombyciferum	B	6–10	golden-yellow	spring	summer
Verbascum chaixii	P	5–10	yellow	spring	summer

Name	Type*	Zone	Color	Planting time	Flowering season
Verbascum thapsus	P	3–9	yellow	spring	summer
Verbena bonariensis	P	7–10	deep purple	autumn, spring	summer–autumn
Verbena × hybrida	P	9–10	red, mauve, violet, white, pink	autumn, spring	summer–autumn
Verbena rigida	P	8–10	pale violet to magenta	autumn, spring	summer
Veronica austriaca	P	6–10	bright blue	autumn, spring	late spring
Veronica gentianoides	P	4–9	pale blue, white	autumn, spring	late spring
Veronica spicata	P	3–9	blue	autumn, spring	summer
Viola cornuta	P	5–9	blue-violet	spring	spring–summer
Viola odorata	P	6–10	violet, white, rose	spring	winter–spring
Viola pedata	P	4–9	violet	spring	spring, summer
Viola, Perennial cultivars	P	6–10	all colors except true blue	spring	most of year
Viola tricolor	P	4–10	yellow, blue, violet, white	spring	autumn–winter
Viola × wittrockiana	A	5–10	all colors	spring	winter–spring
Xeranthemum annuum	A	7–10	white, pink, mauve	spring	summer
Yucca filamentosa	P	4–10	white	spring	summer
Yucca glauca	P	4–9	greenish white	spring	summer
Zantedeschia aethiopica	P	8–11	white	winter	spring–autumn
Zantedeschia elliottiana	P	8–11	yellow	winter	spring–autumn
Zantedeschia rehmanii	P	8–11	mauve, rose-purple	winter	summer
Zephyranthes candida	A	9–10	white	autumn, spring	summer–autumn
Zephyranthes grandiflora	A	9–10	white and pink	autumn, spring	summer
Zinnia elegans	A	8–11	white, red, pink, yellow, violet, orange, crimson	spring	summer–autumn
Zinnia haageana	A	8–11	yellow, orange, bronze	spring	summer–autum

Type: A = annual
   B = biennial
   P = perennial

INDEX